Counting Ants While The

Elephants March By

Thoughts on Church and State, Poverty and Terrorism, War and Peace

Wayne Lavender

Ithaca Publishing

Passing the Peace Inc.

Published by Ithaca Publishing

www.ithacapublishing.org

First published in 2007 by Ithaca Publishing, a subsidiary of Passing the Peace, Inc.

All proceeds from the sale of *Counting Ants* will go to Passing the Peace Inc. All profits from the book will go to projects with the goal to build a world of peace and justice for all of God's people. See www.passingthepeace.org for a detailed breakdown of projects funded by Passing the Peace.

10   9   8   7   6   5   4   3   2   1

Library of Congress Cataloging-in-Publication Date

Lavender, Wayne.
    Counting ants while the elephants march by:
    thoughts on church and state, poverty and terrorism, war
    and peace / by Wayne Lavender.
      p. cm.
    Includes bibliographical references.
    LCCN 2007925602
    ISBN-13: 978-0-9794656-4-2
    ISBN-10: 0-9794656-4-8

    1. Church and social problems. 2. Church and social
    problems--Methodist Church. 3. Mission of the church.
    I. Title.

    HN31.L38 2007   261.8
                    QBI07-600108

Printed in the United States of America

Cover design by Robert Aulicino, cover photo by Deborah Rose-Dempster.

This book is dedicated to Linda
&
Aaron, Andrew, Candido and Adam

Special appreciation to those along the journey who have lent a helping hand:

George, Clayton, Bonnie, Deborah, Don, Janet, Barbara, Karen, Laura, Peg, Christine, Samuel, Rita, Lucille, Margaret, Wendell, Karen, Robin, Dieudonne, Sara and the class members of the Kerhonskon Community Church, Walt and the class members of the West Hartford UMC, Glen and the class members of the South Britain UCC.

CONTENTS

FOREWORD

Bishop C. Dale White

It is a privilege to write the foreword to this testimony from a faithful pastor who is living into a clear and life-altering call to be a disciple who, above all else, preaches peace and justice. His story of years in parish ministry as pastor, priest, and prophet, now driven to focus on peacemaking, is both inspiring and challenging. With courageous clarity, he prods the slumbering church he knows all too well to come awake once again to its true mission, to live into the words of Jesus: "The Spirit of the Lord is upon me, because he has anointed me to bring good news to the poor. He has sent me to proclaim release to the captives and recovery of sight to the blind, to let the oppressed go free, to proclaim the year of the Lord's favor" (Luke 4:18–19).

In reconnecting with Wayne Lavender fifteen years after I left the New York Annual Conference, I was reminded that I had ordained him an elder in the United Methodist Church in 1986. That was the same year the United Methodist Council of Bishops released the study *In Defense of Creation,* in which we declared: "We say a clear and unconditioned No to nuclear war and to any use of nuclear weapons. We conclude that nuclear deterrence is a position that cannot receive the church's blessing." As the leader of that initiative, I am especially gratified to see Wayne's commitment as a sign of a new generation of peacemakers emerging at a critical time in the history of the nation.

As I read this text, I observe the strong influence of the founder of the Methodist movement, John Wesley. A look back at the Wesleyan revival reveals that Wayne writes out of a long heritage of Christian peacemakers.

Who was John Wesley?

John Wesley was an accomplished Bible scholar, a strict priest in the Church of England, and a highly disciplined man spiritually. But he felt a great inner emptiness, until on one occasion he entered a little chapel on Aldersgate Street in London, where, he reports: "I felt my heart strangely warmed. I knew that Christ died for the sins of the world; now I knew Christ died for my sins." The late Wesley scholar Albert Outler said that the Aldersgate experience changed Wesley from a "harsh zealot of God's judgment to a winsome witness to God's grace." God moved him from a passionate scholar of the Bible to a compassionate lover of the people.

What was the sign of that conversion? Wesley left the high Anglican pulpit to go out to the fields, the factories, and the mine heads to bring the message of God's love to the poor, who were seldom seen in the churches. His scriptural message was the love of life and the life of love. He often quoted 1 John 4:7: "Beloved, let us love one another, for love is from God; everyone who loves is born of God and knows God."

Scholars often speak of the "Wesleyan Synthesis." A scholar not only of the Protestant Reformation, Wesley honored eternal truths in the Roman Catholic and Orthodox traditions as well. He was impatient with divisive arguments over the fine points of theology. We might recall his famous invitation: "If your heart is as mine, give me your hand." Mr. Wesley insisted on trying to maintain a wholesome balance among several dimensions of ministry, while many church groups stressed one or another facet and largely ignored the others. Wesley insisted that effective ministry should hold in creative tension a concern for outreach evangelism, the nurture of the people for a lifetime of spiritual growth, and social witness and action.

An outstanding revivalist whose life was transformed in a dramatic conversion experience, Wesley had little to say for religion that concentrates only on conversion. Conversion is the first halting step toward a life maturing in grace through spiritual discipline. He used to say, "Converts are like still-born babies." They must be nurtured through "the means of grace:" prayer, study of the Scriptures, worship, and Holy Communion.

While hardly a social radical, Wesley knew the Scriptures. The rule of his Societies, or small covenant groups of disciples, was "Continue to evidence your desire for salvation, first by doing no harm, second, by doing all the good you can . . . by attending upon all the ordinances of God." Wesley never separated the "spirituals" from the "temporals." The Wesleyan revival issued in labor reforms, in prison ministries, in the abolition of the slaves. Wesley created medical services, advocated for the poor, and cried out against slavery and all forms of injustice. He was deeply influenced by the pietistic Moravians, yet he broke ranks with them at one point. They insisted, "Do not go out to minister to the poor until your heart is right; be sure you are doing it from pure motives." Wesley responded, "Begin now to live the life of serving love. This will help to bring about the inner transformation that will make your heart right." That "roll up your sleeves" pragmatism has characterized Methodists at their best.

Methodism jumped the Atlantic during the colonial revolution, as lay preachers from England, Ireland, and Scotland gathered congregations together in the New World. As George Washington was being inaugurated as president in the Wall Street section of New York City, the Methodist preachers were meeting nearby at John Street Church, which is still active today as Methodism's oldest congregation. The preachers sent a delegation to Washington offering support to his presidency and to the new nation. They announced their purpose: "To reform the continent, beginning with the church, and to spread Scriptural holiness across the land."

Over my twenty-one years in supervisory roles in Methodism, five as a district superintendent and sixteen as a bishop, I have struggled against the reticence among our congregations to become active in peace and justice ministries. I have often asked, "What has happened to us that peace has become a dirty word among the followers of the Prince of Peace?" During the years of the Second World War and the following Cold War, so many of our clergy and laity became thoroughly intimidated by attempts to stifle their witness. My own attempts to be a faithful peacemaker have been met with a range of familiar charges: "You must be a Communist, or at the very least, a Com-simp! You are giving comfort to the enemy! You are not a true American! You are hopelessly naïve! You are uninformed!"

I was bishop of the New York Annual Conference for eight years. My episcopal territory included both Long Island and the western half of Connecticut, two areas that lead the nation in the volume of government defense contracts. On not a few occasions I heard as I challenged the growing militarization of America: "Where do you think the money comes from to support those beautiful churches you serve?" The question illustrates the way in which all of us, even the churches, have become thoroughly imbedded in a permanent war culture.

Are we true to our faith if we allow ourselves to be intimidated and silenced by fear mongering on the part of political leaders and propaganda spread through the media at the call of the military-industrial complex? As United Methodists, how can we justify turning our backs on the clear teaching of our founder, John Wesley? In his "The Moral State of Mankind," he writes:

> There is a still greater and more undeniable proof that the very foundations of all things, civil and religious, are utterly out of course in the Christian as well as the heathen world. There is a still more horrid reproach to the Christian name, yea, to the name of man, to all reason and humanity. There is war in the world! War between men! War between Christians! . . . Now, who can reconcile war, I will not say to religion, but to any degree of reason or common sense?

Mr. Wesley goes on to demonstrate how completely irrational war is as we look at its causes, such as the ambition of princes, or the corruption of their ministers, or arguments over minor details of religion, or popular taste:

"Nor are there any wars so furious as those occasioned by such difference of opinions." He quotes from Jonathan Swift's *Gulliver's Travels:*

> Sometimes two Princes make war to decide which of them shall dispossess a third of his dominions. Sometimes a war is commenced because another Prince is too strong; sometimes, because he is too weak. . . . It is a reason for invading a country if the people have been wasted by famine, destroyed by pestilence, or embroiled by faction; or to attack our nearest ally if part of his land would make our dominions more round and compact. Another cause of making war is this: a crew are driven by a storm they know not where; at length they make the land, and go ashore; they are entertained with kindness. They give the country a new name, set up a stone or rotten plank for a memorial, murder a dozen of the natives, and bring away a couple by force. Here commences a new right of dominion; ships are sent, and the natives driven out or destroyed. And this is done to civilize and convert a barbarous and idolatrous people.

> But, whatever be the cause, let us calmly and impartially consider the thing itself. Here are forty thousand men gathered together on this plain. What are they going to do? See, there are thirty or forty thousand more at a little distance. And these are going to shoot them through the head or body, to stab them, or split their skulls, and send most of their souls into everlasting fire as fast as they possibly can. Why so? What harm have they done to them? O, none at all! They do not so much as know them. But a man, who is King of France, has a quarrel with another man, who is King of England. So these Frenchmen are to kill as many of these Englishmen as they can, to prove the King of France is in the right. Now, what an argument is this! What a method of proof! What an amazing way of deciding controversies! What must mankind be, before such a thing as war could ever be known or thought of upon earth! How shocking, how inconceivable a want must there have been of common understanding, as well as common humanity before any two governors, or any two nations in the universe, could once think of such a method of decision![1]

[1] John Wesley, "The Moral State of Mankind," *Living Thoughts of John Wesley* (Whitefish, MT: Kessinger Publishing, 2003), 78–79.

Given this heritage, it is not surprising that Methodists have for generations steadfastly struggled against war making in all of its forms. In its *Social Principles,* the United Methodist Church declares:

> We believe war is incompatible with the teachings and example of Christ. We therefore reject war as an instrument of national foreign policy, to be employed only as a last resort in prevention of such evils as genocide, brutal suppression of human rights, and unprovoked national aggression. We insist that the first moral duty of all nations is to resolve by peaceful means every dispute that arises between or among them; that human values must outweigh military claims as governments determine their priorities; that the militarization of society must be challenged and stopped; that the manufacture, sale, and deployment of armaments must be reduced and controlled; and that the production, possession, or use of nuclear weapons be condemned. Consequently, we endorse general and complete disarmament under strict and effective international control.[2]

Methodists are not alone in this struggle. Religious communities of every faith have made notable contributions to nearly every major social reform movement in the history of the United States and beyond—slavery, child labor, women's right to vote, the civil rights movement, opposition to torture, not to mention the struggle for freedom against Soviet domination in Eastern Europe and the independence movement in India.

The secret is in joining together with other kindred spirits in the exercise of our political ministry through informed, consistent, and timely public witness. As individuals our voices are weak; as congregations it is hard to get attention; as people of faith banded together with like-minded citizen organizations, we have a chance. More and more, courageous people are forming coalitions to stand up against the powerful corporate interests that ravage the earth, militarize societies, and create poverty.

As I have written elsewhere, looking at the vast power and mind-boggling complexities of the social systems of injustice and destruction, it is all too easy to fall into a mode of cynical resignation. "What can I do about all this?" is the ready refrain. Ironically, just as we allow ourselves to fall into a stupefied paralysis we look around to see the impressive new energies bubbling up from grassroots activists. An exciting number of coalitions that seek a just

---

[2] *The Book of Discipline of the United Methodist Church* (Nashville, The United Methodist Publishing House, 2004), 123.

peace are networking on a global basis. They are unifying the combined passion and expertise of many diverse sectors of society.

At first glance, people confronting massive corporate conglomerates seem a David and Goliath contest, with Goliath holding the most powerful weapons. We need to recall, however, that David won the battle. Civil society has the capacity to redirect the life energies of masses of people. Citizen groups can analyze issues from many perspectives and draw on the best minds to propose solutions. They can organize rapidly with the flexibility to change methods of social change as situations evolve. They have many leaders acting independently; if one is silenced, others take up the struggle. They can use the same electronic communication methods corporations use. Attacks upon citizen networks often expose the brutality of the "principalities and powers," giving these networks new visibility and drawing new organizations to the cause.

What do communities of faith bring to the struggle? History is rich in illustrations of the vital role that church groups have played in awakening civil society. As a result, we have learned the following:

- We are well equipped to confront the false theology of idolatrous institutional systems.
- We are skilled in articulating coherent visions for new futures, guided by the wisdom of the ages illuminated in sacred Scriptures.
- We symbolize in our very being the finest values of the human experience.
- We can call upon a host of committed and courageous persons of goodwill.
- Constant litanies of repentance and forgiveness keep us in touch with the sinfulness of the human condition and the wonders of God's grace.
- Most of all, prayer focuses our attention on the hurts of the human family, softens our attitudes toward even our "enemies," and empowers us both to expect and to envision new futures.[3]

Walter Wink of Auburn Seminary was right on target when he wrote, "Churches, which continually complain about their powerlessness to induce change, are in fact in a privileged position to use the most powerful weapon of all: the power to de-legitimate. But it is a spiritual power, spiritually discerned and spiritually exercised."

---

[3] For a fuller discussion, see my book *Making a Just Peace: Human Rights and Domination Systems* (Nashville: Abingdon, 1998).

The Council of Bishops of the United Methodist Church agreed: "The Church of Jesus Christ, in the power and unity of the Holy Spirit, is called to serve as an alternative community to an alienated and fractured world—a loving and peaceable international company of disciples transcending all governments, races, and ideologies; reaching out to all 'enemies;' and ministering to all the victims of poverty and oppression."[4]

It is fitting that Wayne and I first discussed his evolving book at the National Conference in Building a Wesleyan Theology of Peace for the 21st Century. Meeting for several days in San Francisco in late September 2006 and guided by a number of outstanding scholars and noted peace activists, we discussed in depth the message and spirit of John Wesley. Now as a United Methodist bishop I honor the work of a United Methodist pastor who is committed to reviving the spirit of Wesley in the church in our time.

---

[4] *In Defense of Creation* (Nashville: Graded Press, 1986), 37.

Chapter 1
Redefining the Landscape

The world we have made, as a result of the level of thinking we have done thus far, creates problems we cannot solve at the same level at which we created them.   — Albert Einstein

Then he entered the temple and began to drive out those who were selling things there; and he said, It is written,
"My house shall be a house of prayer;
  but you have made it a den of robbers."   —Luke 19: 45 - 46

I left halfway through the four-day session of the New York Annual Conference of the United Methodist Church in June 2002. I left not because I wanted to—the debates and arguments were, as usual, lively; the food and fellowship were fine; the keynote speaker was excellent. I left because in less than forty-eight hours I would be leading a group of church members on a Volunteer in Mission (VIM) trip to Mozambique, one of the poorest nations in the world.

About a hundred hours after I departed the comforts of Hofstra University where lay representatives and my clergy colleagues were intent on conferencing, I found myself in Maputo, the capital city of Mozambique. The ride from the airport to the bishop's guesthouse was as eye opening, disheartening, and discouraging as it had been on my initial trip there in 1998. We drove past scenes of poverty unimaginable anywhere in the United States. Open sewers were flowing through the streets; desperate men were picking through the trash at one of the city dump sites looking for food or the rare item that could be sold for cash; many sick men, women, and children were lying on the ground, death hovering nearby. In a city with an estimated 100,000-orphaned street children, we could not travel a single block without seeing their faces—the sad, distressed, hopeless look of those who knew they were doomed to a life of desperate poverty and a struggle to survive.

The topics being debated back at the New York Annual Conference of the United Methodist Church paled in the presence of the abject poverty of which I was in the midst. I was reminded of the statistics that a child dies as the result of extreme poverty in a Third World nation approximately every three seconds, and that an average of 20,000 children die *daily* from preventable diseases or a general lack of food and clean water.

During the two-hour debate the conference members had over the possible ordination of gays and lesbians, roughly 2,000 children worldwide had died; while we discussed our changing health care program and pension benefits, developing nations were losing the struggle against issues like mounting foreign debt, cyclical famine, food shortages, the HIV/AIDS epidemic, unemployment, and extreme poverty. The conference's impressive worship services took place against the ongoing reality that the events of September 11, 2001, had set our nation on a course of preemptive and permanent war, and the church of Jesus Christ had done virtually nothing to prevent these wars.

The dining room at Hofstra offered conference delegates three choices of entrees, a fantastic salad bar, fresh fruit and vegetables, a wide selection of desserts, and unlimited access to beverages including six brands of soda, four kinds of milk, three fruit drinks, decaf or regular coffee, and bottled water. While delegates contemplated leaving the plenary sessions early to avoid a fifteen-minute wait in the food lines, about 2.8 billion people—some 45 percent of the world's total population—were forced to survive for another day on the equivalent of two US dollars or less. Some 1.2 billion of those people live on one dollar a day or less. Roughly two-thirds of those living on one dollar a day or less are female. Worldwide, the poorest 20 percent have access to only 1 percent of the total Gross World Product (GWP). I was reminded of the prophet's abrasive words:

> I hate, I despise your festivals,
>
> and I take no delight in your solemn assemblies.
>
> Even though you offer me your burnt offerings and grain offerings,
>
> I will not accept them;
>
> and the offerings of well-being of your fatted animals
>
> I will not look upon.
>
> Take away from me the noise of your songs;
>
> I will not listen to the melody of your harps.
>
> But let justice roll down like waters,
>
> and righteousness like an everflowing stream.
>
> Amos 5:21–24

* * * * * *

A trip to a foreign continent challenges our senses. Sights, sounds, tastes, and smells bombard us in unimaginable ways. In Mozambique, thatched roofs covered mud-brick homes in the midst of coconut, banana, and palm trees. Smoke from small cooking fires filled the sky and our nasal passages mornings and evenings as the women prepared their meals. Lean meals of fish, rice, bread, and fresh fruit—prepared daily and free of preservatives and chemical additives—filled our stomachs. The many four-to-six-foot-tall dirt mounds scattered throughout the country particularly struck me. Our hosts told us they were anthills; as we observed them in person we marveled at the engineering skills of these tiny creatures.

During my first African trip, I had the opportunity to visit a South African game park and was able to see "The Big Five:" rhinoceroses, lions, buffaloes, leopards, and elephants. I saw many other large (giraffes, hippopotamus) and small animals (impalas, baboons). There were beautiful birds (eagles, storks), reptiles (turtles, lizards), and insects. The large anthills we saw in Mozambique were also a common sight in the game park. The sight of an elephant walking right through an anthill particularly struck me. The elephant hardly noticed that it had destroyed the temporal home for hundreds, perhaps thousands, of ants. It flattened the anthill with a few simple steps, and then continued its journey. After the elephant had moved on, I asked the driver to move closer to the destroyed anthill. He did so, and we saw the survivors scurrying about, intent, we surmised, on the process of rebuilding their world.

Epiphanies—experiences of God's presence, moments of clarity—can come to any person at any time and anywhere. Throughout my life there have been a handful of instances when I believe God was speaking to me. These experiences were exhilarating and humbling, exciting and scary, comforting and challenging. Gaining perspective about ourselves, our faith, and the world in which we live can be a painful but necessary experience if we are determined to be faithful disciples of Jesus Christ.

During my trip to Africa in 2002 I had an epiphany. Back in New York, the annual conference had just ended, with its lay and clergy members headed back to their local churches after four days of discussions and debates, fellowship and fun, worship and recreation. The topics at the annual conference—our health care benefits, our pension plan, the salaries of the district superintendents, the overall budget of the conference, the election of officers to serve the conference, even the heated debates on how we interpret the Scriptures regarding such controversial issues as abortion and homosexuality—can be perceived as anthills in comparison to the more pressing global challenges. Life and death subjects—war and poverty, the haves and the have-nots, thousands of children dying each day from preventable diseases—are the elephants of our day that are being largely ignored by comfortable, middle-class American Christians.

Where were the discussions and debates about the widespread poverty experienced by 45 percent of the world's population? Where were the discussions and debates about the ongoing war in Afghanistan and the growing movement toward a war in Iraq? Where were the discussions and debates about our military/industrial/political establishment's move further toward a society of permanent war? Where were the discussions and debates about how this establishment had entrenched itself into our society in such profound ways that to speak against it was and is considered unfaithful, unpatriotic, and unwise? Where were the discussions and debates about what true stewardship is and about the incredible and growing disparity between the world's rich and poor? The members of the annual conference, myself included, were thrusting our moral lances at ants and anthills while the elephants marched boldly onward, redefining the landscape and leaving the survivors to pick up the pieces of their shattered lives.

I look at my spiritual journey as a long and winding road that has taken some interesting and surprising twists and turns. I have not always looked at the sessions of annual conference with as much sadness and disappointment for its misplaced passion and energy as I do now. Like so many others, I have caucused and plotted, spoken from the floor, and from the stage. I have made presentations and objected to motions. I have voted by raising a hand, standing up, and writing on a paper ballot. I have been a member or chairperson of dozens of district and conference committees and have done my best to serve these positions faithfully. I have served the institutional church on local, district, and conference levels, and I continue to do so today. My service, however, is moving in a new direction.

Not everyone has the opportunity to travel to a Third World nation. My trips to Mozambique brought me face to face with extreme poverty and destitution unimaginable to most Americans. Although I had read about world poverty, I needed to see it in person before I could believe it. The stark reality I have witnessed has shown the way to my conversion.

Reflecting on my twenty years of experience as a United Methodist pastor, I am constantly amazed at the passion church members have for the secular, non-disciple-making programs and activities in which our churches participate. Attend worship at nearly any of the 36,000 United Methodist churches throughout the United States and you will read in the bulletin announcements or hear in person about the coming tag sales, crafts events, Victorian teas, bake sales, holiday pageants, musical events, car washes, and breakfasts or dinners. In addition to the barrage of fund-raisers the church engages in, church members are encouraged to join church committees, where they get bogged down in planning and organizing inwardly focused activities and programs. Serving on a committee and staffing fund-raisers are poor substitutes for practicing the true radical and challenging servant life (discipleship) of Jesus Christ.

I have witnessed passionate debates in local churches over the type of carpet to be placed in the sanctuary, the color of the walls in a Sunday school classroom, the physical location of the baptismal font, or where the choir should sit for the worship service. I have even seen members leave the church over issues such as how often the Apostles' Creed should be read during Sunday morning worship, or in anger over the selection of a particular person to serve in a position of "power." Far too often and for far too long the church has fought the wrong battles at the wrong times—attempting to kill the ants while the elephants are rampaging through the land. Put another way, Jesus said:

> Woe to you, scribes and Pharisees, hypocrites! For you tithe mint, dill, and cummin, and have neglected the weightier matters of the law: justice and mercy and faith. It is these you ought to

have practiced without neglecting the others. You blind guides! You strain out a gnat but swallow a camel! (Matt 23:23–24)

Of course, not all churches are merely *playing* church; not all are missing the greater message of the gospel while arguing over minor matters. Some churches, to various degrees of success, participate in building God's kingdom here on earth via peace and justice ministries. Congregations that serve the least, the last, and the lost by offering or supporting food pantries and meal programs, long- or short-term shelters or housing, counseling services, and mission teams enable the Word to become flesh through good deeds and actions. John Wesley knew the true purpose of the church when he wrote:

> The Gospel of Christ knows no religion but social, no holiness but social holiness. You cannot be holy except as you are engaged in making the world a better place. You do not become holy by keeping yourself pure and clean from the world but by plunging into ministry on behalf of the world's hurting ones.[5]

Sadly, the majority of churches I have observed tend to focus a vast amount of their time and energy on issues that, from God's perspective, must be ants in comparison to the real elephants of our day. We spend more time and energy coordinating and setting up fund-raisers than we spend on feeding the hungry. We fret more about the church's committee structure and polity than we concern ourselves with the growing antagonism between the world's major religions. We are more concerned with the pros and cons of gay marriage than we are with our nation waging an unjust war. We *fight* about theology more than we *practice* our faith. Parochial attitudes dominate the mindset of local pastors and church members, reversing Wesley's catchphrase from "I see the whole world as my parish" to "I see the parish as my whole world."

I often wonder what Jesus would think of his church were he to return today. How disillusioned would he be that his church through the centuries has concentrated on tiny issues while forfeiting its prophetic voice of peace and justice? What would Jesus say about the current world situation? What, indeed, would Jesus do?

---

[5] John Wesley, Preface to Hymns & Sacred Poems (1739), as reprinted in *The Works of John Wesley* (London: Wesleyan Conference Office, 1872; reprinted: Grand Rapids, Mich.: Zondervan Pub. House, 1958), 14: 321.

I am reminded of three quotes that speak to today's issues with great wisdom:

> The task of the Christian is at least to make the thought of peace once again seriously possible.   —Thomas Merton[6]

> A church that is not able to take a firm stand against war is not a church which deserves to be believed. —Harvey Cox[7]

> If you can keep a cool head in these times, perhaps you don't understand the situation.   —Words painted on a subway car, New York City

The military budget of the United States for 2007 is $520 billion. This figure does not include the ongoing costs of the wars in Iraq and Afghanistan, which already have exceeded $400 billion.[8] In 2007 the military budget of the United States will be greater than the combined military budgets of all the other nations in the world combined!

The average American is convinced the United States donates over 20 percent of federal tax dollars to overseas development and relief. The total budget of the federal government for 2007 is approximately $2.3 trillion. If the average citizen were correct in how much money the United States spends on foreign aid, the total amount to provide food, health care, and education in developing nations would be over $400 billion. The facts show, however, that our foreign and development aid amount to *less than 1 percent* of the federal budget; the reality is that we give only $16 billion for foreign aid to all of the nations of the world combined.

Many Americans also believe that Africa is a hopeless continent, destined to continue down its path of extreme poverty forever. Over and over again, we ignore the suffering of our brothers and sisters in Africa and soothe our consciousnesses by placing the blame for conditions there on corruption and incompetence. We say Africa is a money pit, that the billions and billions of aid and support given to Africa through the years has simply

---

[6] Thomas Merton, *Peace in the Post-Christian Era* (New York, Orbis Books, 2007), 7.

[7] Peace Quotes, found on line at www.ecapc.org/peacemakerquotes.asp

[8] In chapter 11 we will review the work of Joseph Stilglitz, and Linda Bilmes, who estimate that the true cost of the war in Iraq will be more than $1 trillion and will probably exceed $2 trillion.

made the situation worse and that we ought to cut our losses and move away. This "money down the drain" reasoning is used as an excuse for not giving more aid to developing nations in Africa and other parts of the world. A closer look reveals some interesting information. In 2002, the United States gave $2 billion in aid to sub-Saharan Africa. With a population of 650 million people, this amounted to an average of about three dollars per person. How much good can this pitiful amount of money can achieve?

But the situation is even worse than we think. The average African did not receive three dollars. As economist Jeffrey Sachs explains, "Taking out the parts for U. S. consultants, food and other emergency aid, administrative costs, and debt relief, the aid per person came to the grand total of six cents."[9] Regardless of the level of corruption, can we really expect any long- or short-term results when only six cents is finding its way through the agencies and getting to the people in need? There is corruption in Africa as on every other continent, but the West is hardly in a position to preach morality to Africa. Three centuries of a brutal slave trade was followed by one to two centuries of cruel colonial rule and exploitation that has not ended yet. The corruption found in some African nations is a minor nuisance when compared to the real problems this continent is suffering from, and the aid the developing nations could send would go a long way toward ending the poverty cycle and propelling Africa into the twenty-first century.

I have a bumper sticker that reads, "Peace begins when the hungry are fed." Poverty and oppression lead to despair and depression; those without hope have nothing to lose. Revolutions do not occur when people are happy and content, but where there is injustice, inequality, and corruption. Poor nations have become the incubator for international terrorism; they provide sanctuary for drug traffickers and arms dealers, and are at the center of the current HIV/AIDS epidemic.

A child dies somewhere around the world every three seconds from a preventable or treatable disease. Using this three-second interval of time, one can see where our priorities lie:

Period of Time	Event
3 seconds	A child dies from a preventable or treatable disease
3 seconds	The United States spends $49,467.27 for military purposes
3 seconds	The United States spends $1,522.07 for humanitarian aid programs

---

[9] Jeffrey Sachs, *The End of Poverty* (New York, The Penguin Press, 2005), 310.

It has been consistently said by some Americans that the United States does not have enough money to help the 2.8 billion people living so far below the poverty level that their daily existence is threatened. The truth is that everything simply boils down to a question of priorities and goals. Do we want to feed the world's hungry, thereby promoting peace? Do we have the desire to provide clean drinking water to all of God's children? Do we like to help educate and provide health care for the least, the last, and the lost?

The 2005 Human Development Report from the United Nations Development Program claimed that a total of only $7 billion annually for the next ten years will provide 2.6 billion people with access to clean drinking water, saving 4,000 lives a day. The same report noted that a doubling of our foreign aid, from $16 to $32 billion per year, could *eliminate* global poverty by the year 2025!

The money, however, needs to be spent more wisely! Merely doubling the aid to Africa without changing the way the aid is distributed would only increase the amount of money getting to those who need it most from six cents to twelve cents. Jeffrey Sachs and William Easterly are academic rivals who each propose solutions to the current inefficient systems and whose plans, if implemented, would result in saving millions of lives.

It seems so simple. Why not shift resources from weapons of death and destruction to an arsenal of life-sustaining exports such as food, shelter, education, and health care? Why not gradually reduce our military spending while increasing our foreign aid, thereby making friends and eliminating the need for a massive military? Why not "beat our swords into plowshares and our spears into pruning hooks" or, in contemporary terms, convert our rifles into rakes and transform our tanks into tractors? Why not invest in projects and mission ventures that have a proven track record?

The Fertile Crescent gave birth to the world's first civilizations, but from the time of Abraham, the Middle East has been a battlefield, with a history of warfare unparalleled anywhere else on earth. It is ironic that in the birthplace of three of the world's great religions, no one has learned the lesson that violence begets violence, that warfare leads to more warfare, and that killing leads to resentment, anger, and despair, with an intense passion for revenge.

It is not surprising that today's Middle East is a boiling cauldron of resentment, anger and despair. The War on Terror has failed to bring peace to the Middle East; it is clear that killing won't win this war. From the decision to invade Iraq to the detention centers at Guantanamo Bay and the prisoner abuses at Abu Ghraib, the United States has lost the sympathy of the world we held on September 12, 2001. Our blatant disregard for the Geneva

Conventions through the use of physical torture and cruel treatment, as well as attacks on personal dignity through humiliating and degrading treatment, offers terrorist organizations all the publicity they need to be successful. The civilian massacre at Haditha, the raping and killing of a woman and her family at Mahmoudiya, the pictures of innocent men, women, and children killed by our misguided bombs, and the issues raised by Guantanamo Bay and Abu Ghraib have unleashed levels of resentment and rage against the United States unprecedented in our history.

Our leaders apparently fail to understand that the War on Terror is in reality a publicity war. This war is a war of ideas and perceptions. We are desperately losing this battle and have yet to grasp the rules of engagement. Al-Qaeda, Hezbollah, and Hamas understand all too well that the winner of this war will be the one who can capture the hearts and minds of the local and global populations.

Clearly, we need a new strategy. Shock and awe will not win this war. Neither will overwhelming force. Smarter and larger bombs will not provide the answer. Iraq is in ruins. Afghanistan is politically, socially and economically living in great chaos. The infrastructure of Lebanon has been destroyed. Military activities have created economic and social instability. The killing of so-called insurgents and terrorists is creating martyrs and war heroes. Fundamentalist Islamic clergy are using these wars to increase and expand their influence throughout the Muslim world and to become more entrenched in their reactionary thinking. Fundamentalist Christian and fundamentalist Jewish clergy are doing the same. The unchecked growth of these fundamentalists provides the feeding ground for current and future warfare and conflict.

The events of September 11, 2001, changed the course of history in the United States and the world. Can any one person say he or she was not affected by those horrible events? On her morning commute, my own sister watched from across the Hudson River as the planes struck and the buildings collapsed; it took many hours for us to hear that she was safe and was on her way home. As in the bombing of the federal building in Oklahoma City and the school shootings in communities such as Littleton, Colorado, Americans saw the face of evil and terrorism, the innocent slaughtered by angry individuals.

Like Pearl Harbor, the surprise attacks against the United States on September 11, 2001, unified our nation and "awoke a sleeping giant." The unleashing of death and destruction against us created great pain and suffering; these emotions quickly gave way to feelings of hatred and revenge. Our government chose the path of war, turning our thirst for revenge and retribution first on the Taliban government and the terrorists of Afghanistan before moving its sight to Iraq. Our nearly blind march toward war in Iraq came even though most of our international allies had serious reservations and objections to military action and in stark contrast to the fact that Iraq was not involved in the events of 9/11 despite the desperate attempts by the Bush administration to find evidence linking the two.

Where have these wars taken us? If the attacks on the United States steeled our resolve for revenge and led us to war, do not the same principles reside within the people of the Middle East? What did we think our bombings and invasion would bring to the people of Iraq? Did we really believe we would be greeted as liberators? Were we hoping for thank you notes? The invasion and occupation of Iraq have only served to unite the Arab nations and many Islamic people in their hatred of the United States and have steeled their resolve to carry on this war at any cost.

We Americans need to be asking ourselves these questions: What kind of nation are we? Why do so many people and so many nations around the world hate us? Why are people willing to take their own lives in their efforts to kill us? What can we be doing to reduce their hatred and animosity toward us? How can we become a better neighbor?

We Christians need to ask ourselves these additional questions: Who was Jesus Christ? What does it mean to call Jesus the Prince of Peace? Are we being faithful to his call to discipleship? What kind of church do we want to be a part of? In the days following 9/11, we should have been asking ourselves these questions: How do we combat evil without becoming evil ourselves? How can we destroy a monster without becoming the monster ourselves? Given the complex geopolitical realities of our world, what would Jesus have us do?

I am concerned about the moral compass of the United States. Years ago President Eisenhower warned of the dangers of the "permanent war machine" and its potential to take over our country. According to John Graham:

> We're ignoring his admonition. Congress won't let us close military bases to save money. Worse yet, Congress is spending trillions of dollars on weapons systems, the next fighter jet, national missile defense, more aircraft carriers and nuclear missile submarines. The justification for this gorging on weaponry is to defend against the dangers of $1.49 box-cutters.

We have become a more violent, aggressive society; we are a nation moving toward empire. John Kennedy declared in June 1963, "The United States, as the world knows, will never start a war." We have replaced our defensive, "strike only after we have been struck" philosophy with a preemptive, "hit them before they hit us" war strategy. Still worse, there are those in our churches and in our government who believe we are doing these things in the name of Jesus Christ.

I am also concerned about the moral compass of the church of Jesus Christ in the United States. Although initially there was some well organized opposition to the war in Iraq, since the start of the war the church has been silent or, even worse, supportive of the war effort. With the exception of a brave voice here or there crying out in the wilderness, and excluding the faithful witness of the traditional peace denominations (i.e., the Quakers, Mennonites, and Brethren), the church of Jesus Christ has silently abdicated its responsibility to stand up and forge a different path, a path of peace and justice for all. I am concerned that the church has lost its prophetic voice and vision. To recover them, we must boldly proclaim a sea change ideology of preemptive peace as opposed to preemptive war; we must preach that to have peace is to be at peace. There is no way to peace—*peace is the way.*

Finally, I am concerned about my own moral compass. According to Luke, Jesus instructed his new disciple Simon Peter to travel into "the deep water and let down your nets for a catch" (Luke 5:4). Too many of us are trolling the shallow end of the world's waters, concerning ourselves with minnows while the larger fish swim safely beyond our reach. I want to go into the deeper waters! On Judgment Day I will not be asked how many committee meetings I attended or what church social and fund-raising programs I participated in; I will be asked to describe the deep waters I let my nets down in.

I wrote this book because I needed a reality check. The thoughts and feelings I had and was sharing with friends—was I the only person to believe these things? Am I the only Christian who believes the church of Jesus Christ has lost its way? Am I the only one who is concerned our clergy and church members are getting lost counting ants while the elephants are marching by? Why are we more upset by the theological discussions that divide us than by the death of 20,000 children die each day from preventable causes? Why do we fight over control and power in the church when our country spends forty times more money on our military than we do on Third World development? American Christians worry, fret, agonize, and fight to defend our health care insurance, salaries, pensions, and standard of living more than we worry, fret, agonize and fight to assist the 2.8 billion people who live on less than two dollars per day. I wrote this book to hear from you, my readers, and know that someone else shares my fears and concerns and is interested in exploring with me a more faithful path.

I wrote this book because it had to be written. The people in our churches need a wakeup call, a call to action as disciples of Jesus Christ.

Why has the church lost its voice in the presence of war and injustice? Where are the prophets of our day? I know pastors and church members who can quote paragraph, line, and verse from the United Methodist Church's *Book of Discipline* and who can turn a session of the annual conference or any church meeting inside out with motions and amendments to motions from Robert's Rules but who do not know the peace and grace of Jesus Christ. Where is the sacrificial spirit of Jesus Christ in the church today? Where are those persons willing to take up their crosses and follow the Prince of Peace?

I wrote this book because as a Christian living during these dark times I had no choice but to speak up and speak out, to declare the emperor indeed has no clothes on. Our government and military contractors have formed an unholy alliance that feeds our armed forces' insatiable appetite, hurtling us down a pathway of permanent war and permanent profits at the expense of the world's poor.

John Lennon once said, "Life is what happens to you while you're busy making other plans." And we are busy making other plans. We race from task to task, from appointment to appointment, from errand to errand. Between work and family obligations, who has the time to ponder important questions: How well is your soul? How faithful is the church? Are our government and its workers behaving in the manner we would like them to?

I know clergy who diligently labor in the field, preparing sermons, visiting the sick and elderly, writing newsletter articles, performing weddings and funerals, counseling those in need, and overseeing the business of the church. I worked fifty to seventy hours per week for two decades performing these and many other tasks. All of these duties, and a thousand others, are good activities. They need to be done. Yet it is so easy to lose sight of the challenging, prophetic call of the gospel while serving the institutional church.

Like clergy, church members become distracted by trivial issues while neglecting the weightier matters. We indulge our desires and appetites while ignoring the gospel mandates. Demonic forces at work within our churches, our nation, and our world continue unchecked by the good Christian men and women who have lost sight of the vision of our Lord and Savior, Jesus Christ.

As individuals and as the church, we are called to a time of repentance and confession. It is clear, as the prayer of confession reads, that

> we have not loved you with our whole heart.
>
> We have failed to be an obedient church.
>
> We have not done your will,

we have broken your law,

we have rebelled against your love,

we have not loved our neighbors,

and we have not heard the cry of the needy.[10]

Beyond our period of confession and repentance there must be a time of action. We will need to revisit the Gospels and review the message of Jesus Christ, the Prince of Peace. We will need to learn again who we are, who our neighbors are, and what it means to be "good" to them. We will need to think creatively and with ideas and thoughts that are "out of the box." We will have to look at new paradigms, both within the church and within our nation, in order to provide adequate education, housing, health care, and education to all of God's children. We will need to return to Christ's message of love and grace, mercy and peace.

* * * * * *

A baby born two thousand years ago was placed in a manger at a stable in the ancient village of Bethlehem. That child grew to be a man who was eventually nailed to a cross in Jerusalem, the city of peace. Throughout the centuries people have spoken of this person using various titles: Messiah (or Christ), teacher, redeemer, Lord, Savior, King of Kings, Lord. My favorite title has always been "Prince of Peace."

The Prince of Peace's keynote address can be found in the Sermon on the Mount, which appears in the Gospel of Matthew, chapters five through seven. Reading it years ago, I felt the call to ministry. I return to it often for meditation and reflection. My favorite verse in the entire Bible can be found there: "Blessed are the peacemakers, for they will be called children of God" (Matt 5:9). In these troubled times, the world needs the message of Jesus Christ more than in any other time in human history.

---

[10] "A Service of Word and Table I," *The United Methodist Hymnal* (Nashville: United Methodist Publishing House, 1989), 8.

Chapter 2

Jesus as Peacemaker

Thoughts on Neighborliness

Then Jesus said to him, "Put your sword back into its place; for all who take the sword will perish by the sword."—Matt 26:52

Nothing in Jesus' life or teaching can be twisted in support of killing or warfare. —Robert McAfee Brown

For twenty-five years the Rev. Fred Rogers, a.k.a. Mister Rogers, opened his television show with a simple song titled "Won't You Be My Neighbor?" *Mister Rogers' Neighborhood* introduced millions of children to a safe, cozy, and friendly neighborhood; his daily guests included artists, musicians, writers, carpenters, plumbers, engineers, teachers, doctors, and nurses—men and women who shared what they were doing to make the world a better place. His show was a gift—a place of grace—in contrast to the fast-paced, consumer-oriented shows that have grown to dominate commercial television.

From time to time, I think of Mister Rogers and the wonderful neighborhood he was able to create for the children of this nation and beyond. I think of my neighborhood and the kind of neighbor I have been. During the past forty years I have lived in thirteen different communities—from apartments in cities to private homes and parsonages in suburban and rural neighborhoods. I think of some of the neighbors I have had the pleasure and displeasure of knowing through these years. Every neighborhood seems to have at least one home that practices an "open door policy," a place where children and adults are equally welcomed and provided with food and drink, entertainment and conversation. These are the homes you turn to when you find yourself short an egg, cup of sugar, or splash of vinegar. Equally so, every neighborhood has a house that is strictly "off limits," where no trespassing signs are prominent and a snarling, fierce dog works in tandem with fences and security systems to let you know that you had better think twice before dropping in for a visit.

In a simplified but nevertheless true sense, we can summarize the outward expression of one's faith by how well each person treats his or her neighbors. While we are saved by faith, our faith reveals itself in works of love, grace, mercy, and peace toward others. Jesus Christ was the greatest peacemaker the world has ever seen—a man who taught peace, who preached peace, and who lived a life of peace. His deep faith in God led him to a life of service to those around him. He fed the hungry, healed the sick, gave sight to the blind, and provided hope to thousands, millions, even billions of human beings who found in his words the strength to face each day with the courage and determination to walk the same path he chose. He was keenly aware of the human condition—the desperate search for meaning in a world filled with pain, violence, suffering, and warfare—and did what he could to bring peace and justice to the world. In short, Jesus was a great neighbor.

Jesus as a Great Neighbor

Jesus was an itinerant preacher/teacher/rabbi who used many different forms of communication to convey his message. His primary teaching mode was that of the parable. The parable is a short, simple story that draws a parallel to real-life issues and helps the hearer to understand his or her faith in a new and different way. Parables often contain a twist, that is, they challenge our conventional thinking about the world and God's kingdom. Jesus used parables to present his vision of the kingdom of God, including this one, the parable of the Good Samaritan:

> Just then a lawyer stood up to test Jesus. "Teacher," he said, "what must I do to inherit eternal life?" He said to him, "What is written in the law? What do you read there?" He answered, "You shall love the Lord your God with all your heart, and with all your soul, and with all your strength, and with all your mind; and your neighbor as yourself." And he said to him, "You have given the right answer; do this, and you will live."
>
> But wanting to justify himself, he asked Jesus, "And who is my neighbor?" Jesus replied, "A man was going down from Jerusalem to Jericho, and fell into the hands of robbers, who stripped him, beat him, and went away, leaving him half dead. Now by chance a priest was going down that road; and when he saw him, he passed by on the other side. So likewise a Levite, when he came to the place and saw him, passed by on the other side. But a Samaritan while traveling came near him; and when he saw him, he was moved with pity. He went to him and bandaged his wounds, having poured oil and wine on them. Then he put him on his own animal, brought him to an inn, and took care of him. The next day he took out two denarii, gave them to the innkeeper, and said, 'Take care of him; and when I come back, I will repay you whatever more you spend.' Which of these three, do you think, was a neighbor to the man who fell into the hands of the robbers?" He said, "The one who showed him mercy." Jesus said to him, "Go and do likewise." (Luke 10:25–37)

This is perhaps the most well known of Jesus' parables. Throughout the world there are hospitals named "The Good Samaritan Hospital." Many states have laws called "Good Samaritan laws," which protect civilian laypersons who stop to help the sick or wounded. The "Good Sam" van, which is sponsored by a local bank, drives up and down I-95 in Southern Connecticut during rush hour helping commuters with car problems. *The American Heritage Dictionary of the English Language* gives this definition of *Good Samaritan:* "1. In a New Testament parable, the only passer-by to aid a man who had been beaten and robbed. Luke 10:30–37. 2. A compassionate person who unselfishly helps another or others."

It is bitter irony that such a well-known parable has lost its powerful, challenging message. Like the Lord's Prayer, familiarity has bred complacency through the years. The Lord's Prayer is the perfect prayer, but it has been said so often that for many it has become nothing more than a chore, a rote collection of words that have lost their strength and power.

The real message of this parable stems from the hatred and bitter feelings between Judeans and Samaritans. The negative feelings between the Jewish audience Jesus addressed and the Samaritans he spoke of date back nearly a thousand years before the time of Jesus. The Samaritans were perceived as racially and religiously inferior to the "true and pure" Jews of Jesus' time. Perhaps this can best be understood through analogy by reflecting on the racial tension and division between blacks and whites in the United States in the 1950s. The embittered relationship between the races in the Deep South only a generation ago can provide a framework for understanding the dynamics between the Jews and Samaritans in Jesus' time.

That a Samaritan would aid an injured Jew after the priest and Levite passed by on the other side of the road was radical neighborliness, a paradigm-shifting concept, something that flew in the face of conventional wisdom and forced the hearers to reconsider who their neighbors were and what it meant to be a good neighbor. The despised Samaritan exceeded all expectations for the victim: he treated the injured man's wounds with oil and wine, bandaged them, and took the man to an inn with payment for a few days' stay and promises of future reimbursement, if necessary.

Jesus then follows up with a question for the lawyer: "Which of these three, do you think, was a neighbor to the man who fell into the hands of the robbers?" The question is asked of the lawyer in a multiple-choice format; the answer would have to be the priest, the Levite, or the Samaritan. What an easy question to answer! No one, not even a lawyer, could possibly choose the priest or Levite, who each crossed to the other side of the road to avoid the wounded man. The only answer is, of course, the Samaritan. Yet this answer is so offensive that the lawyer cannot even utter the word *Samaritan;* instead, he replies, "The one who showed him mercy." While the lawyer avoids saying the word *Samaritan,* he concedes that to be good neighbors we must show mercy.

The reviled Samaritan acted godly by practicing mercy—he is the model neighbor, a person of grace.

Like his contemporaries, Jesus could have despised the Samaritans. He could have echoed what others were saying about the perceived inferiority of these "half-breeds." He could have acknowledged how the Samaritans were racially and religiously unclean because they did not follow the commands and ordinances of the Bible in the same way as the "true, faithful" Jews had. He could have sympathized with the priest and Levite who passed on the other side of the road, knowing that because the priest and Levite were professional worship leaders, they would be forbidden to lead worship if they had come into contact with the blood from the victim's wounds. Jesus could have spoken about maintaining the status quo in preserving the separation of the Jews and Samaritans; he could have told a story about a Jew helping another Jew in need. Instead, he *challenged* his audience to look at others in a new and different light.

Imagine the good deeds and acts of compassion and charity this parable has generated through the centuries. One can imagine those who heard Jesus himself tell this parable returning to their homes with a new understanding of human nature, of seeing the Samaritans in a new way. One thousand years of bitter hatred and animosity were swept away through the actions of grace and kindness in Jesus' story. The story is pure brilliance. The story is pure grace. The story reveals its teller as divine.

Now imagine the peace, prosperity, and goodwill this parable could have generated had Christians really heard and understood its message. While it is wonderful to honor and praise the Good Samaritan in Sunday school classes and from church pulpits, it is far harder to practice this story in the real world, where mean-spirited neighbors, real enemies, and terrorists are present. It is part of human nature to demonize those who are different from us; this allows us to justify our hatred and animosity for individuals and nations who do not share our beliefs and values. This capacity to dehumanize takes place on an individual and communal basis, pitting person against person, religion against religion, and nation against nation.

Jesus had a rare gift. He was able to distinguish between ants and elephants; he was able to differentiate between the trivial issues and the essential truths of our faith. The leaders of the Jewish people of Jesus' day wanted to lead faithful lives and wanted their people to do the same. The path they took was a path of total allegiance to the laws of the Torah, a rigid position that sometimes, as shown through the example of the priest and Levite, excluded mercy and grace. One's faithfulness was recorded by how well one kept the commandments, and not just the Ten Commandments but also the entire 613 commandments given within the first five books of the Bible. These commandments included dietary restrictions and regulations, rules about what is clean and what is not clean, regulations governing relationships between the sexes, and the worship rules and orders of the temple in Jerusalem.

What Jesus stressed, above and beyond simple allegiance to an outward adherence to these laws, was the spirit of love, grace, mercy, and peace. The law is to be understood as a guide for an inner transformation of our hearts and lives. The law is a tool for our faith; it is not faith itself. Jesus broke the ant-like rules of the day by, for example, healing the sick on the Sabbath and allowing physical contact between a Samaritan and a Jew. He installed a focus on the spirit of the law and how God's grace and love for all people shines in and through the spirit of the law. Jesus was interested in the spirit of the law and how it illustrates God's grace and love. Jesus' faith in grace trumped the Pharisees' religion of doctrine; the ideas of love, grace, mercy, and peace eclipse the concept that rules and regulation, laws and dogma are the most important elements of being faithful to God.

Jesus was consistent throughout his ministry with the simple message of love, grace, mercy, and peace toward all as the true expression of the law. This message is to be understood on both an individual and corporate level, as seen in the remarkable tale of the Judgment of the Nations. It is yet another story of how we treat our neighbors:

> When the Son of Man comes in his glory, and all the angels with him, then he will sit on the throne of his glory. All the nations will be gathered before him, and he will separate people one from another as a shepherd separates the sheep from the goats, and he will put the sheep at his right hand and the goats at the left. Then the king will say to those at his right hand, "Come, you that are blessed by my Father, inherit the kingdom prepared for you from the foundation of the world; for I was hungry and you gave me food, I was thirsty and you gave me something to drink, I was a stranger and you welcomed me, I was naked and you gave me clothing, I was sick and you took care of me, I was in prison and you visited me." Then the righteous will answer him, "Lord, when was it that we saw you hungry and gave you food, or thirsty and gave you something to drink? And when was it that we saw you a stranger and welcomed you, or naked and gave you clothing? And when was it that we saw you sick or in prison and visited you?" And the king will answer them, "Truly I tell you, just as you did it to one of the least of these who are members of my family, you did it to me." Then he will say to those at his left

hand, "You that are accursed, depart from me into the eternal fire prepared for the devil and his angels; for I was hungry and you gave me no food, I was thirsty and you gave me nothing to drink, I was a stranger and you did not welcome me, naked and you did not give me clothing, sick and in prison and you did not visit me." Then they also will answer, "Lord, when was it that we saw you hungry or thirsty or a stranger or naked or sick or in prison, and did not take care of you?" Then he will answer them, "Truly I tell you, just as you did not do it to one of the least of these, you did not do it to me." And these will go away into eternal punishment, but the righteous into eternal life. (Matt 25:31–46)

A striking feature of this scripture passage is that it is a judgment story of the "nations." In this story Jesus does not suggest individuals alone will be held accountable for their actions but we will be judged together as a group of people. Jesus joins the tradition of the prophets of the Old Testament who described the judgment of the nations and what would happen to each country if it did not repent, turn around, and act in accordance to God's will and spirit.

Reading Gospel stories such as the Good Samaritan and the Judgment of the Nations challenges us to look honestly at our nation and ourselves and forces us to ask hard questions. Where do we stand in terms of the final judgment? Has the United States, the richest nation in the history of the world, done all that it can to feed the hungry? Have we provided clean water, welcomed strangers, supplied clothing and shelter to those in need, cared for the sick, and visited the incarcerated? Have we done these acts of mercy for those who are living within our nation? For the "neighbors" who live in the depths of poverty within our inner cities? For those who go to bed hungry every night in Appalachia? For those trapped in the cycle of poverty in single-parent homes where the income generated from minimum wage jobs can never meet the demands necessary to provide food and shelter to a family? Have we been good neighbors to those who are unemployed, homeless, uninsured, ill, or battered? Looking beyond our nation, have we met there the needs of God's people? Have we followed the spirit of Jesus Christ by caring for the least, the last, and the lost on a global scale, where 2.8 billion people live on less than two dollars a day and thousands die daily of preventable or treatable diseases?

It is obvious the citizens of the United States of America can do much more. It is equally apparent that the federal government can do much more. The questions, then, become: Do we, as individuals and as a nation, want to do more? Are we willing to become better neighbors? Can we share the crumbs from our table with those who need a helping hand?

I believe the American people are a generous people. Every day I meet warm, friendly, caring individuals, many of who want to grow in their faith, knowledge, and relationship with God through Jesus Christ. But these people have stumbled, in part because they are trapped in a consumer-driven society that compels us to spend ceaselessly on ourselves. The priorities we have set for ourselves are out of line with the priorities Jesus established for members of his church. We provide tips to the religious institutions we are members of rather than tithes; we provide pennies where dollars are demanded; we give limited amounts from the abundance we enjoy to those in need. We need to, as Mother Teresa said, "give until it hurts and then give some more until it feels good."

Let us return to Jesus himself. Born in a stable and raised as a carpenter (a noble profession, but certainly not one designed to provide wealth and security to oneself or one's family), Jesus had no bank account and no pension or health insurance. Of course, people in Jesus' day did not enjoy these benefits of modern living, but the image has emerged in the past decade of Jesus as the "peasant messiah," a man of limited material resources who had to borrow a coin when asked about whether it was lawful to pay taxes to the emperor (Matt 22:15–22). Jesus warned us of the danger of material possessions and the grip wealth can have on our lives. He taught us to give—not just tips from our wealth but sacrificial, abundant, generous works of grace and love, because "where your treasure is, there your heart will be also" (Matt 6:21).

The same can be said about our nation as a whole. While it is true the United States gives more actual dollars in foreign aid than any other nation on the planet, the *percentage* of what we give is lower than any other developed nation in the world except for Italy. We are like the prosperous Jewish patrons (Mark 12:41–44) who flouted their giving to the temple so others would see their wealth and what they were giving. This was in contrast to the poor widow, whose sacrificial gift of two mites demonstrated her total commitment to God's kingdom. Giving miserly and meagerly from our disposable incomes does not reflect the values and ways of life Jesus calls us toward.

The USA Practicing What It Means to Be a Good Neighbor

The best example the world has ever seen of one nation reaching out to others as good neighbors was the Marshall Plan. On June 5, 1947, Secretary of State George C. Marshall delivered an address at Harvard University and outlined what would become known as the Marshall Plan. Europe, coming off the devastating destruction of World War II, had just experienced one of the worst winters in its recorded history. It was Marshall's belief something immediate and substantial needed to be done to prevent further suffering and the spread of Communism to Western Europe. His plan was to provide up to $20 billion in relief. The goal was to have the European nations work together on how they would best use the aid. Marshall's original plan included aid to all of Europe, including the Soviet Union and its Eastern European satellites. Marshall's vision was to be the "Good Samaritan" to nations in need, even if those nations were or had been our enemies. Therefore, aid was to be provided to Germany and Italy, our enemies from World War II, as well as to the emerging enemy, the Soviet Union. It was an international policy that would help show the world what a good neighbor the United States could be. It was a plan of love and grace, mercy and peace.

Unfortunately, the Soviet Union rejected the aid. Joseph Stalin saw the proposal as an opportunity for the United States to spy on his nation and perhaps to undermine his rule. His rejection prevented aid from the United States going to either the Soviet Union or the other Soviet-controlled nations of Eastern Europe.

The Marshall Plan, limited now to Western Europe, quickly passed through the Unites States Congress.[11] Marshall's strategy not only benefited the people of Western Europe but also the United States, because American food and supplies were used. The Marshall Plan was the most important factor in the United States' conversion from a wartime economy to a peacetime economy. American goods were produced in the United States and shipped across the Atlantic on American ships. American businesses, scientists, laborers, and contractors were hired to feed, clothe, and shelter those in need. The United States created work and income for thousands of Americans while being a good neighbor to the nations of Western Europe.

By 1953, at the conclusion of the Marshall Plan, the United States had spent $13 billion on aid and development. Western Europe was again standing on its feet. Aid was distributed equitably to the nations of Western Europe devastated by the war including, of course, Germany and Italy. We had defeated the Nazis and Italian Fascists, and now in victory we became their good neighbors.

The Golden Rule reads, "In everything do to others as you would have them do to you" (Matt 7:12). In 1947 the citizens of the United States understood the true meaning of this text. Ignoring the distinction between who had been our allies and who had been our enemies, we became a good neighbor to Europe. We had embraced the words of Franklin D. Roosevelt's final inauguration speech from January 1945, when he said, "We have learned

---

[11] Many historians believe that Stalin's announcement to reject the aid was a positive force in Congress's approval of Marshall's plan.

that we cannot live alone, at peace; that our own well-being is dependent upon the well-being of other nations, far away. . . . We have learned the simple truth, as Emerson said, that 'the only way to have a friend is to be one.'"

It is relatively easy to be a good neighbor to those who are our own good neighbors. We smile and wave and are happy to provide them with eggs or a cup of milk when they come knocking at our door. But how do we treat the not-so-nice neighbors, the ones with the "no trespassing" signs and growling dogs? Mister Rogers' neighborhood was a fantasy, a utopian village created through the delightful power of television. It was a safe place for children to watch and learn, but it did not represent the real world. It did not include the not-so-nice neighbors, the self-interested people who can and do hurt other people. What do we do with these individuals in real life? What do we do with nations that present a threat, perceived or real, to our nation or to other innocent, weaker nations?

Jesus told us we needed to love the not-so-nice neighbor too. He told parables like the Good Samaritan so we could see the potential for good within all people. He invited everyone, regardless of race, sex, class, moral reputation, or national background to approach the table of grace. But Jesus went beyond even this with his extraordinary claims about enemies and foes. In the Sermon on the Mount, Jesus lays out the blueprint for life in the kingdom of God, focusing on a new teaching, a new ethic, a new way of being in relationship with each other:

> You have heard that it was said, "An eye for an eye and a tooth for a tooth." But I say to you, Do not resist an evildoer. But if anyone strikes you on the right cheek, turn the other also; and if anyone wants to sue you and take your coat, give your cloak as well; and if anyone forces you to go one mile, go also the second mile. Give to everyone who begs from you, and do not refuse anyone who wants to borrow from you. (Matt 5:38-42)

Jesus provides here three examples of how we are to replace current world values and embrace a new way of thinking. Jesus commands us to go beyond simple passive resistance. He gives us a way to break the cycle of hatred and turn it into love. He teaches us to love the unlovable, to offer no resistance to those in power, to refuse to conform to the ways of the world. The person being struck in the face, the person being sued for his or her coat, and the person being compelled to walk a mile (to carry the pack of a Roman soldier, which was the law wherever the Romans were in control) are all victims; they are the injured party in Jesus' preaching. The one who slaps, the one who sues, and the one who forces the other to go a mile are all in positions of power and authority, and they are abusing that power. They are the neighbors we do not want in our neighborhood! But Jesus does not teach us to hit back, or to struggle to retain possession of our coat, or to deny the oppressor the power to force us to walk a mile. Instead, Jesus encourages us not only to accept these actions but to give even more—to offer the other cheek, to hand over the cloak, and to walk a second mile. *We disarm our oppressors by offering actions of love.*

But Jesus is not finished yet. He continues with these words:

> You have heard that it was said, "You shall love your neighbor and hate your enemy." But I say to you, Love your enemies and pray for those who persecute you, so that you may be children of your Father in heaven. (Matt 5:43–45)

The idea of loving your enemies and praying for those who persecute you is perhaps the most difficult of all of the teachings of Jesus. Nevertheless, loving your enemies and praying for those who persecute you go to the heart of the gospel message and form an essential teaching of Christianity. And what is the alternative? As Gandhi pointed out so well, "An eye for an eye and tooth for a tooth will only leave the world blind and toothless."

The cycle of violence knows no end. Jesus offers the world an alternative, a path away from revenge and retribution. Jesus offers us the opportunity to practice love and grace, mercy and peace on a person-to-person and nation-to-nation basis. We know from the history of the world that unless someone is willing to stop the cycle of violence, it will not stop on its own. Jesus puts forward a proposal that can lead to a world of peace, and suggests his followers accept his plan.

It is time—indeed, it is well past the time—for the church of Jesus Christ, every follower of Jesus Christ in the world, to say a loud and clear "No more!" to war, to violence and destruction. Of all the distortions, heresies, fallacies, and misunderstandings of Jesus through the years, the making of war in the name of Jesus, the Prince of Peace, must be the greatest sin and misplaced devotion of all.

How Will We Fight Today's Enemies?

The current War on Terror can be fought in two radically different ways—with the "eye for an eye" policy or a "good neighbor" policy.

Following the "eye for an eye" policy, we can fight the War on Terror by eliminating or killing anyone who is an enemy or a terrorist. We can fight with guns and bullets, bombs and missiles, soldiers and civilians, helicopters and fighter jets. But do we really believe we can kill every one of the terrorists out there and live in peace? I believe following the path of "an eye for an eye" will only produce more enemies, more terrorists, and more war and will take us further from Christ's teachings and increase the chasm between God's children.

The second way to fight the War on Terror would be to become a good neighbor to these nations and people who we perceive to be not so neighborly and break the cycle of violence by learning to coexist. This "good neighbor" policy recognizes that the cycle of violence, of "an eye for an eye and tooth for a tooth" will not work. It also recognizes that for every terrorist who is killed another two are created. This "good neighbor" policy acknowledges that poverty, oppression, the lack of fundamental rights, and the absence of hope for the future are the cradles of international terrorism and provide the foot soldiers for those movements committed to paths of violence. To eliminate the areas of extreme poverty throughout the world should be the goal of every person of faith and of every civilized nation in the world. To do this would be true to the gospel, and would help eliminate the breeding grounds for terrorists.

Toward this end, I am convinced that we need a new Marshall Plan. The original Marshall Plan helped show the entire world what a good neighbor we could be and helped to stabilize an area that could potentially have caused great problems. Europe was on the verge of economic, social, and political collapse. The Marshall Plan was an integral piece preventing this collapse from happening.

Jesus' good neighbor policy is currently needed in the Middle East, in Africa, in Central and South America and in other regions of the world. The new policy could stabilize these areas as the Marshall Plan steadied Europe, create more goodwill and, reduce the motivation to join terrorists' organizations.

Are We Missing Something?

There are those within the Christian church who argue *against* the portrayal of Jesus as a pacifist and peacemaker. It is difficult, if not impossible, they argue, to turn the other cheek when real violence has been committed, when family members, neighbors, or friends have been hurt or killed. We live in the real world, with some really bad people. There are rapists, murderers, and terrorists who have, and will again, hurt people. Revenge is human nature, and it makes perfect sense to return to an eye-for-an-eye theology.

In fact, we can find support for a violent Jesus. After all, some of his parables include the use of violence and force and seem to portray God as a God of wrath and judgment (see the parable of the Wedding Feast in Matt 22:1–14). In the same Gospel where Jesus says that he came to bring peace (John 14:27), he also says, "I came into this world for judgment" (John 9:39). Matthew records these harsh words:

> Do not think that I have come to bring peace to the earth; I have not come to bring peace, but a sword.
>
> For I have come to set a man against his father,
>
> and a daughter against her mother,
>
> and a daughter-in-law against her mother-in-law;
>
> and one's foes will be members of one's own household. (Matt 10:34–36)

How do Christians understand these words? Simply put, does Jesus call his disciples to open warfare, to gather swords and engage in strife and violence? These are severe words: "I have not come to bring peace, but a sword." Is Jesus telling us we are to pick up our swords and fight, to usher in the kingdom of God through the use of force and violence? Is Jesus asking his followers to engage in a holy war against the opponents of Christianity, even if these include close members of our families? Is this a call to arm ourselves and prepare for physical battle?

I do not believe this is a literal call for Christians to take up arms. The real question, it seems to me, is this: Who will wield the sword that Jesus brings? The sword that Jesus brought was aimed at Jesus! The sword Jesus brought will be wielded against his followers by those who are against the Christians precisely because the words of Jesus are so unwelcomed by those who gravitate toward the sword!

If Jesus were alive today, would he replace the sword with modern weapons? Can you imagine Jesus in a military uniform? Can you see him with a rifle? Driving a tank? Ready to shoot a missile? The Prince of Peace flying a fighter jet into combat?

Indeed, Jesus is nothing short of a revolutionary. His love of God and love of neighbor led to a radical faith of love, grace, mercy, and peace. He never lost sight of the bigger picture. He preached this message, he taught this message, and he lived this message—a life obedient to God right up to the cross.

Jesus' Moment of Truth

Of course, Jesus did more than just preach and teach this way of life. He practiced it. He ate with his neighbors, including sinners, tax collectors, prostitutes, and Samaritans. He healed a Roman centurion's daughter. He practiced a radical understanding of God's love for all people. He lived the life of a good neighbor, welcoming everyone in the world with an open door policy and open arms.

During the last week of his life, Jesus entered Jerusalem triumphantly, on the back of a donkey, a symbol of humility.[12] As Jesus rode into Jerusalem, he rode toward his death. Jesus could have avoided this situation. He could have fled Jerusalem. He could have organized his followers to defend him. He could have led an armed revolt against the Roman soldiers. But Jesus was true to his core values; his spoken words of "love your enemies." We can see this clearly in Matthew's account of Jesus' arrest in the garden of Gethsemane:

> Jesus said to [Judas], "Friend, do what you are here to do." Then they came and laid hands on Jesus and arrested him. Suddenly, one of those with Jesus put his hand on his sword, drew it, and struck the slave of the high priest, cutting off his ear. Then Jesus said to him, "Put your sword back into its place; for all who take the sword will perish by the sword. Do you think that I cannot appeal to my Father, and he will at once send me more than twelve legions of angels? But how then would the scriptures be fulfilled, which say it must happen in this way?" (Matt 26:50–54)

Each of the Gospels recounts this same story with slightly different variations (Mark 14:43–52; Luke 22: 47–53; John 18:2–11), but it is only in the Gospel of John that the attacker of the high priest's slave is identified as Peter. Writing some two centuries later, a church theologian named Tertullian understood that "when Christ disarmed Peter in the garden, he disarmed all Christians."

The disarming of Peter in the garden is perhaps the most important turning point in the story of Jesus. When his life was on the line, Jesus could

---

[12] By the beginning of the first century, Jerusalem had seen many "triumphant entrances," from King David— who danced before the ark of the covenant—to Nebuchadnezzar, Alexander the Great, and Pompey. Historian Paul Brooks Duff has written about Greco-Roman entrance processionals in *The March of the Divine Warrior*. Traditionally, the conqueror/ruler rides into the city on a great warhorse, accompanied by his army.

have chosen a different path—but he did not. He did not offer evil for evil but chose to practice what he preached and taught, offering the other cheek and avoiding violence. He chose the path of love, grace, mercy, and peace.

In Luke an extra verse appears that is not present in the other Gospel narratives: "But Jesus said, 'No more of this!' And he touched his ear and healed him" (Luke 22:51). The healing of the slave's ear demonstrates the good neighbor policy. Like the United States' decision to enact the Marshall Plan nearly two thousand years later, Jesus chooses healing over warfare. He provides aid and comfort to the enemy. He chooses love over hatred and thus remains true to what he preached and taught.

Following his arrest, Jesus was beaten, interrogated, and tried. Once again, Jesus remained faithful and "on message." He remained true to his preaching and teaching in his appearances before the high priest, Herod, and Pilate. He offered the world a better way, as recorded by John:

> Pilate asked him, "So you are a king?" Jesus answered, "You say that I am a king. For this I was born, and for this I came into the world, to testify to the truth. Everyone who belongs to the truth listens to my voice." Pilate asked him, "What is truth?" (John 18:37–38)

I am awed by the courage and grace that Jesus showed in the final hours of his life. Pilate, standing face to face with "the way, the *truth,* and the life," does not see it. Looking into the eyes of the Prince of Peace, he cannot see or understand who or what is before him. What is the truth? The truth is the pathway to God is through love, grace, mercy, and peace. The truth is we show our love to God and our neighbor by being good neighbors to all people, regardless of their race, religion, sex, or nationality. Throughout his passion, trial, and crucifixion Jesus continued to practice what he preached. He disarmed Peter in the garden of Gethsemane, he healed the ear of the slave that Peter had wounded, he turned his cheek time and time again after being struck, he did not return evil for evil, he loved his enemies and prayed for those who persecuted him, and he asked forgiveness for those who were responsible for his death. His preaching and teaching became incarnate, his words made flesh in these final days.

I believe the church of Jesus Christ, much like Pilate, is unable to see the truth, even when it is standing right in front of us. Jesus Christ, the Prince of Peace, offered the world an alternative to its obsessive thirst for war, violence, and killing, yet we have continued to turn our back to his way. We ignore his emphasis on love and grace, mercy and peace, and continue to focus on petty rules and regulations, arguing and debating over issues like the "right" way to worship, who should be ordained and who denied, and when going to war or participating in actions of violence is appropriate. The church all too often continues to bless and sanctify war, even going so far as to claim that many wars are holy wars fought in God's name!

Jesus offered his followers the cross as the means for overcoming evil. Through his death on the cross he opened the way to salvation for all of humanity. His soul remained pure and spotless; he fulfilled God's plan for his life and attained eternal life. Imagine what would have happened had Jesus encouraged his disciples to fight back, to defend themselves and himself? Imagine if Jesus had not been captured that fateful night in Jerusalem but instead led an armed escape from the Roman authorities. Imagine if Jesus had led an armed revolt aimed at Roman control of Israel.

The image I have of Jesus today is with a bowl of water in his hands and a towel around his waist, preparing to get on his knees and wash the feet of any who come before him. The call to a life of service in the name of Jesus Christ is a life that demands our total loyalty, a life of resistance to violence and warfare, of feeding the hungry, providing drink to the thirsty, welcoming the stranger, providing clothing to the naked, caring for the sick, and visiting those in prison. It is to be the good neighbor. These are the appropriate responses to the call of Jesus Christ, a call that is still coming down through the ages to those who are able to listen.

Chapter 3
The Church as the Body of Christ

Then the LORD answered me and said:
Write the vision;
    make it plain on tablets,
    so that a runner may read it.
For there is still a vision for the appointed time;
    it speaks of the end, and does not lie.
If It seems to tarry, wait for it;
    it will surely come, it will not delay.
                    —Habakkuk 2:2–3

The church is of God,
and will be preserved to the end of time,
for the conduct of worship
    and the due administration of God's Word and Sacraments,
the maintenance of Christian fellowship and discipline,
the edification of believers,
and the conversion of the world.
All, of every need and station,
    stand in need of the means of grace which it alone supplies.
                    —Baptismal Covenant III,
                    United Methodist Hymnal

Walt Disney, born on December 5, 1901, was a creative genius. In 1955, in the midst of a successful career as an animated moviemaker, he opened Disneyland in Anaheim, California. The opening of Disneyland fulfilled his dream of offering Americans a family-based, Disney-character theme park. But Disney always regretted he could not buy enough land in the vicinity to keep out the cheap hotels, shops, and restaurants that soon surrounded his theme park.[13] For the next decade he considered many options to solve this problem; his solution was to build another park with enough land to fulfill his original dream. He selected a largely undeveloped area just south of Orlando, Florida. On November 15, 1965, a press conference was held with Walt and Roy Disney and the governor of Florida, Haydon Burns, to announce the purchase of 27,500 acres for this new vacation resort.

Unfortunately, Walt Disney died on December 15, 1966. It was widely believed that Disney World would never be completed because of Walt's untimely death, but his brother Roy postponed his planned retirement and took over the Disney organization. The construction of Disney World became his top priority. Five years later, on October 1, 1971, Disney World opened; the official dedication took place later that month on October 29.

Following the fantastic, two-hour dedication ceremony featuring many Disney characters and celebrities, an interviewer reportedly mentioned to Walt's widow how it was a shame that her husband had not seen Disney World. Mrs. Disney responded, "He did." Walt Disney had an incredibly vivid mental image of what his new theme park would be, his wife explained, he had *seen* it in his mind. The Magic Kingdom, geographically located at the center of this park, would become the symbolic and spiritual heart of Disney World. His image was so real and tangible that others could see it, feel it, touch it, and ultimately, catching his vision of the park, build it.

Today Disney World is the number one vacation destination in the United States, having replaced Washington, DC, with this distinction earlier this decade. It seems safe to say Walt Disney, the dreamer and visionary, would be pleased with what has taken place in that former swampland in the middle of Florida. His vision is complete.

Walking the countryside of Israel some two thousand years ago, a holy, passionate man with a vision and a dream shared his thoughts and ideas with a small group of followers and anyone else willing to listen. He used simple stories and parables in his preaching and teaching to share his dream of the kingdom of God. Jesus, like Walt Disney, died before his kingdom was built. But his set of instructions were later recorded in the Gospels and other New

---

[13] Disneyland sits on approximately 300 acres in Anaheim, California. Today Disney World covers over 30,000 acres near Orlando, Florida.

Testament documents. These blueprints showed how God's kingdom would be constructed not of brick, wood, and stones but from love and grace, mercy and peace. Jesus invited his followers to see the big picture, the beautiful kingdom of God. He showed us a better way.

Looking down from heaven, I wonder if Jesus is pleased with what his followers have done with his vision, his set of plans for the kingdom of God. Would Jesus be as happy with what we have done with the construction plans he left as Walt Disney must be with Disney World? If Jesus were to issue a report card for the universal church based on the instructions he gave to us, what grade would we receive? Have we, his disciples, been true to the vision he saw? Has the church been faithful to the man who went to the cross for us? Would he be proud to call the institutional church the body of Christ?

Jesus was fully human; Jesus was fully divine. This is one of the great mysteries of the Christian faith: "The Word became flesh and lived among us" (John 1:14). He lived an earthly life—within a biological body with the same physical needs and limitations as any other human being. But Jesus, equally divine, was able to personify God through his life of love, grace, mercy and peace. He fully and completely gave of himself to others, sacrificing his own wants and wishes, eventually laying down his own life on the cross for the benefit of humanity.

Following Jesus' death and resurrection, the church he left behind became the body of Christ. We became Christ's arms and legs, we became his muscles and skeleton, we became his voice and mind. The church became the means through which Jesus entrusted his vision to the world.

It is my guiding principle that when the church of Jesus Christ participates in actions of love and mercy, of grace and peace, it is acting faithfully as the body of Christ. When we perform selfless activities to feed, clothe, shelter, and nurture those in need, when we let our "light shine before others, so that they may see [our] good works and give glory to [our] Father in heaven" (Matt 5:16), then we are adding flesh and muscle to the body of Christ. When we worship, when we celebrate the sacraments, when we witness to our faith through praise and thanksgiving, we are building God's kingdom. In these circumstances, we are acting divinely.

Conversely, when the church of Jesus Christ acts to gain power or control, we no longer act as the body of Christ. When we exploit people, when we foster hatred, unkindness, cruelty, and anger, when we bless or condone war and violence, death and destruction, we are acting truer to our human, sinful nature. When we remain silent in the presence of dark forces that strip human dignity or take life, when we walk away from injustice, intolerance, torture, discrimination, and evil, we fail as the living embodiment of Christ's vision.

Through the history of the church there have been great moments when individuals and the institution itself have risen to meet the challenges of the day with Christ like grace and love, and other times when the church has failed to be faithful. Indeed, many times the church itself has been the cause of pain, persecution, death, and suffering. This chapter will briefly review the history of the church and see where it has acted divinely in carrying out Jesus' vision of a heavenly kingdom, and where it has come up short and made decisions reflecting our fallen humanity. By looking into the past we may determine how to better become the church of Jesus Christ in the future.

The Church of Jesus Christ Acts Divinely

The history of the church begins with the book of the Acts of the Apostles, which was written by the same author who wrote the Gospel of Luke. The Gospel of Luke is centered on the life of Jesus Christ. Acts, in contrast, tells the exciting story of the early church from the ascension of Jesus into heaven to Paul's preaching from his prison cell in Rome. Reading Acts has been compared to holding both ends of a powerful electrical current—you can feel the energy flowing through the disciples and leaders of the early church. Chapters unfold to tell the powerful stories of Peter and Stephen, Paul and Barnabas, Dorcas and Lydia. The story of Acts, which starts in Jerusalem with Jesus' resurrection now spreads like ripples in a pond toward Damascus, Asia Minor, Egypt, Macedonia and, finally, to the capital city of Rome.

Acts is filled with descriptions of the early Christians who dedicated themselves completely to Jesus' vision. We read about the first Christians who gave their lives for their faith in the stories of the stoning of Stephen (Acts 7) and martyrdom of James (Acts 12:2). We also read about the tremendous transformation that comes to Saul of Tarsus, who is confronted by the risen Christ on the road to Damascus. Seeing Jesus himself, Saul converts to Christianity and begins using the name Paul. Paul's transformation is incredible: he shifts from being a persecutor of the Christian church to one of the church's greatest evangelists and biblical writers. Paul endured unbelievable hardships, including beatings, imprisonment, a shipwreck, and deportation to Rome as a prisoner, because of his decision to be a faithful disciple of Jesus Christ.

The Spread of Christianity

The church continued to grow rapidly throughout the first centuries. How it developed from the ministry and vision of one person and his hand-chosen group of twelve, to a few thousand during the time of the Acts of the Apostles, to an estimated *six million people* by the year 300 is an extraordinary story.

Steeped in the tradition of Judaism, Christianity presented to the world the perspective of human redemption through God's own sacrifice on the cross.

The early church cared for the elderly, the sick, widows, and orphans, and offered the world hope in the midst of pain and suffering. The early Christians preached the good news of Christ's resurrection and conquest of death. As the church reached out to the least, the last, and the lost, and shared their faith in eternal life, new converts were attracted and Christianity grew dramatically. During this same time period, Christianity came under intense persecution. The more the church grew by being faithful to Christ's vision of God's kingdom, the more those in power saw it as a threat and used their power to suppress this new movement.

The Persecuted Church

A great fire in Rome occurred in the year 64 CE. The emperor Nero's failure to take action has been immortalized with the phrase "Nero fiddled while Rome burned." In fact, Nero was at his seaside villa in Anzio and delayed his return to Rome when told of the raging fires. His apparent apathy about the fire and the suffering of his people led to the rumor he had started the fire himself. To deflect responsibility, Nero needed someone else to blame—and found it in the Christians. According to the Roman historian Tacitus:

> Nero created scapegoats. He punished with every kind of cruelty the notoriously depraved group known as Christians. Mockery of every sort accompanied their deaths. Covered with the skins of beasts, they were torn by dogs and perished, or were nailed to crosses, or were doomed to flames and burnt, to serve as nightly illumination, when daylight had expired.[14]

By the fifth century, church tradition accepted ten persecutions of Christians by the Romans. These ten persecutions were under the following emperors:

1. *Nero* (c. 64–68). Traditional martyrdoms of Peter and Paul.
2. *Domitian* (r. 81–96)
3. *Trajan* (112–117). Christianity is outlawed, but Christians are not sought out.
4. *Marcus Aurelius* (r. 161–180). Martyrdom of Polycarp.

---

[14] Tacitus, *Annals* 15:44.

5. *Septimus Severus* (202–210). Martyrdom of Perpetua.
6. *Decius* (250–251). Christians are actively sought out by requiring public sacrifice. Martyrdoms of bishops of Rome, Jerusalem, and Antioch.
7. *Valerian* (257–259). Martyrdoms of Cyprian of Carthage and Sixtus II of Rome.
8. *Maximinus the Thracian* (235–238)
9. *Aurelian* (r. 270–275)
10. *Diocletian and Galerius* (303–311). Severe.

The early church leader Tertullian also wrote about the persecutions of the Christians, including this now-famous comment: "The oftener we are mown down by you, the more in number we grow; the blood of Christians is seed."[15] Converts flocked to the new religion, seeking the same faith and courage they saw in those willing to give their lives to the God of Jesus Christ. The early Christians were convicted, and they endured, with great perseverance, these persecutions. Paul understood this phenomenon when he wrote:

> I want you to know, beloved, that what has happened to me has actually helped to spread the gospel, so that it has become known throughout the whole imperial guard and to everyone else that my imprisonment is for Christ; and most of the brothers and sisters, having been made confident in the Lord by my imprisonment, dare to speak the word with greater boldness and without fear. (Phil 1:12–14)

The body of Christ, on the whole, acted divinely throughout this period of history by accepting suffering, turning the other cheek, serving the poor, and placing their own physical needs aside while striving to serve God by being good neighbors to others. There were moments of greed and corruption among church leaders and members,[16] but the overall impression of the church through the first centuries was its faithfulness to the vision of its leader, Jesus Christ.

Perhaps the greatest irony of church history is how Christianity came to be the dominant religion in the Roman Empire and, subsequently, throughout

---

[15] Tertullian, *Apology,* in *The Ante-Nicene Fathers,* vol. 3, ed. Alexander Roberts and James Donaldson (repr., Peabody, MA: Hendrickson, 1994), 102.

[16] See Acts 5:1–11, the story of Ananias and Sapphira, who lied about how much money their field had been sold for.

Western civilization, and then how the church used its position to persecute others. Christianity changed from being a religion of the down and out and instead became the religion of the rich and powerful.

Once in the position of power, the church used the same tactics used against it for centuries: social pressure,[17] military strength, capital punishment, and financial penalties (including the seizure of property) to suppress divergent opinions within itself and to stifle and restrain the growth of different faiths and traditions. Christian authorities did to so-called heretics what had been done to Jesus and early Christians by the religious and political authorities of their day.

The Union of Church and State under Constantine

Christianity emerged from its time of persecution and became the dominant religion of the Roman Empire during the reign of Constantine (r. 306–337 CE). Constantine came to power when an estimated six million persons within the Roman Empire were Christians. He took control of the Roman Empire after defeating the army of his rival Maxentius at the battle of the Milvian Bridge. On the eve of this battle Constantine reportedly had a vision; he later told church leaders Jesus had appeared to him in a dream. Jesus' message was for Constantine to convert to Christianity and as a sign of this conversion place a Christian symbol on his soldiers' shields. If Constantine did these things, he would be victorious and win the battle over Maxentius. Constantine did as the vision had suggested; he had his soldiers paint crosses on their shields, he won the battle, became emperor, and moved to establish Christianity as the official religion of the Roman Empire.

The major step in this process of establishing Christianity as the official religion of the Roman Empire was the Edict of Milan. Issued in the year 313 CE, it officially granted religious toleration and acceptance to the church and brought an official end to the persecutions. Christianity was no longer persecuted and soon became the government-sanctioned religion of the Roman Empire.

At this time in its development, Christianity was doctrinally fragmented and disjointed. Although the church had grown dramatically during the three centuries of its existence, there was no central authority, no clearly accepted tradition, and no established standards or approved rules and guidelines for the faith that was now the state religion. To correct this doctrinal weakness, a great

---

[17] The power of the church to excommunicate those it deemed a threat or those it believed fell outside of accepted orthodoxy cannot be overemphasized for the impact it had for all Christians.

council was convened in the year 325 CE. Three hundred bishops of the church gathered at Nicea, the modern city of Iznik, Turkey, near Constantinople. The Council of Nicea was presided over by Constantine himself. Imagine a major church council today being presided over by the secular leader of any nation. The union of church and state had been established! This link between state power and Christianity created what has come to be known as the Constantine Era, a period of some 1,600 years in which the interests of the state and religion were often identical.

The council adopted a creed (known today as the Nicene Creed), defined baptismal and ordination services, and established the official doctrines of the church. This council, the first "official," systematic gathering of the leaders of the Christian church, defined what orthodoxy was to be, thereby also establishing what it meant to be a heretic. "Orthodox" was the name given to the accepted theology and doctrines of the church; "heresy" was defined as any theology that was believed to include errors or contradictions to the thoughts and beliefs of orthodoxy. A person who held beliefs that were declared heretical was called a "heretic." Heresy came to be defined not only as an error but also as a crime that needed to be punished. The church that had once been the persecuted now became the persecutor.

The Church as Persecutor

Constantine, a professed Christian, conquered and gained control of the Roman Empire by means of conquest and the sword. His conversion to Christianity and the union of the church and state brought about a profound shift in the way the church operated. No longer was the church's primary concern of building God's kingdom on earth through the tools of love, grace, mercy, and peace; instead, church and state leaders worked to build earthly kingdoms, using the tools of armies, warfare, violence, and aggression. *This was a paradigm shift that transformed the cross of Jesus Christ from a symbol of selfless sacrifice and radical love into an offensive sword of power and force.* The church moved from being a religion of the meek to being a religion of the mighty.

From the time of Constantine through the Middle Ages and into the modern era, kings, emperors, prime ministers, and presidents have used the blessing of the church to establish and maintain their policies. Church and state have worked together to maintain their power base and serve their common interests. This union reached its zenith during the Middle Ages when popes actually fielded armies and led them into battle! Thomas Merton understood this paradigm shift:

> But the fact remains that a warring and warlike Christendom has never been able to preach the Gospel of charity and peace with

full conviction or full success. As Cardinal Newman so rightly said, the greatest victories of the Church were all won before Constantine, in the days when there were no Christian armies and when the true Christian soldier was the martyr, whose witness to Christ was nonviolent. It was the martyrs who conquered Rome for Christ with a conquest that has been stable for twenty centuries. How long were the crusaders able to hold Jerusalem?[18]

Under Constantine, civil punishment followed religious offenses: Severe penalties against the Donatists were carried out,[19] and all Arian books were ordered to be burned.[20] Further, those who refused to have these "heretical" books destroyed were themselves given the death penalty! The persecutions were not limited to Christian heretics. Beginning at this time, followers of other faiths, especially Jews and later Muslims, were sought out and punished. The Crusades, the Inquisition, the pogroms of Eastern Europe, the Holocaust, and the conquest, colonization, and conversion of the Americas, Africa, and India are the worst examples of Christianity's use of the sword to spread its message and mission.

The Crusades

The Crusades, a series of nine military expeditions that lasted several centuries, represent one of the Christian church's darkest hours. The Crusades were launched from a combination of religious, political, economic, and social reasons and their impact is still felt today. The First Crusade (1096–1099) was called by Pope Urban II to take back the Holy Land and establish a Christian government in Jerusalem. The pope promised indulgences (the forgiveness of penalties from sins committed during a church member's lifetime) to those who participated, thereby linking military service to religious rewards.

---

[18] Thomas Merton, *Peace in the Post-Christian Era* (Maryknoll, NY: Orbis, 2004), 129.

[19] The Donatists were a schismatic group that appeared in North Africa and named for one of their leaders, Donatus. Simply stated, the Donatists thought that many of the leaders of the church were corrupt and impure. They also had a distinctive worship style, emphasizing mystical union of the righteous inspired by the Holy Spirit and instructed by the Bible. For more information see Maureen A. Tilley, *The Bible in Christian North Africa: The Donatist World* (Minneapolis: Fortress, 1997).

[20] The Arians were another schismatic group, under the teaching of Arius, who maintained that Jesus was not necessarily eternal. In fact, the beliefs of the Arians were one of the leading causes of the Council of Nicea and were dealt with in the Nicene Creed with the word homoousios, meaning "of the same substance" or "of one being." For more information see J. N. D. Kelly, *Early Christian Doctrines* (Princeton, Princeton University Press, 1978).

The First Crusade was carried out by a poorly organized mob that, before setting out from Europe, turned its wrath and fury on Jews. They burned synagogues, destroyed Jewish homes, and killed thousands before departing for the "Holy Land." Along the way, the crusading army randomly fought with many Christians through whose land they traveled and, after capturing Jerusalem in December 1099, slaughtered some 40,000 persons who had surrendered. This massacre was a total annihilation of all the citizens of Jerusalem—the Jews, Muslims, and Christians who had lived peacefully together for centuries. Reports indicate that the blood from the slaughtered ran in the streets like rivers and crusaders made their way to give thanks to God for the victory after wading waist deep through pools of blood.

The Christians held Jerusalem for approximately one hundred years until its conquest under the leadership of Saladin. After the Christians lost control of the Holy City, other crusades were launched to re-conquer it. Because of the internal conflict and tension between the European kingdoms, some of the crusades (such as the Fourth Crusade) never made it to the Holy Land and instead were diverted to the destruction of Christian cities, such as Constantinople. Death and destruction, sanctioned by the Church, is the legacy of the Crusades.

The Inquisition

The Inquisition was the official name given to Roman Catholic courts established to deal with heresies and heretics. In 1199 Pope Innocent III declared heresy was a *capital offense.* In 1220 the Dominicans took control of the Inquisition and immediately began purging the church of persons whose theology deviated from the accepted orthodoxy. In so doing, the church executed members of its own clergy and laity. In 1252 Pope Innocent IV authorized the use of torture upon those accused of heresy.

The Inquisition reached its nadir with the infamous Spanish Inquisition, aimed primarily to convert Jews and Muslims, witches, and pagans of Spain in the late fifteenth early sixteenth centuries. Spain's first grand inquisitor, Dominican Tomas de Torquemada (1483–1498) imprisoned a hundred thousand persons and executed thousands. The church, acting in partnership with the state, seized the victims' properties and announced during public worship services the judgments and punishments on those found guilty.

Pope Paul III created the Holy Office of Inquisition to fight theologically and physically against the Protestant Reformation. Excommunication and executions were common. War broke out between Roman Catholic Christians and their Protestant brothers. The worst periods were under the leadership of

Popes Paul IV (1555–1559) and Pius V (1566–1572). The Inquisition existed until 1834 when it was finally discontinued, but was revived in 1908 and given the new name of the Congregation for the Doctrine of the Faith. Mercifully, this newer organization does not use torture and execution as the means of defining orthodoxy, although excommunication is still practiced.

Anti-Semitism

Anti-Semitism has been a trademark of Christianity since the earliest days of the church. Roman Catholic theologian Hans Küng has said of the two thousand years of tension between Christianity and Judaism: "It is precisely between those closest related that the bitterest rivalries will exist." The Gospels were written thirty to seventy years after the death of Jesus during a time when the church was trying to define itself as a distinct entity from Judaism. Are the Gospels anti-Semitic? This is a complicated question that has been debated in many books. I would argue there are negative, stereotypical statements made in the Gospels that have contributed throughout the centuries to the way Jews have been portrayed by the church. "Christ killers" is an appalling name that has been given to the Jewish people, and the hatred Christians have fostered toward their Jewish brothers and sisters have led to numerous acts of violence.

Anti-Semitism reached its height with the Holocaust under Nazi Germany—a state-sponsored program designed to eliminate the entire Jewish population of Europe. In many cases, the church and theologians supported Hitler's programs and policies, including the attempt to exterminate the Jews. In his book *Theologians under Hitler,* Robert Ericksen documents the support given to the Nazi government and anti-Semitic propaganda by three great German theologians: Gerhard Kittel, Emanuel Hirsch, and Paul Althaus.[21] These three, and many others, provided the intellectual and theological arguments for Hitler's policies. A movie of the same title shows actual footage of German bishops proudly offering the Nazi salute and enthusiastically shaking Hitler's hand. The churches and Christian leaders who supported the ideas and plans of the Nazis stands "as the climax of Christendom's shame," says Baylor theologian Michael Hanby.[22]

---

[21] Robert Ericksen, *Theologians under Hitler* (New Haven, CT: Yale University Press, 1985). The movie version was released in 2006.

[22] Quoted in Jason Byassee, "Theologians and Nazis," *Christian Century,* May 30, 2006, 11.

Colonization and Evangelism

Africans tell a short parable that describes their impression of the colonization of their continent:

> When the white men arrived on our shores, they held a gun in one hand and a Bible in the other. They invited us to close our eyes and join them for a prayer. We did so. When the prayer was over and we opened our eyes, we were holding their Bible and they were holding our land. And they were still holding on to the gun.

Matungi, an East Congo villager, wrote:

> I have tried hard to understand the white man and his ways, but I can only see harm. What happiness have they brought us? They have given us a road we did not need, a road that brings more and more foreigners and enemies into our midst, causing trouble, making our women unclean, forcing us to a way of life that is not ours, planting crops that we do not want, doing slave's work. At least the BaNgwana left us our beliefs, but the white man even wants to steal these from us. He sends us missions to destroy our belief and to teach our children to recite fine-sounding words; but they are words we believe in anyway, most of them. And we live according to our beliefs, which is more than the white man does.[23]

North and South America, Africa, India, and the islands of the South Pacific were conquered and settled by many who were Christians, some of whom were escaping religious persecution in their homelands. Ironically, once again, many of these same Europeans who fled their homelands to pursue religious freedom now became the persecutors of those whose land they descended upon. The native inhabitants of these lands were labeled as pagans, and systematic campaigns of conversion and/or annihilation were begun. Encounters with native populations were generally hostile, and it was

---

[23] Colin Turnbull, *The Lonely African* (New York: Simon & Schuster, 1962), back cover.

common for the natives to be given the choice of conversion to Christianity or death by the sword. Diseases the Europeans brought with them devastated the native populations, whose people had not been exposed to these diseases prior to contact with the Europeans.[24] There are documented cases of the Christian European settlers purposely giving to the Native Americans clothing, rugs, or other items they believed contained lethal diseases in the hopes of further reducing the native population.

The Church as a Peacemaking Body

But this chapter is not all about the evil committed in the name of Jesus Christ through the centuries. Many sincere and genuine efforts have been made through the years to build God's peaceful kingdom. As we have seen, the church grew dramatically in the first three centuries through its mission and outreach. Throughout the centuries, individuals and the church itself have made tremendous sacrifices in the name of Jesus Christ. Additionally, the church has from time to time taken stands against war and the use of force. This chapter now turns again to times, places, and people who have attempted to build Jesus' vision of the kingdom of God through words and deeds of love and grace, mercy and peace.

There is no evidence that in the first two centuries following Jesus' death any Christians were involved in military service. There are no known Christian writers who approved of Christian participation in warfare from the time of Jesus' death until at least the year 313. In fact, all who wrote on this subject disapproved of the idea of Christians serving as soldiers. However, a profound change took place in the years following the Edict of Milan (313 CE) allowing Christians to serve in the military. By 416 this shift was so complete a soldier had to be a Christian to serve in the Roman army.

The first known Christian conscientious objector to military service was a Roman centurion named Marcellus. Marcellus was a soldier who then converted to Christianity. After his conversion, he refused to fight. He was brought before the emperor and forced to choose whether he would fight for Rome or not. He said these words: "I cannot inflict wounds on another human being. I serve only Jesus Christ." Because of his beliefs and conviction, he was executed.

---

[24] In *Guns, Germs, and Steel* (New York: Norton, 1997), Jared Diamond extensively documents how those from Eurasia were able to conquer and exploit the other areas of the world.

There have been many conscientious objectors since Marcellus, including one of my Christian heroes, Jesse Lee. Jesse Lee was born in Virginia and raised a Methodist. As a young man he became an active lay speaker. In 1778 he was drafted by the Continental Army and required to report to camp. Upon arriving, Lee made it clear that as a Christian he would not fight. His commanding officer argued and debated with Lee to no avail, finally trying to force the stubborn young man into fighting by leaning a gun against him. Lee reports that he merely stepped aside and allowed the gun to fall harmlessly to the ground, an action that visibly angered his commanding officer enough to have Lee arrested and thrown into prison. But Lee was undaunted and began singing and preaching from his small cell. After two days he and the commanding officer worked out a compromise in which Lee agreed to drive the ambulance wagon and tend to the wounded. Lee performed these tasks for two months until the fighting left that area of the country. Lee was released from his service and, as he wrote in his journal years later, was nearly as happy as his captain that his service was completed.

At the same time the Crusades were taking place, peace movements were also spreading throughout Europe, including one called the "Great Alleluia" that involved some 400,000 persons in Northern Italy in the twelfth century. Nearly a century later a second peace movement erupted called "Bianchi," in which over 200,000 persons marched on Rome. These events, organized by the local clergy and church members, were designed to demonstrate the church of Jesus Christ was first and foremost a church of peace.

Special, holy individuals have come and gone throughout church history, such as Mother Teresa of Calcutta. Her faith, piety, and devotion to the least, the last, and the lost earned her fame and recognition in life, and the process toward her canonization as a saint has already begun. I myself can think of hundreds of church members, colleagues, friends, and associates who could be lifted up as advocates for peace. Former president Jimmy Carter is an example of a man of faith who has devoted his life to peace, and in 2002 the Norwegian Nobel Committee recognized his efforts with its highest award.

Surprisingly, there is no patron saint of peace in the Roman Catholic Church. While there have been thousands of witnesses to the life, preaching, and teaching of the Prince of Peace, my nomination for the patron saint of peace would be Francis of Assisi. Francis gave up a life of wealth, power, and status to follow his call to serve Jesus Christ. He established the Franciscan Order and became the patron saint of animals, birds, and the environment. He is also recognized by the church as a great promoter of peace, simplicity, and harmony. His name has been associated with the following prayer,[25] which has always been one of my favorites:

PAX POTIOR BELLO (Peace is more powerful than war)

Lord, make me an instrument of Your peace!

Where there is hatred, let me sow love;

Where there is injury, pardon;

Where there is doubt, faith;

Where there is despair, hope;

Where there is darkness, light;

Where there is sadness, joy.

O Divine Master, grant that I may not so much seek to be consoled, as to console;

To be understood as to understand;

To be loved as to love;

For it is in giving that we receive;

It is in pardoning that we are pardoned;

And it is in dying that we are born to eternal life.

The Future

Walt Disney had a vision—a theme park centered on his Disney characters where families could vacation in a safe, clean, wholesome atmosphere. The Walt Disney Company, who through the years has overseen the expansion and growth of Disney World with an eye toward Walt's vision, has faithfully maintained that vision. New hotels, restaurants, rides and exhibitions are continually being added—all based around Disney's incredible dream.

Jesus Christ also had a vision—a revelation of God's kingdom here on earth, built with love, grace, mercy, and peace. From time to time, the church has been faithful to that vision. Equally, however, there have been times of sin and error, when the church has acted in concert with the forces of darkness to

---

[25] Recent scholars and theologians have questioned Francis's authorship of this prayer. Whether or not Francis wrote it, however, it does capture the spirit of his ministry of peace.

bring about pain and suffering. During these times, the church has failed to act faithfully to the vision of its leader.

Martin Luther King Jr. was concerned about the role of the church in his day. After his arrest in Birmingham for participating in a march that had been declared illegal, King wrote a letter from his jail cell in response to a published letter from members of the Birmingham clergy who were critical of his presence and activities in their city. The following excerpt from this letter, dated April 16, 1963, comes toward the end:

> There was a time when the church was very powerful—in the time when the early Christians rejoiced at being deemed worthy to suffer for what they believed. In those days the church was not merely a thermometer that recorded the ideas and principles of popular opinion; it was a thermostat that transformed the mores of society. Whenever the early Christians entered a town, the people in power became disturbed and immediately sought to convict the Christians for being "disturbers of the peace" and "outside agitators." But the Christians pressed on, in the conviction that they were "a colony of heaven," called to obey God rather than man. Small in number, they were big in commitment. They were too God-intoxicated to be "astronomically intimidated." By their effort and example they brought an end to such ancient evils as infanticide and gladiatorial contests.
>
> Things are different now. So often the contemporary church is a weak, ineffectual voice with an uncertain sound. So often it is an archdefender of the status quo. Far from being disturbed by the presence of the church, the power structure of the average community is consoled by the church's silent—and often even vocal—sanction of things as they are.
>
> But the judgment of God is upon the church as never before. If today's church does not recapture the sacrificial spirit of the early church, it will lose its authenticity, forfeit the loyalty of millions, and be dismissed as an irrelevant social club with no meaning for the twentieth century.

Like King in his day, we must recapture and recommit ourselves to the original vision of Jesus Christ. Returning to his love, grace, mercy, and peace is the only real hope for the church and the greatest prospect the world has for moving forward in this day. To do so, we must return to the blueprints of our architect, the Prince of Peace, and build with his plan in mind. We need to return to the Scriptures constantly as the source of that vision, and make them applicable to the modern world.

Chapter 4

Interpreting the Scriptures

Serious and Responsible Biblical Study

I believe the Bible as it is.

—W. J. Bryan

The Bible is true, and some of it happened.

—Roman Catholic priest

In *Romeo and Juliet,* William Shakespeare pens these words for his star-struck lover, Romeo:

> But, soft, what light through yonder window breaks?
>
> It is the east, and Juliet is the sun. (Act 2, scene 2, lines 2–3)

What is the image Shakespeare wants his audience to understand in this passage? Is Romeo telling us Juliet, his love, is a large, gaseous ball of fire? That she is extremely distant from him, at a range of approximately 90 million miles? That she burns with an external temperature of 6,000° C, with an inner fire estimated at 15,000° C? That approximately 98 percent of the mass in the entire solar system is within her being and 1.3 million earths could fit inside her interior? That too much exposure to her could lead to significant third-degree burns and she is absent 50 percent of the time?

The answer to these questions is, of course, no. What Shakespeare is telling us is when you find your soul mate, when you find that true and special person, he or she appears to you as a bright light, the center of your existence, the warmth that provides life with meaning. Juliet offers Romeo life-sustaining qualities. Just as humans cannot exist without the life-giving properties of the sun, so Romeo cannot live without Juliet. *Shakespeare is using the sun as a metaphor for Romeo's love of Juliet.*

The tale of Romeo and Juliet is fiction. Yet the story of Romeo and Juliet is true. If you want to understand what true love is, if you want to know what people experience when they find their soul mates, if you want to appreciate the lengths human beings will go through to be with a loved one, read *Romeo and Juliet.* It is an inspired work about love and grace in our fallen world.

The tragedy of Romeo and Juliet is also true in its depiction of humanity's fall from grace. If you want to understand intolerance, hatred, and narrow-minded, fanatical prejudice, read Shakespeare's portrayal of the Montagues and Capulets. Caught up in their petty personal conflict, they retreat to an unholy and ignorant motto: "It is us against them." Only Romeo and Juliet can see the fundamental truth: they are in love with each other, and the conflict created by their families cannot keep them apart.

Shakespeare, like all great literary masters, used a variety of writing techniques to capture the essence of human nature. Students of his works find metaphors, allegories, symbolism, and similes liberally sprinkled throughout his writings. Interestingly, *Romeo and Juliet* is so powerful and moving that "in Shakespeare's own time the story passed from legend into 'history,' and the events were stated to have actually occurred in Verona in the first years of the fourteenth century."[26]

I wonder what Shakespeare thought about these contemporaries, men and women who actually believed his plays to be historically true narratives. Would he have been amused? Astonished? Nearly four hundred years after his death Shakespeare's literary works are still read and studied. And even though we know and acknowledge his works are fiction, scholars nevertheless argue over the proper interpretation and meaning of a particular passage, scene, act, or play.

Just as literary scholars debate and discuss the proper interpretation of Shakespeare's works, so too do we in the church spend a great deal of time discussing how the Bible should be read and interpreted. Nearly two thousand years after the last books of the New Testament were written and the canon closed, there are those who believe all of the stories and events of the Bible actually took place. Furthermore, those who read the Bible literally have developed an exclusive and narrow understanding of God's kingdom. In many instances, their literal reading of specific verses, chapters, or books has led to hatred and prejudice. If you believe, for instance, that God stopped the sun from setting so that Joshua and the children of Israel could have more daylight to slaughter the Amorites at Gibeon (Joshua 10), you are more likely to believe God takes sides in partisan conflicts and even provides aid and support to win military victories.

There is an intense battle being waged within Christianity over how the Bible is to be interpreted. On one side are these literalists, those who read every word of the Bible as the inerrant, infallible word of God. On the other side are those who read it through the lens of modern scholarship, who understand the Bible through the use of symbols, metaphors, and allegories. This debate goes to the heart of what it means to be a Christian; it defines who we are. Our entire theology depends upon which side of this great chasm we sit. Our theological perspective then goes on to shape our outlook on life, from politics, to domestic and foreign policy, opinions on science, evolution, global warming, the rapture, global population planning, stem cell research, the justification of war, whether or not there is an exclusive truth and pathway to God, and so forth.

Christianity is centered in its sacred Scriptures; the Bible is at the heart of our tradition. In this chapter we will look at how the literalist-fundamentalists have developed and grown within Christianity, Judaism, and Islam through the years, and why their emergence and expansion during the twentieth century presents a great threat to world peace and security. Above

---

[26] *The Complete Works of William Shakespeare* (Boston: Houghton Mifflin, 1906), 834.

all else, this chapter will encourage Christians to read the Bible with an eye toward love, grace, mercy, and peace as the divine message of Jesus' life and teaching.

The Historic Bible

The Bible comes to Christians in two parts: the Old Testament and the New Testament. There are a total of 67 books in the Bible; in fact, the word "Bible" is derived from the Greek word *biblia,* meaning "books." This is the same root we use in our word "bibliography." The Old Testament contains more books (39) than the New Testament (27), and the Old Testament encompasses approximately 75 percent of the total Bible. Most of the Old Testament was written in Hebrew, but there are also brief sections of the Old Testament written in Aramaic, a language related to Hebrew. The New Testament was written in Greek.

Ancient Texts

There is no universally accepted and absolute text of the Old Testament in Hebrew; likewise, there is no universally accepted and absolute text of the New Testament in Greek. There are different versions of the ancient books that vary, one from the other, in words, sentences, paragraphs, and chapters. The original letters of Paul, the handwritten documents of the Gospel writers, and the earliest copies of the other books of the Old and New Testaments no longer exist. What we have are copies of the originals and, in most cases, copies of the copies.

Often sentences, paragraphs, and chapters found in the existing copies of the originals are identical to each other; other times, there are variations and discrepancies. How these differences came to be is unknown. Scholars theorize that simple human error may have played a role. In other places, a scribe, assigned the task of copying a scroll, may have injected his own thoughts, opinions, and theological perspectives into the new copy, thus altering the original and leaving us with two versions of the same book.

The existence of conflicting versions of the "original" texts in Hebrew and Greek presents complications for biblical translators. When scholars gather to translate the Bible into English, they must first decide which of the ancient texts to use as the basis of their work. Through the centuries, a general consensus has emerged over which ancient texts are the most authentic and authoritative, although this consensus is somewhat arbitrary and not universally accepted. Biblical translators with integrity include in their footnotes or commentaries how and why they chose certain texts over others, and even include in their footnotes alternative verses when applicable.

English Bibles

There are nearly seven thousand English-language editions of the Bible available today,[27] ranging from the King James Version (KJV) to the translation used most often by mainline Protestant congregations, the New Revised Standard Version (NRSV). The KJV was the first "authorized" and widely produced English translation of the Bible. Published in 1611, it is the work of thirty-seven scholars whom King James assembled to produce an English Bible. Many English-speaking Christians have memorized verses or even whole passages from the King James Bible, and it has held up extremely well after four centuries of use. However, the language used in the KJV, like the language of Shakespeare, is somewhat dated and is difficult at times to understand. The NRSV was published in 1991; it is an updated version of the Revised Standard Version (RSV), which was completed in 1971. These translations corrected many of the errors of the KJV and reduce the use of words such as "thee" and "thou."

When we speak of the Bible, we need to recognize that for those limited to the English language, every word has already been translated from one ancient language into English. Furthermore, with conflicting texts in the original language it becomes difficult at times to know for certain what the writer's original words and intentions were.

The Literalists

The perspective of those Christians who believe in the words of the Bible exactly as they appear can be summarized as "God wrote it; I believe it!" These literalists come in two primary groups: brief history literalists and long history literalists.

Brief History Literalists

The brief history literalists believe in the words of the Bible precisely as they are written. For example, they believe the universe and all within it were created in six twenty-four-hour days and then God rested on the seventh day, exactly as described in Genesis 1. They believe the world is less than ten thousand years old, based on adding the collective ages given in the Bible of various people, from Adam and Eve through Jesus and into the twenty-first century. They maintain humans lived at the same time as the dinosaurs and other ancient animals and these animals became extinct during the flood in Noah's

---

[27] Mark A. Noll, *The Old Religion in a New World* (Grand Rapids: Eerdmans, 2002), 162.

time. The flood accounts for the finding of fossils throughout the world: the floodwaters compressed the bones of these animals and turned them into fossils, leaving them for us to find today.

Source: the Northwest Creation Network.

When confronted with scientific evidence supporting the earth's age of approximately five billion years, brief history literalists deny these claims outright. Their explanation for the results of carbon and radioactive dating and other scientific tests pointing to a universe billions of years old is that Satan created these illusions to steer people away from the biblical truth. They reject Darwinian evolution and other scientific theories challenging their understanding of the universe.

To support their beliefs, the brief history literalists point to God's ability to raise Jesus Christ from the tomb. If God was able to raise Jesus Christ from the dead, then God was certainly able to create the world in six days.

Long History Literalists

The long history literalists also believe in the creation of the world in exactly the order and pattern described in the book of Genesis, but with the understanding a day and night might have been millions or even billions of years. They reject evolution or other scientific theories about the creation of the world, and accept the timeline as outlined in Genesis, even if these events took place over many years: God created the heavens and the earth, separated the light from the darkness, the earth from the sky, and water from the land. God created the fish of the seas, the birds of the air, and then the animals on the land, leading up to the creation of humanity through Adam and Eve. They accept scientific evidence indicating the world may be billions of years old while arguing, in God's eyes, it may have counted as six days.

Both kinds of literalists proclaim if one does not accept the Bible as literally true—if, for example, one doubts the existence of Adam and Eve, or Noah's ability to gather two of every kind of animal on the planet and kept them fed for the duration of the flood—then where does one draw the line? At this point one enters the "slippery slope" where disbelief in one part of the Bible leads to doubt in other areas and, eventually, in all parts of the Bible.

They reason you must therefore accept all of the biblical stories as true and exactly as written.

There Have Always Been Literalists

Literalists are not a new phenomenon. From the time of ancient Israel, through the development of the early church and into the Middle Ages, Jews and Christians had no reason to think that the histories and stories of the Bible were anything but factual. They were aware of the conflicts within the Bible—different accounts of the same event, contrasting stories and inconsistencies within a biblical book and between different books—but they accepted these divergent passages without a great deal of critical evaluation.

The Middle Ages gave way to the Renaissance and subsequently to the Age of Reason. As inquisitive minds began to awaken, they asked pressing questions regarding the church, the Bible, Christianity, and God. New theories, such as the central position in our solar system of the sun, and Darwin's theory of evolution, challenged and threatened traditionally accepted Christian theology. As humanity continued to unlock the mysteries of our wonderful and complex world, these findings tended to clash with the biblical framework.

Additionally, modernity and the Industrial Revolution brought with them new values, new mores, new cultural understandings, and a changing civilization. Coupled with the dramatic advances in science, many thought the church was losing the influence and control it had over its members, its place in society, and its influence within nations and on an international scale. Many feared what would happen to the church in the future.

It was under these general circumstances the world was introduced to fundamentalism.

The Rise of Fundamentalism

The rise of the fundamentalists within many of the world's religions is one of the most dangerous developments to have taken place during the twentieth century. As the number of persons who identified themselves as fundamentalists grew, so did their power and influence, both within their religion and in secular society as well.[28]

---

[28] There is a difference between literalists and fundamentalists. Literalists are those who believe the words of the Bible are true exactly as written. Fundamentalists, always literalists, maintain that there are certain doctrines within their faith that must be accepted as essentially true.

Fundamentalism became a force in Christianity beginning with a series of twelve booklets on Christian theology published and mailed to over three million people from 1910 to 1915 by Lyman and Milton Stewart, wealthy California businessmen. Titled *The Fundamentals,* the pamphlets defined positions on five "fundamental truths" from the Stewarts' perspective:

1. The inerrancy of the Bible

2. The divinity of Jesus Christ

3. The virgin birth

4. The substitutionary theory of the Atonement

5. The physical reality of Jesus' miracles and his physical resurrection

While these five principles have defined Christian fundamentalism, the emphasis has always been on the inerrancy of the Bible. In Christianity, fundamentalists are "born again" and "Bible-believing" Protestants, as opposed to "mainline," "liberal," "progressive" Protestants. Christian fundamentalists generally look upon Christians who are not literalists with the same condemnation they have for atheists, agnostics, or those who practice other faiths. They are a reactionary movement seeking to protect their religion against the values, principles, and morals of the modern world.

Hand in hand with the dramatic rise in fundamentalism within Christianity has been an increase in the number of Muslims and Jews who are also often called "fundamentalists." By definition, all Muslims believe in the "literal" interpretation of the Qur'an, which they maintain is the direct speech of God to his people. Therefore, the term "Islamic fundamentalist" does not quite fit the Muslim worldview. According to Muslim scholar Reza Aslan, "'Islamic fundamentalism' . . . refers to the radically ultraconservative and puritanical ideology most clearly represented in the Muslim world by Wahhabism."[29] It is therefore with this understanding that I use "Islamic fundamentalist" to describe the fanatical Muslims who, under extreme conditions, become committed to terrorist activities, including suicide bombings.

Within Judaism, the Haredi ("Torah-true") Jews represent "fundamentalism." Haredi Jews look at Reform and Conservative Jews with contempt, thinking they ought to know better what the Torah says about being

---

[29] Reza Aslan, *No God but God* (New York: Random House, 2005), 242. Wahhabism is the term used to describe a sect of Sunni Islam that is based on the teachings of Muhammad ibn

observant Jews. They seek to be pure Jews by observing *all* of the laws and commandments of the Torah to the best of their ability, believing this is the correct path to God.

The fundamentalists within each of these faith traditions stress exclusive knowledge and access to God and are intolerant of other perspectives. Their prejudice toward those with different theologies often leads to uncompromising fanaticism and extremist activities, committed, of course, in the name of God. *The emergence of these exclusive, inflexible movements within Judaism, Christianity, and Islam is a recipe for "the perfect storm." Militant Christians, Muslims, and Jews prepared to kill and die for their God is a disaster waiting to happen.*

The Threat of Fundamentalists

In his book *When Religion Becomes Evil,* Charles Kimball identifies "five warning signs" of fundamentalism.[30] He claims when one or more of these qualities are present within a religion, it can become evil and destructive:

1. *Absolute truth claims.* Fundamentalists maintain that they, and only they, know the will of God. Since they know God's will, they believe it is their right and duty to impose their will on others. Derogatory proclamations about other faith traditions or even those within their religion that disagree with them are common, as is the discounting of other sacred texts.

2. The fostering of *blind obedience* to those leading their faith. Cults and other organizations that demand absolute compliance, conformity, and submission are a sure sign of corrupt religion. Often formed around a charismatic leader who claims to understand the absolute truth and know the will of God, no dissent is tolerated within such groups.

3. An emphasis on *establishing the "ideal" time,* that is, the belief that an imminent cataclysm or the end times are fast approaching. One

Abd Wahhab (1703-1792). They accept the Qur'an and hadith as fundamental texts, and see their role to restore Islam back to its original nature that has been corrupted due to innovation, heresies and idolatry.

[30] Charles Kimball, *When Religion Becomes Evil: Five Warning Signs* (San Francisco: HarperSanFrancisco, 2002).

can now visit a Web site (www.raptureready.com) to check on the top indicators signaling the arrival of the Christian rapture! Related subjects include Armageddon, the second coming of Christ, and the arrival of the Antichrist.

4. *The ends justify any means.* Religious fundamentalists will accept war, murder, assassination, and the slaughter of innocents as collateral damage if they believe God's plan is being carried out. Using the ends to justify the means stands in stark contrast to the basic, underlying foundation of the world's great religions—the requirement to love God and love your neighbor as yourself.

5. *Declaring holy war.* Conflicts between religions are as old as religion itself, but when one or both sides declare holy war, religion has turned a corner and become evil. As Kimball writes, "This much is crystal clear: holy war is not holy."[31] The Crusades are Christianity's worst expression of declaring holy war, and the identification of *jihad* in Islam with killing others is another manifestation of religion becoming evil.

How do fundamentalists defend such heinous activities? God is served through actions of grace and mercy, kindness and gentleness. Christian fundamentalists use the Bible as a weapon to intimidate and force compliance with their agenda. Shakespeare condemned such use of the Scriptures in the words of Antonio from *The Merchant of Venice:*

Mark you this, Bassanio,

The devil can cite Scripture for his purpose.

An evil soul producing holy witness

Is like a villain with a smiling cheek,

A goodly apple rotten at the heart.

O, what a goodly outside falsehood hath! (Act 1, scene 3, lines 94–99)

---

[31] Kimball, *When Religion Becomes Evil,* 182.

The citing of Scripture to support one's rationale for acts of war, terror, or murder is a common strategy among Jews, Christians, and Muslims and has been for so long that we now consider it to be routine and normal. National leaders turn to the clergy to provide religious assurance that their military actions are justified and in accordance with God's will, and the clergy turn to selected passages from the sacred texts to validate and rationalize the making of war in God's name.

Literalist and the Book of Revelation

One of the primary texts cited by Christian clergy from the New Testament is the book of Revelation, also known as the Apocalypse of John. Written late in the first century, it presents a sensational, although often bewildering, climax to the New Testament. It has been read, studied, and interpreted from many different angles, including the literalist, which sees it as the prophecy of the end of time. Those who read Revelation this way see in the future a physical, violent war (culminating in the battle of Armageddon), the existence of the Antichrist (whose number is 666) and the triumphant return to earth of Jesus Christ (following the rapture) leading his army to military victory. The literalists look at the restoration of Israel and return of the Jews to the Holy Land as one of the key steps in this process; they believe the Jewish temple will soon be rebuilt, with the return of the royal priesthood and temple sacrifices to follow. These events will usher in the millennium, a thousand-year period of time when Christ will reign in peace.

Almost predictably, this is the plot line of the *Left Behind* series of books by Tim LaHaye and Jerry Jenkins, which Jerry Falwell has called the most influential books since the Bible. Together these books have sold over sixty million copies. Like *The Da Vinci Code,* the *Left Behind* series is fiction; unlike *The Da Vinci Code,* it has received widespread support and encouragement from the literalist-fundamentalists in our nation. Readers discover that the Antichrist is alive today and living in the new Babylon, located outside of modern Baghdad. The Antichrist consolidates global power through the United Nations and has as his primary political ally a French politician.

It has been said that politics creates strange bedfellows. So too does religion. Fundamentalist Jews have developed an unholy alliance with fundamentalist Christians, who are each looking to rebuild the temple in Jerusalem for their own purposes. Fundamentalist Jews know there are 613 laws in the Torah, of which approximately 40 percent concern themselves with the temple. They believe God wants the temple practices to resume and that the Messiah will not arrive on earth until the temple is rebuilt. Fundamentalist

Christians believe the rebuilding of the temple is one of the steps in the process of Christ's second coming.

There is a big problem with this unholy alliance, however: the temple cannot be built because two Muslim buildings, the Dome of the Rock and al-Aqsa Mosque, now occupy the space where the temple is to be built. To deal with this inconvenience, a solution has been found: blow up the Muslim buildings. Incredibly, there have been twelve attempts to blow up the Dome of the Rock and al-Aqsa Mosque, or to kill Muslim worshippers nearby. The documentary *Shrine under Siege* depicts the many Christian and Jewish groups actively working, both collaboratively and independently, to destroy these holy sites.[32] In her book of the same title, *Shrine under Siege,* Grace Halsell reviews the same territory covered in the film but goes further by anticipating what the reaction of the billion Muslims worldwide might be if these sites were destroyed. Anticipating World War III, this would be a combined Pearl Harbor and 9/11 event to spark hostilities.

It is not surprising, but still grossly disturbing, to learn that a great majority (87 percent) of the Christian right supported the president's decision to go to war with Iraq.[33] Their literal reading of the book of Revelation, combined with an acceptance as truth of the fictional narrative from the *Left Behind* novels, convinced them the war in Iraq was part of the great battle of good versus evil. The United States and Christianity, of course, will fight on the side of God, and Iraq and the Muslims, obviously, on the side of Satan. The literalist-fundamentalists' support of this war, along with their ongoing support for the State of Israel (and even radical attempts to rebuild the temple) are done in the hope they will bring to fruition the events described in Revelation and usher in the reign of God.

The acceptance of war as a vehicle to build God's kingdom is in direct opposition to the teachings of most of the New Testament and an elephant running unchecked through the Christian village. Framing the current war in terms of good versus evil is the strategy of all sides; this is the line of defense Jews, Christians, and Muslims all default back to. Selectively using scriptural texts to exegetically prove God is on your side and will lead you to victory is simple ignorance. It is imperative for those with the voice of peace and tolerance, of love and acceptance, of grace and mercy to speak loudly so that their words and message may be heard.

---

[32] Directed by Ilan Ziv and released in 1985, the forty-two-minute video is available for rent or purchase at http://www.frif.com/cat97/p-s/shrine_u.html.

[33] Charles Marsh, "Wayward Christian Soldiers," *New York Times,* January 20, 2006, op-ed page,

My Journey

Literal interpretation of the Bible is not the only path available for Christians to travel. Progressive, contemporary biblical scholarship offers students a rewarding and rich perspective that is honest and rational. It opens up for the biblical student a whole new dimension for understanding the truth and invites a deeper appreciation of the biblical text and the message its writers were attempting to convey. The apostle Paul's words to the Corinthians can guide us in our reading of the Bible: "When I was a child, I spoke like a child, I thought like a child, I reasoned like a child; when I became an adult, I put an end to childish ways" (1 Cor 13:11).

I grew up in the church. As a child, I loved being at church and often dragged my parents along. I strove for perfect attendance and collected pins each year for that achievement.[34] I learned the stories of the Bible and believed them as written. As I matured, I began questioning the authenticity of the biblical account. I began to wonder about the historical accuracy of the stories recorded in the Bible, which caused me to question my faith. After all, I thought, if the stories of the Bible do not describe accurate and factual events, how can I accept this religion?

Fortunately, I had a sensitive and grace-filled pastor who encouraged me to wrestle with my faith and these questions. He shared with me he himself did not accept the Bible as literally true but read it in a broader way, through the use of symbols, allegories, and metaphors. Through high school and college his assurances were enough and, despite the nagging doubts in the back of my mind, I responded to the call to ministry and enrolled in seminary.

In seminary, I learned others shared my concerns and biblical scholars had been wrestling with these same concerns for centuries. Reading the Bible through the lens of symbols, allegories, and metaphors did not mean the Bible was wrong and therefore could be discarded or disregarded as irrelevant. I learned reason and religion were not opposed to each other and Christians could honestly accept the world of modern science and their faith as compatible. These revelations, gained through years of study and prayer, were life changing. My love of the Bible continues to grow as it unfolds in new and surprising ways. Free from defending its historic accuracy, I now concentrate on its life-affirming, grace-filled message. It is indeed the Book of Life.

After three years at seminary I emerged with a growing confidence in the Bible as the heart of my faith. Although this is not primarily a book

---

[34] The truth is that these churches gave out "perfect attendance" pins for those whose attendance was at 90 percent or higher.

about methods of biblical interpretation, it is important to look at the different approaches to Bible study, since our beliefs are anchored in the sacred texts.

Contemporary Biblical Scholarship

In contrast to the literal approach to the Bible is the critical, literary approach. The need to study biblical texts from more than a literal approach can be seen by a simple reading of the following:

He shall judge between the nations,

and shall arbitrate for many peoples;

they shall beat their swords into plowshares,

and their spears into pruning hooks;

nation shall not lift up sword against nation,

neither shall they learn war any more. (Isa 2:4; Mic 4:3)

Proclaim this among the nations:

Prepare war,

stir up the warriors.

Let all the soldiers draw near,

let them come up.

Beat your plowshares into swords,

and your pruning hooks into spears;

let the weakling say, "I am a warrior." (Joel 3:9–10)

The prophecy given in Isaiah is completely opposite the instructions given in Joel. Isaiah speaks of changing weapons of war into farming implements, while Joel, living in a different time under different circumstances, urges the opposite. If we are to believe the Bible exactly as written, what do we do with these texts? Should we prepare for peace, as Isaiah writes, or for war, as Joel says? What does God want us to do?

The commonsense response is different people living in different times under different circumstances wrote the Bible. The writer of Isaiah 2 was writing about a time of peace, when the nations of the world would put an end to war and live in harmony together. In contrast, the author of Joel lived during a time when he thought the best solution to the day's problems was to prepare for war. Different circumstances, different writers, different messages.

Critical, literary scholars attempt to find the historical setting of texts and determine the situation in which they were written before they search for God's will in them. As an example, let us look at how contemporary Christians interpret the following passage from Paul:

> Women should be silent in the churches. For they are not permitted to speak, but should be subordinate, as the law also says. If there is anything they desire to know, let them ask their husbands at home. For it is shameful for a woman to speak in church. (1 Cor 14:34–35)

If we were to accept these words as literally true, as being God's will because they appear in the Bible, we would obviously not continue to ordain women or even, presumably, to allow them to read Scripture or assist in worship. Indeed, there are a growing number of fundamentalist churches that do not allow women this right and privilege.

The prohibition of women speaking in church is not the only text from the Bible that many modern Christians struggle to understand and accept. Consider these verses:

> All who curse father or mother shall be put to death; having cursed father or mother, their blood is upon them. (Lev 20:9)

> If a man commits adultery with the wife of his neighbor, both the adulterer and the adulteress shall be put to death. (Lev 20:10)

> Six days shall work be done, but on the seventh day you shall have a holy sabbath of solemn rest to the LORD; whoever does any work on it shall be put to death. (Exod 35:2)

I do not know anyone who would advocate the literal interpretation of these three verses. While we may well agree children should not curse their parents, married individuals should not commit adultery, and work should not be performed on the Sabbath, the stated penalty for these offenses goes well beyond the crime and is virtually unenforceable. Most of us have not cursed our parents, most of us have not committed adultery, but most of us have, by almost any definition, worked on the Sabbath. How would you like to be executed for having worked on a Sunday? If we are strict fundamentalists, we need to accept all of Scripture as equally relevant and enforceable and not choose for ourselves which texts represent God's words and will and which ones do not.

What's more, even though the word "slave" appears in the Bible 153 times, not a single time is slavery forbidden or outlawed. Many biblical characters owned slaves, and Paul wrote about the proper treatment toward slaves in his letter to Philemon. Yet I can think of no human institution that is more despicable than the ownership of one human being by another.

The interpretation of the Bible is the issue that split churches in the United States in the 1840s and, indirectly, led to the Civil War. The Methodist Church split in 1844 following the election of a slave owning pastor who was elected to the position of bishop. Churches in the southern sections of the United States supported his election; churches in the northern sections of the United States did not. The Baptists split in 1845 over a similar issue. The Presbyterians split in two stages, in 1837 and 1857. Following the Methodist and Baptist splits, politicians Henry Clay and John C. Calhoun wondered how long the United States could stay united when its people were no longer willing to sit in the same pew.[35]

As northern clergy and church members increased their attacks on the institution of slavery, southern clergy and church members defended their position with biblical quotations, including the following:

When you buy a male Hebrew slave, he shall serve six years, but in the seventh he shall go out a free person, without debt. If he comes in single, he shall go out single; if he comes in married, then his wife shall go out with him. If his master gives him a wife and she bears him sons or daughters, the wife and her children shall be her master's and he shall go out alone. But if the slave declares, 'I love my master, my wife, and my children; I will not go out a free person,' then his master shall bring him before God. He shall be brought to the door or the doorpost; and his master shall pierce his ear with an awl; and he shall serve him for life.

---

[35] Randall M. Miller, Harry S. Stout, and Charles Reagan Wilson, *Religion and the American Civil War* (New York: Oxford University Press, 1998), 79.

When a man sells his daughter as a slave, she shall not go out as the male slaves do. If she does not please her master, who designated her for himself, then he shall let her be redeemed; he shall have no right to sell her to a foreign people, since he has dealt unfairly with her. . . .

When a slaveowner strikes a male or female slave with a rod and the slave dies immediately, the owner shall be punished. But if the slave survives for a day or two, there is no punishment; for the slave is the owner's property. (Exod 21:2–8, 20–21)

A disciple is not above the teacher, nor a slave above the master. (Matt 10:24)

Slaves, obey your earthly masters with fear and trembling, in singleness of heart, as you obey Christ; not only while being watched, and in order to please them, but as slaves of Christ, doing the will of God from the heart. (Eph 6:5–6)

Do we prepare for war, or peace? Should women be allowed to speak in church? Do we apply the death sentence to those who curse their parents, commit adultery, or work on the Sabbath? Should slavery be allowed? These and many other questions could be asked of the fundamentalists who read the words of the Bible as literally true.

Over 150 years ago, mainline churches in the United States split over whether the Bible was literally true in regard to one human being owning another. Southern bishops, clergy, and lay members defended the practice of owning slaves and turned to the Bible to advance their cause. Today many look to the Bible to address controversial topics, such as homosexuality, the most contentious and divisive issue before the church. Those with a literal interpretation see this issue in simple black and white terms: homosexuality is forbidden!

Taking a literalist perspective can lead to absurd ends, as depicted humorously in this open letter to Dr. Laura Schlessinger, a radio personality who quoted Leviticus 18:22 ("You shall not lie with a male as with a woman; it is an abomination") to defend her labeling of homosexuals as biological mistakes. The following letter demonstrates, with great sarcasm, the danger of taking the Bible literally. It is, unfortunately, anonymous.

Dear Dr. Laura,

Thank you for doing so much to educate people regarding God's Law. I have learned a great deal from your show, and I try to share that knowledge with as many people as I can. When someone tries to defend the homosexual lifestyle, for example, I simply remind him that Leviticus 18:22 clearly states it to be an abomination. End of debate.

I do need some advice from you, however, regarding some of the specific laws and how to best follow them.

a) When I burn a bull on the altar as a sacrifice, I know it creates a pleasing odor for the Lord (Lev 1:9). The problem is my neighbors. They claim the odor is not pleasing to them. Should I smite them?

b) I would like to sell my daughter into slavery, as sanctioned in Exodus 21:7. In this day and age, what do you think would be a fair price for her?

c) I know that I am allowed no contact with a woman while she is in her period of menstrual uncleanliness (Lev 15:19–24). The problem is, how do I tell? I have tried asking, but most women take offense.

d) Lev 25:44 states that I may indeed possess slaves, both male and female, provided they are purchased from neighboring nations. A friend of mine claims that this applies to Mexicans, but not Canadians. Can you clarify? Why can't I own Canadians?

e) I have a neighbor who insists on working on the Sabbath. Exodus 35:2 clearly states he should be put to death. Am I morally obligated to kill him myself?

f) A friend of mine feels that even though eating shellfish is an abomination (Lev 11:10), it is a lesser abomination than homosexuality. I don't agree. Can you settle this?

g) Lev 21:20 states that I may not approach the altar of God if I have a defect in my sight. I have to admit that I wear reading glasses. Does my vision have to be 20/20, or is there some wiggle room here?

h) Most of my male friends get their hair trimmed, including the hair around their temples, even though this is expressly forbidden by Lev 19:27. How should they die?

i) I know from Lev 11:6–8 that touching the skin of a dead pig makes me unclean, but may I still play football if I wear gloves?

j) My uncle has a farm. He violates Lev 19:19 by planting two different crops in the same field, as does his wife by wearing garments made of two different kinds of thread (cotton/polyester blend). He also tends to curse and blaspheme a lot. Is it really necessary that we go to all the trouble of getting the whole town together to stone them? (Lev 24:10–16) Couldn't we just burn them to death at a private family affair like we do with people who sleep with their in-laws? (Lev 20:14).

I know you have studied these things extensively, so I am confident you can help.

Thank you again for reminding us that God's word is eternal and unchanging.

Your devoted disciple and adoring fan.

Celebrating the Richness of the Bible

For centuries, Christian scholars have wrestled with the Bible, diligently working to hear God's voice through the writings of two historic communities: ancient Israel and the early Christian movement. Using modern, critical tools, these scholars have demonstrated the importance of understanding the practical, theological, and historical perspectives of the particular writer whose words are being studied. This approach allows us to harmonize faith and reason and allows us to understand the Bible on multiple levels. It is an honest and responsible method; it will help stem the tide of millions of Christians who have left the church in the past few decades because they cannot accept biblical literalism, and it will help us create a world of peace and justice for all of God's children by focusing on the building of God's kingdom instead of trying to trigger the second coming by starting World War III.

The Bible was written during five cultural periods: the Bronze Age, the Iron Age, the Persian Period, the Hellenistic Period, and the Roman Empire. Additionally, it was written in three languages and is filled with cultural idioms, etiologies, and local flavor. It contains parables, allegories, metaphors, and other symbols, in texts that offer tremendous challenges to those who dip into them. One of the reasons we read the Bible through the lens of symbolism is because so many parts of it fall so completely within the definition of symbolism. Who, for example, could dispute Jesus was talking metaphorically when he called his followers to be the "salt of the earth" (Matt 5:13)? It would be silly to argue otherwise. What about when John the Baptist calls Jesus the "lamb of God" (John 1:29, 36) or when John the evangelist uses images of bread and water to define Jesus? The Bible often tells us that God has hands, feet, ears, and eyes, but of course, God does not. The use of these symbols and metaphors helps us to understand our faith in rich and profound ways.

The Bible was written over a period of approximately a thousand years by an inspired group of historians, poets, artists, creative writers, prophets, theologians, and preachers. Each group used the literary skills it specialized in. Historians, for instance, used their understanding of history to document a particular event or time period. The two-part books of Samuel and Kings are the best examples we have of Old Testament history. The poets creatively used words to express beauty, passion, and inspiration; the Psalms are a tribute to the collective genius of their writers, and sections of poetry can be found throughout the Old New Testaments. Creative writers used various symbolic images in their writings. Metaphors are prominent in the book of Jonah, where the author uses them to express the truth that God loves all people. The prophets often used visual aids to make their case, while the theologians used theology. The preachers' concern was to convict and convert the hearers of their message. The Gospel writers can be seen as preachers, using a variety of homiletic tools to polish their message. Collectively, the biblical writers have left us with a great work of literature.

An End to Childish Ways

As we have seen, there are certain passages from the Bible that defy modern sensibilities, deter millions from faith, and challenge the belief that our God is a God of love and grace, mercy and peace. We could, like the literalist-fundamentalists, accept these passages, along with the rest of the Bible, as the absolute, inerrant Word of God. Choosing this would lead us away from the findings of the scientific communities throughout the centuries and toward a narrow, limited understanding of God and our place in the universe.

Or we could adopt the line of thought that holds that human beings developed and wrote the words of the Bible, trying to convey their conception of God and Satan, good and evil, life and death, and the righteous life. There was a time when "an eye for an eye and a tooth for a tooth" was an enlightened philosophy because it prevented "justice" from exceeding the initial crime. There were times when slavery was widespread throughout the planet. There were times when women were considered inferior to men. There were times when humans thought of God as a God of retribution and vengeance. There were times when humans thought God encouraged hostilities and fought against those of different faiths.

Of course, there are still those who believe the times have not changed, that an "eye for an eye" justice system still applies today, that slavery, sanctioned by the Bible, is justified. There are those who still believe women are inferior to men, that God does punish the wicked and fights on the side of "truth, justice, and the American way." But we need to understand as cultures change, so do our perspectives. The Bible explains how our spiritual ancestors understood God, humanity, and the relationship between the two. The Bible is divinely inspired but filtered through the lens of human experiences.

Interpreting the Bible through the use of symbols is not inferior to the literalist method. Stories, narratives, and myths have meaning, even when the events described did not literally take place. When I read the Bible, I read it as though it were a mirror reflecting God's light back toward my soul, my life, my family, my community, and my church. It leads me toward the truth as I gain more wisdom and insight into life. Instead of spending great amounts of time and energy trying to defend the literalism of the Bible, reading it through the lens of contemporary scholarship allows me to see, with honesty and integrity, the kingdom of God from the perspective of the biblical writers.

I do not worry, for instance, whether the heavens and earth and all within were created over a six-day time frame. Putting the literal interpretation aside allows me to focus on the truth of this story, namely, that it was God who created the heavens and the earth. The narrative is dramatic, the scope cosmic, the results spectacular. God continually steps back to observe his creation and "see" it is good. The created universe is indeed good. The truth is we are to be co-creators with God, taking the love and grace that built the universe and using it to improve, enhance, and perfect, to the best of our ability, the world we live in.

In the same way, it would be a waste of time for me to ponder how Jonah could have spent three days in the belly of a whale. Instead, I look at Jonah's call and response: called to preach judgment and destruction to the people of Ninevah, Jonah flees on a boat headed in the opposite direction. We, like Jonah, avoid responsibilities and tasks we are called to undertake. Following his encounter with the great fish, Jonah repents, turns around, and heads for Ninevah. Astonishingly, the people there repent and are spared judgment. Depressed by God's demonstration of mercy, Jonah pouts. Later God gently reminds Jonah that he had received a second chance; why not a second chance for the Assyrians? The story is about second chances—God's grace, mercy, and forgiveness for all of God's children.

Freed from a literal reading, I need not be concerned with how and where Jesus was born. More important is the question of why Jesus was born. I read the truth of these stories through their rich symbolism: Bethlehem was the hometown of King David and translates into English as "house of bread." Jesus is from the family of King David. A manger is the place where animals feed. Jesus came to be the King of Kings, to feed people spiritually through his sacrificial love. The visit of the shepherds and the birth in the stable indicate that God came to humanity in a humble form and not as a king or celebrity. The visit of the magi reminds us that Jesus came as the savior for all people. The star the magi followed indicates that Jesus came as the light of the world.

Like the Old Testament prophets, the book of Revelation is filled with secret meanings, wild symbols, and mysterious animals and beasts. A literal reading of the book was never its author's intent. Written during the end of the reign of Emperor Domitian (r. 81–96 CE), who persecuted Christians, the book was written in code to prevent the Roman authorities from recognizing this book was a call to the persecuted church. It encouraged the persecuted Christians to remain faithful. The Apocalypse reminds its readers that God reigns and Christ lives. In his book *Peace in the Post-Christian Era,* Thomas Merton describes human history as the continual struggle within individuals to find spiritual peace. The combat described in Revelation takes place on a deeper, spiritual level. Believing that the early Christians were all pacifists, Merton does not read the book as a prophecy of the cataclysmic final war but as a spiritual struggle for the meek to inherit the earth by remaining faithful to the Lamb of God, Jesus Christ.[36]

I read the Bible as a continuing narrative, from the grand opening of Genesis to the mysterious, enigmatic conclusion in Revelation. Along the way are some ups and downs, with chapters and chapters of obscure rules and laws, pages of unknown names and seemingly insignificant genealogies, and upsetting stories of war and destruction. But the strongest continuing theme flowing throughout this great book is the love, grace, mercy, and peace God gives to his people and expects them to replicate. *This is the dominant message of the Bible.* It calls me to be more than I am: to give of myself in thought, word, and deed. To share my gifts of time, talent, treasure, and service. I learn I receive more when I give. The Bible teaches me when I am able to give it all away, I find my true self and follow in the footsteps of Jesus Christ.

Buddhist theologian and teacher Thich Nhat Hanh understands this dilemma: "People kill and are killed because they cling too tightly to their own beliefs and ideologies. When we believe that ours is the only faith that contains the truth, violence and suffering will surely be the result."[37] The great battle being fought now over the proper interpretation of the Bible will not be solved within the pages of this book. I know, however, which side will bring to the world an approach that favors God's peace and justice.

---

[36] Thomas Merton, *Peace in the Post-Christian Era* (Maryknoll, NY: Orbis, 2004); see especially 29–31.

[37] Thich Nhat Hanh, *Living Buddha, Living Christ* (New York: Riverhead, 1995), 2.

Chapter 5

Different Spokes for Different Folks

There is only one God and He is God to all; therefore it is important that everyone is seen as equal before God. I've always said we should help a Hindu become a better Hindu, a Muslim become a better Muslim, a Catholic become a better Catholic.

—Mother Teresa

Man is the religious animal. He is the only religious animal. He is the only animal that has the True Religion—several of them. He is the only animal that loves his neighbor as himself and cuts his throat, if his theology isn't straight. He has made a graveyard of the globe in trying his honest best to smooth his brother's path to happiness and heaven.

—Mark Twain

Thurman Munson was the catcher for the New York Yankees from his Rookie of the Year season in 1970 until his untimely death in a plane crash in 1979. He was a favorite of the fans and named captain of the team. Until he signed with the Cleveland Indians in 2007, Trot Nixon was the right fielder for the Boston Red Sox. First drafted in 1993, he joined the Red Sox in 1999 and was a key player in helping them win the World Series in 2004.

I have lived forty of my forty-eight years in Connecticut near the so–called Munson-Nixon Line, the porous border separating the fans of the New York Yankees from the fans of the Boston Red Sox. The Red Sox– Yankees rivalry is as competitive as any in all of sports, with the spirited enmity dating back to the early decades of the 1900s. Babe Ruth played for the Red Sox and contributed to three World Series titles before being sold to the Yankees in December 1919. His sale set off the "Curse of the Bambino,"

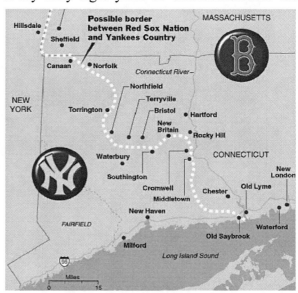

Source: New York Times, August 18, 2006

the inability of the Red Sox to win another World Series while the Yankees accomplished this twenty-six times. The curse was finally lifted in 2004 with the Red Sox's first World Series victory since 1918.

There are New York Yankees fans. There are Boston Red Sox fans. Many Yankees fans have friends who are fans of the Red Sox, and vice versa. They have learned to live as friends with strong loyalties to rival teams.

I have never met a Yankees fan who converted to become a Red Sox fan. Likewise, I have never met a Red Sox fan who converted to become a Yankees fan. A fan who would leave one of these teams to root for the other side would be considered a traitor. I have heard rumors of a few "conversions," but I have no firsthand experience of anyone crossing this chasm. Conversions are considered so unlikely that no resources, no time and no energy is expended by either the Yankees or the Red Sox to sway fans from the other city to switch allegiance to their team. Converted fans would be treated as apostates. By and large, the mentality of these fans is one of, "I'll root for my team, you root for your team, and may my team win."

I am convinced that the effort religions put toward converting persons of different religious backgrounds to their faith is a misguided undertaking that has had far more serious and tragic consequences than any sporting rivalry. Efforts to convert generate tremendous malice between individuals and religions. Sadly, many Christians put more emphasis on converting non-Christians to Christianity that they do in leading Christ-like lives. Christians have killed persons of other faiths because they would not convert to Christianity; likewise, Christians have been killed because they would not give up their Christianity.

Members of the world's religions would do better in seeking greater conversation, rather than conversion, with persons of different faiths. Interfaith conversations can lead all spiritual seekers to a deeper sense of awe and appreciation at the diverse ways God has been revealed to humanity and how God is experienced, encountered, praised, and worshipped. Interfaith communication builds bridges between people of different religious backgrounds, drawing participants closer to each other and closer to God as we realize how vast and infinite God's grace truly is.

Approximately 50 percent of the world's population is Jewish, Christian, or Muslim. We all look to Abraham, the father of monotheism, as our spiritual ancestor, but we fight like immature children. History shows us that there have been times of tolerance and respect between members of these religious communities when they have lived, worked, studied, and played together. Similarly, there have been times of conflict between followers of these religious traditions. These conflicts have often led to violence and even warfare. We are living in such a time today.

It is unfortunate, but perhaps inevitable, that these three great monotheistic, sibling faiths would clash. This conflict comes partly as a result of monotheism itself. Monotheistic religions make the claim that there is only one God—hence the tendency to claim that there is only one path to that God. Religions that postulate the existence of many gods do not have the same absolute answers to the ultimate questions of life and death, good and evil, righteousness and truth. The adherents of polytheistic traditions seem to have a "live and let live" philosophy. Reza Aslan writes, "If there is only one God, then there may be only one truth, and that can easily lead to bloody conflicts of irreconcilable absolutisms."[38]

The Palestinian-Israeli conflict is, in many ways, a "conflict of

---

[38] Reza Aslan, *No God but God* (New York: Random House, 2005), xxiv.

irreconcilable absolutisms." It is a religious struggle between Jews and Muslims over who will control Jerusalem, who will control the Holy Land, and who has the one "true" faith. The men who planned and carried out the attacks of September 11, 2001, did so, in part, because of their absolute belief in the one true religion of Islam. The United States responded to the 9/11 attacks with the War on Terror, which led to the invasions of Afghanistan and Iraq— decisions made, in part, from our leaders' Christian beliefs and convictions. Jews defend their small piece of land at the center of the Middle East with a fierce determinism based, in part, on their religious conviction that God gave it to them.

For religious fanatics, there always seems to be someone or some group within their own tradition who pollutes or teaches falsely and whose voice must be purged. Christian extremists hate and kill other Christians with whom they disagree, as evidence in the wars between Protestants and Roman Catholics through the past five centuries. Muslim extremists hate and kill other Muslims with whom they disagree, as seen in the brutal and ferocious battles between the Sunni and Shi'a factions. Jewish extremists hate and kill other Jews with whom they disagree, as seen recently in the threats and murders of moderate Jews who participate in the "land for peace" proposals by those who maintain that God has given the Jews the land of Israel and that to negotiate it away is contrary to God's will.[39]

Of course, wars are not fought exclusively for religious purposes. Political, economic, and social issues often drive nations to war. But even when these factors are the guiding forces behind a war, religion is often used as a supplemental moral motivation. They say there are no atheists in foxholes, which derives from the fact no one wants to be killed in the trenches so all are busy praying to their God for survival. So too, no wars are fought without an appeal to God to smite the enemy and lead one's own forces to victory.

Throughout the centuries, an unholy, symbiotic alliance has developed between clergy and politicians, each providing the other with the support and encouragement needed to achieve or maintain power and authority. Hymns, prayers, sermons, and worship services devoted to supporting the troops and religious justification for military action go back as far as Homer and have provided countless governments and military leaders with the religious and moral foundation to wage war.[40] In exchange for their support of particular

---

[39] Israeli Prime Minister Yitzhak Rabin was assassinated by a Jewish nationalist militant in 1995 because he sought a comprehensive peace proposal with his neighbors and signed the Oslo Accords with the PLO.

[40] Homer was a legendary Greek poet traditionally credited with *The Iliad and The Odyssey;* it is assumed that he lived in the eighth century BCE.

wars, clergy have received gifts of status, access to the inner sanctums of power, and resources denied those who speak against war.

No area of the world has experienced as much warfare and conflict as the Middle East. In the region known as the Fertile Crescent, soldiers and armies have moved north and east from Egypt and south and west from the Tigris-Euphrates River valley since the beginning of recorded history. A list of the generals and commanders who have led troops through the region reads like a "Who's Who" of military leaders and includes pharaohs, kings, rulers, and emperors.

The center of the Fertile Crescent lies in Israel, the birthing ground for Judaism and Christianity and an important locale in Islam. Historians often group a series of battles and armed clashes together around a central name— for example, the Peloponnesian War (431–404 BCE), the Thirty Years' War (1618–1648), the French and Indian War (1754–1763) and the Napoleonic Wars (1803–1815). I propose naming the three thousand years worth of warfare and violence that have taken place from Egypt to modern Iraq "the Holy War." Fought by faithful Jews, Christians, and Muslims, this war has been carried out with the blessings and encouragement of religious leaders. Collectively, this ongoing religious violence has done more damage to religion and faith than can ever be calculated, and can best be understood as gross distortions of God's will and purpose for humanity.

If we are to have peace in the twenty-first century, we must make an attempt to break down the barriers separating the world's religions, particularly between Jews, Christians, and Muslims. This chapter will attempt to provide a different interpretation of how the world's religions can be understood as complementary traditions and pathways toward God. As persons of faith see and understand the harmonizing role different religions can bring to the world, competition, conflict, and a desire to convert others will diminish, leading us toward peace and justice.

Who Is Right?

Abraham: A Journey to the Heart of Three Faiths by Bruce Feiler, is a wonderful, thought-provoking book about Judaism, Christianity, and Islam.[41] It allows Jews, Christians, and Muslims to understand Abraham's role within all three traditions claiming Abraham as their spiritual father. Feiler estimates that one-third of the Jewish people believe salvation is possible only through Judaism, that approximately half of Christians believe salvation is possible

---

[41] Bruce Feiler, Abraham: *A Journey to the Heart of Three Faiths* (New York: Morrow, 2002).

only through being Christian, and perhaps two-thirds of Muslims believe salvation is possible only through Islam.

This is the heart of the problem. Many faithful Jews, Christians, and Muslims see their religion as the only legitimate path to God. In their zeal for conversions and new members, religious leaders and followers who believe they have the exclusive path to God lose respect for the divine and sacred found within other traditions. When humans proclaim that their religious tradition is the sole way to God, they discredit other faithful traditions. Historically, when the exclusive claims become the dominant theological perspective, periods of intolerance, discrimination, persecution, and war have followed. As we observe what is happening in the world at the beginning of the twenty-first century, it becomes apparent that we are in the midst of another period of conflict and warfare caused, in part, by religious bigotry and extreme narrow–mindedness.

The Wisdom of a Buddhist Teacher

There is another way. I am reminded of the story of a student I knew from college. Following our graduation he set out for India because he had developed in college an obsession with Buddhism. He wanted to achieve enlightenment. He went to a monastery and began practicing meditation. After staying there for about three months he had the opportunity to visit with the guru for a private session. The spiritual guide mentioned how dedicated and serious the young American seemed was to become a Buddhist monk and achieve enlightenment. The conversation then turned in a new direction. The sage asked the student what his faith had been in the United States.

"I was an Episcopalian," was his answer.

"And how long were you an Episcopalian?"

"My whole life, really, up to going to college. Once I went to college I only attended church once or twice a year."

The guru then suggested something quite unexpected. He told the young college graduate to go back to the United States and return to his religion. Become a Christian again, the guru told him. Go back to your faith.

"Spirituality is like climbing a mountain," the guru continued. "As a Christian, you have been climbing your whole life. Even though you do not know it, you are already well on the way up your mountain toward the summit. If you want to become a Buddhist, you will be starting all over now at the bottom of this mountain. Go back to Christianity. Climb the mountain that you have already started on. Then, when you get to the top, you will rise above the fog and the clouds and see the sun and the sky, and then you will see other mountaintops, for all of the world's great religions lead to mountaintops. On the top of the mountain you will see what all of the great religions see from the summit—truth, wisdom, love, grace, compassion, justice, understanding, and peace. Go back to Christianity. Climb your mountain. Get to the top, and I will wave to you from my mountain!"

I have always been moved by the wisdom of this Buddhist guru, and the faith he had in the other world religions. It seems this wisdom derived in part from his lack of interest in converting the young Christian before him into a Buddhist. More important to this teacher was to see the young Christian grow as a child of God. The Buddhist believed there are different pathways to God and these pathways all lead up to a mountaintop from whence other mountains can be seen.

The Golden Rule in World Religions

While it is correct that the differences between the world's religions help define whom we are, our common humanity and the truths that run through all of the world's great faiths agree on the importance of love, compassion, mercy, and peace. I find it fascinating that many of the world's religions have a version of the Golden Rule. Below is the Golden Rule as it appears in different religious traditions. I believe the founders and leaders of these religions knew intuitively and/or through revelation that the pathway back to God begins by treating others with the same respect, courtesy, and love one expects for oneself.

Christianity

In everything do to others as you would have them do to you. (Matt 7:12)

Baha'i

Blessed are those who prefer others before themselves. (Tablets of Baha' U' llah 71)

Buddhism

Hurt not others in ways that you yourself would find hurtful. (Udana-Varqu 5:18)

Hinduism

This is the sum of all duty: treat others as you yourself would be treated. (Mahabharata 5:1517)

Islam

No one of you is a believer until you desire for another that which you desire for yourself. (Sunnah)

Jainism

In happiness and suffering, in joy and grief, regard all creatures as you would regard your own self." (Lord Mahavir, 24th Tirthankara)

Judaism

Rabbi Hillel said: "What is hateful to you, do not do to your neighbor: that is the entire Torah; the rest is commentary; go and learn it." (Talmud Shabbat 31A)

Zoroastrianism

Human nature is good only when it does not do unto another whatever is not good for its own self." (Dadistan-i-Dink 94:5)

God's Wheel

The image I like to use when thinking of the world's religions is of a wheel. I see God at the center, or hub, of the wheel. Humanity is located out in the area we would define as the tire itself. There are different spokes leading toward the center, toward God. One spoke, my spoke, is Christianity, and even more specifically, the United Methodist Church. But I believe many spokes lead back to the center and back to God. There are spokes for Confucianism, Hinduism, Buddhism, Judaism, Islam, and many more. I believe God has provided humanity with a variety of ways for us to approach him. To recognize these paths seems to be a step toward the divine; we move from intolerance toward acceptance, grace, and love.

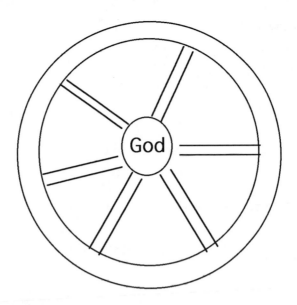

Jesus: The Only Way?

Of course, not all Christians accept that there are multiple paths to God. Adherents of this view like to quote several favorite biblical texts, including the following:

> All things have been handed over to me by my Father; and no one knows the Son except the Father, and no one knows the Father except the Son and anyone to whom the Son chooses to reveal him. (Matt 11:27)

> Go therefore and make disciples of all nations, baptizing them in the name of the Father and of the Son and of the Holy Spirit, and teaching them to obey everything that I have commanded you. And remember, I am with you always, to the end of the age. (Matt 28:19–20)

> There is salvation in no one else, for there is no other name under heaven given among mortals by which we must be saved. (Acts 4:12)

The primary biblical text used by Christians to maintain the exclusive trail to God, however, is this verse from the Gospel of John:

Jesus said to him [Thomas], "I am the way, and the truth, and the life. No one comes to the Father except through me." (John 14:6)

On one level, these texts are clear and indicate the only legitimate pathway to God goes through the teachings, preaching, and life of Jesus Christ. But there are a variety of ways to interpret the Bible, from the literal to the symbolic, and the Bible has texts conflicting with and even contradicting each other. Focusing on these passages as the absolute, authoritative answer to whether Christianity has exclusive access to God is not the only way we have to understand our faith.

One of the troubles with the exclusivist line of thinking is all biblical texts must be taken as literally true as well, including texts that contradict the passages that seem to identify Christianity as the only pathway to God. For instance, in Genesis 17, God makes an *everlasting* covenant with Abram:

When Abram was ninety-nine years old, the LORD appeared to Abram, and said to him, "I am God Almighty; walk before me, and be blameless. And I will make my covenant between me and you, and will make you exceedingly numerous. . . . No longer shall your name be Abram, but your name shall be Abraham; for I have made you the ancestor of a multitude of nations. I will make you exceedingly fruitful; and I will make nations of you, and kings shall come from you. I will establish my covenant between me and you, and your offspring after you throughout their generations, for an everlasting covenant, to be God to you and to your offspring after you. And I will give to you, and to your offspring after you, the land where you are now an alien, all the land of Canaan, for a perpetual holding; and I will be their God." (Gen 17:1–2, 5–8)

The covenant that God established with Abram (now Abraham) was affirmed under the leadership of Moses at Mount Sinai (Exod 20–24), and renewed following the conquest of Israel by Joshua at Shechem (Josh 24).

Paul affirms the everlasting quality of the covenant that God has made with the Jewish people in his letter to the Romans:

I ask, then, has God rejected his people? By no means! I myself am an Israelite, a descendant of Abraham, a member of the tribe of Benjamin. God has not rejected his people whom he foreknew. . . . But as regards election they are beloved, for the sake of their ancestors; for the gifts and the calling of God are irrevocable. (Rom 11:1–2, 28–29)

Paul is saying the covenant God established with the Jewish people is still valid, still applicable, and still in effect. How then can the literalist claim the path through Jesus Christ is the exclusive path to God when the Bible, in both the Old and New Testaments, clearly affirms the covenant God established with the Jewish people? If we want to say only Christians get to heaven, if we want to argue we have the exclusive and sole connection to God, then what are we to do with these contradictory passages affirming the eternal place Judaism has in covenant with God?

Furthermore, biblical texts from both the Old and New Testaments describe God's grace and love for all of the world's people. This is true of Deutero-Isaiah (Isa 40–55), an amazingly universal and pluralistic book, and of Jeremiah and Jonah, which treat non-Jews as equals with the Jews. Luke stresses God's grace and freedom to do anything. Luke makes it clear the primary reason why Jesus offended so many people in his day was his reading of the Old Testament stories stressing God as the God of all people. We can see this in the description of Jesus' sermon at Nazareth (Luke 4:16–30), and this pattern continues throughout the entire Gospel. Luke presents the freedom of God in such strong terms that grace is freely offered to persons outside of the Jewish faith, an issue putting Jesus at odds with the religious leaders of his day.

Did Jesus believe he was the only route to God? Theologians have long debated if Jesus intended to start a new religion. Jesus was born a Jew, lived as a Jew, and died on the cross as a Jew. His teaching and preaching was done not to convert his Jewish listeners to a new religion but to help draw them closer to God. He showed humanity the way to God through his acts of love, grace, mercy, and peace. As an embodiment of God's grace and love, surely Jesus could find and appreciate the variety and wonders of God's love in and through different people, different cultures, and different religions.

The Qur'an is as complex and open to discussion and interpretation as the Bible. Christians do a great disservice to Muslims when we denounce their faith as violent and aggressive. The Qur'an maintains that war is either just or unjust, but *never* "holy." The idea of killing individuals who will not convert to Islam violates one of the most important principles from the Qur'an: "There can be no compulsion in religion" (2:256). The Qur'an also states, "The truth is from your Lord, believe it if you like, or do not" (18:29). It also includes the phrase "To you your religion; to me mine" (109:6), and asks rhetorically the question "Can you compel people to believe against their will?" (10:100). The implied answer to this question is no, an answer confirmed through the centuries countless times by individuals who refused to believe as directed, even in the face of torture and death.

A Different Approach

Those with an open mind can look at sacred texts from a variety of angles. Fundamentalists who claim Christianity is the exclusive pathway to God point to John 14:6 as the definitive passage supporting their claims. We will therefore look at this text closer and as representative of the other exclusive texts.

Most biblical scholars consider the Gospel of John to be the last of the Gospels written, having been put into writing probably sixty to eighty years after Jesus had died. John is thought to be the least historically accurate of the four Gospels; John is not as interested in history as he is with theology. He has a radically different time frame for events than in the Gospels of Matthew, Mark, and Luke. For instance, Matthew, Mark, and Luke place the cleansing of the temple by Jesus in the final week of Jesus' life, whereas John places this important event near the beginning of Jesus' public ministry (John 2:13–22).

"I am the way, and the truth, and the life. No one comes to the Father except through me" does not appear in Matthew, Mark, or Luke. Of course, there are no recordings of Jesus making this statement. Most non-literalist scholars believe Jesus did not say these words at all but they were the thoughts of the evangelist John or of the early church. The words fit the overall theological perspective of the Gospel of John, namely, Jesus came as the savior of the whole world. The Gospel of John was written at a time when church leaders were attempting to distinguish Christianity from other religious traditions, especially from Judaism, from which it developed. Converting Jews and gentiles to the new religion of Christianity seems to have been the goal of John and many early church leaders.

Having said this, the text does allow for some interpretation. Leo Tolstoy, the famous Russian novelist, was a devout Christian. Tolstoy worked to understand this verse of Jesus and translated the original Greek into his native Russian in a slightly different manner. Translated again to English, Tolstoy's translation looks like this: "Jesus said to him, 'I am the way, and the truth, and the life. No one comes to the Father except through *the way that I have come.*'"

What a big difference this slight variation can make! Now the door to God is not exclusively through Jesus Christ, but through the way Jesus took. Jesus lived a life of selfless sacrifice, feeding the hungry, healing the sick, welcoming the stranger, and giving himself completely on the cross. The way to God is through love, sacrifice, and giving—the way Jesus lived his life.

I do not believe anyone knows the will of God, and I am skeptical of those who appear to be the surest in their statements of who God is and what God wants from humanity. But I do not believe in a God who would condemn anyone for failure to believe in Jesus Christ as the only pathway to God's throne. I know many faithful Jews, Muslims, and Buddhists who are practicing their faith in ways that humble me. To exclude them from heaven based on their rejection of Christianity seems illogical. Would God ban Gandhi from heaven? Confucius? The Buddha? Elie Wiesel? Space would not allow in all the books of the world to list the faithful, peaceful followers of the world's great religions who each deserve a place at God's table.

There is an old story of a group of parishioners who tragically die in a bus accident together. They are met at the pearly gates by St. Peter himself, who welcomes them and escorts them to an elevator for the ride to their eternal destination. As they approach the twenty-fifth floor, Peter encourages them to be quiet: "We are about to go by the floor of the United Methodists. Please do not make any noise, because they think they are the only ones who have made it to heaven."

Which city, New York or Boston, has the best baseball team? It depends, of course, on whom you talk to. It does not matter how many games or championships either team wins or who the players are. What matters is which team you root for, which team you love. But we know there will be precious few fans of the New York Yankees who convert and become fans of the Boston Red Sox; likewise, conversions of Red Sox fans becoming Yankees fans will be few and far between.

Similarly, there will be few conversions in the twenty-first century of Jews to Christianity or Islam; few Christians will give up their faith traditions to become Jews or Muslims, and only a small number of Muslims are likely to convert to Judaism of Christianity. Given this reality, persons of faith should consider their options. We can continue to live with the goal of converting others to our religious tradition, or we can choose a different path. We can learn to live with tolerance and acceptance.

Christianity is a faith that asks its followers to become partners with God in building the kingdom. We do so through our acts of love, grace, peace, and mercy. The most important thing for Christians is to live out faith-filled lives, and in so doing we will be amazed at how others perceive us. Gandhi once said that he would be willing to convert to Christianity if he could find just one congregation that, as a whole, was living out the Gospel of Jesus Christ.

I am a Christian. My pathway to God is through Jesus Christ. I witness to this faith through my serving the least, the last, and the lost. I am responsible for my own actions, and when I stand before the judgment throne God will ask me how I lived out my faith and my life as Wayne Lavender. If I were to believe my pathway was the only legitimate pathway back to God, I would be guilty of the first deadly sin, which is pride. Pride has been called the sin from which all others arise. Judging the pathway that others are on is God's job, not mine. When I am more concerned with the salvation of my neighbor than I am with my own place at God's table, I am guilty of evaluating others' souls. Playing the role of God is inappropriate for humans. Extending the invitation to heaven and condemning others to hell is God's responsibility, not ours. Gandhi said, "Like the bee gathering honey from the different flowers, the wise person accepts the essence of the different scriptures and sees only the good in all religions."

Serving God through Jesus Christ is, for me, the most fitting and proper way to live my life. When I serve God through Jesus Christ, I allow my light to shine so others too may see the light. This is what it means to be dancing, with joy, with the elephants. Find your pathway to God and let your light shine, and together we shall approach the throne of God through service and love, peace and justice.

Separation of Light and Darkness, 1511
Michelangelo, Sistine Chapel

Chapter 6

The Children of Light and the Children of Darkness

Thoughts on Good and Evil

The light shines in the darkness, and the darkness did not overcome it. There was a man sent from God, whose name was John. He came as a witness to testify to the light, so that all might believe through him. He himself was not the light, but he came to testify to the light. The true light, which enlightens everyone, was coming into the world.

—John 1:5-8

What is needed to exorcize these evil spirits? Light, and still more light. No bat can face the dawn. We must flood that underworld with light.
—Victor Hugo, *Les Miserables*

Good and evil, light and darkness, right and wrong, and sacred and sinful form dramatic, thematic opposites. Countless writers, authors, theologians, and artists have used these themes in their work to portray the reality of existence and its dual nature. One of the world's greatest artists, Michelangelo, portrayed this distinction in his fresco on the Sistine Chapel ceiling titled *Separation of Light and Darkness.*

One of my favorite writers is J. R. R. Tolkien (1892–1973). Tolkien, an Oxford University professor, philologist, and writer, was a devout Roman Catholic and close friend of C. S. Lewis. He is best remembered as the author of *The Hobbit* and *The Lord of the Rings.* In these and other works, he created a fantasy world inhabited by elves, dwarves, orcs, ents, wizards, hobbits, and humans. The tension between the forces of good and the forces of evil builds throughout *The Lord of the Rings* trilogy, culminating in the final book, *The Return of the King,* where the White Wizard Gandalf, risen from the dead (sound familiar?), leads the forces of good against the Dark Lord Sauron.

Tolkien himself described *The Lord of the Rings* to his friend Robert Murray, a Jesuit priest, as "a fundamentally religious and Catholic work, unconsciously at first, but consciously in the revision."[42] Indeed, Christian themes dominate the work. In addition to the theological themes of good versus evil, the author writes about death and resurrection, mercy and grace, salvation, repentance and forgiveness, justice, free will, and self-sacrifice. Tolkien himself was a soldier in World War I and wrote most of *The Rings* trilogy during World War II.

Although Tolkien's characters tend to be either good or evil, he portrays the internal struggle between these two polarities through dynamic personalities and psychological insights. One character in particular, Gollum, is deeply divided, acting both on good and evil impulses as this timeless battle is carried out in his soul. Even Frodo and Bilbo, the heroes of *The Lord of the Rings* and *The Hobbit,* respectively, are seduced by the powerful ring and tempted to try and possess its power.

But *The Lord of the Rings* and *The Hobbit* are fictional works, divorced from the world of reality. We cheer when the Dark Lord is overthrown and good triumphs through the selfless deeds of a small fellowship of friends, but the real world is not so simple. We cannot simply write off the forces of evil, nor expect the good to triumph so easily.

The attacks of 9/11 can be considered evil by any civilized standard. The Holocaust in Europe was evil, as were the ethnic killings in Cambodia, Bosnia, Rwanda, and Darfur. Equally so, the school attack in Columbine,

---

[42]Tolkien, *The Letters of J. R. R. Tolkien.* (Boston: Houghton Mifflin, 1981).

Colorado, and the assault on the Federal Building in Oklahoma City by Timothy McVeigh represented the face of evil. Acknowledging that evil, in one form or another, exists on earth, we must come to grips with its insidious nature. The pressing questions are: How do we address evil without becoming evil ourselves? Will good people commit themselves to lives filled with actions of love and grace to combat and offset the evil around us, regardless of the evil perpetrated against us? Will the forces of light unite and become as organized as the forces of darkness? Will the church of Jesus Christ come together to negate the forces of evil in the world, or will we continue to divide and debate, sabotage and undermine each other over trivial ant-like issues, allowing ongoing war, destruction, violence, and pain to continue unabated?

I have titled this chapter "The Children of Light and the Children of Darkness," the same title as a book written by twentieth-century theologian Reinhold Niebuhr in 1944. His research and work were completed during the bloodiest period in human history, with major battles taking place throughout Europe, Africa, and Asia, and Jews and other enemies of the Nazis being systematically murdered. During this time, soldiers and civilians committed countless atrocities. It seemed as though the spiritual struggle between good and evil was being waged dramatically on the global stage through the armies of the nations involved. Niebuhr's book became an instant Christian classic and is still read and studied by Christians throughout the world.

Niebuhr's basic premise is that the world is divided into people who *tend* to be either children of light or *tend* to be children of darkness. Children of light are persons who are loving, selfless, and benevolent. These are persons who reflect the love of God in their lives. The children of darkness are persons who are self-centered and bitter. They are men and women who are filled with anger, hatred, and evil. Niebuhr was writing during the lifetime of some of history's greatest polar opposites: a child of light named Mohandas Gandhi and a child of darkness named Joseph Stalin, a child of light named Oskar Schindler and a child of darkness named Adolf Hitler. More recently we have seen the faces of good and evil on the global scale through the lives of Mother Teresa and Osama bin Laden.

Of course, human beings live in the gray areas, with no one totally a child of light or a child of darkness. Niebuhr argues that humans are continually at odds with themselves; we have two impulses standing in perpetual contradiction to each other. Simply stated, each of us internally experiences a battle between the forces of good and evil, altruism and selfishness, and human love, creativity, self–denial, and self–sacrifice versus human lusts and desires, ambition and greed. I have the potential to be a child of light, or a child of darkness.

Taking this a step further, I have the capacity to move constantly between light and darkness—to perform an action of grace and love, mercy and peace one moment, and then to act in a cruel and mean-spirited way the next. It is easy to be a self-serving jerk, which takes no training, no practice, and no discipline. It is much harder to accept the yoke of Christ and be focused on your neighbor's needs. As Jon Stewart once said, "Have you ever tried to live exactly as Jesus wanted us to live? You can do it for about an hour, and then you need some 'me-time.'"[43]

We all have choices to make in life, which we make moment by moment, day by day, week by week, and year by year until the sum total of our lives is calculated. I would hate to be judged solely on my worst moments; equally, it is unreasonable to assume that I will be remembered exclusively on the basis of my most altruistic actions. One would have to assume that child-of-darkness Adolf Hitler was capable of acts of love, just as we might imagine that child-of-light Mother Teresa might have had days when "she woke up on the wrong side of the bed."

Further clarifying this point, Russian writer Aleksandr Solzhenitsyn wrote:

> If only it were all so simple! If only there were evil people somewhere, insidiously committing evil deeds, and it were necessary only to separate them from the rest of us and destroy them. But the line dividing good and evil cuts through the heart of every human being. And who is willing to destroy a piece of his own heart?
>
> During the life of any heart this line keeps changing place; sometimes it is squeezed one way by exuberant evil and sometimes it shifts to allow enough space for good to flourish. One and the same human being is, at various stages, under various circumstances, a totally different human being. At times he is close to being a devil, at times to sainthood. But his name doesn't change, and to that name we ascribe the whole lot, good and evil.[44]

Martin Luther King Jr. also recognized the existence of good and evil, light and darkness within each person. Preaching at the Dexter Avenue Baptist Church on Christmas Day 1957, he spoke these words:

---

[43] Jon Stewart, host of *The Daily Show,* spoke that line in an episode in October 2005.

[44] Aleksandr I. Solzhenitsyn, *The Gulag Archipelago* (New York: Harper & Row, 1973), 168.

There is some good in the worst of us and some evil in the best of us. When we discover this, we are less prone to hate our enemies. When we look beneath the surface, beneath the impulsive evil deed, we see within our enemy-neighbor a measure of goodness and know that the viciousness and evilness of his acts are not quite representative of all that he is. We see him in a new light. We recognize that his hate grows out of fear, pride, ignorance, prejudice, and misunderstanding, but in spite of this, we know God's image is ineffably etched in his being. Then we love our enemies by realizing that they are not totally bad and that they are not beyond the reach of God's redemptive love.

Reinhold Niebuhr, Aleksandr Solzhenitsyn, and Martin Luther King Jr. all recognized and acknowledged the existence of good and evil within each of us. I am, fortunately, a child of light some of the time; sadly, I am also a child of darkness at other moments. My personal goal is to nurture that child of light inside of me so it becomes my dominant personality, the person I most want to be. Furthermore, it is my hope the religious institutions of our country and world will work toward increasing the light within all of their members. As individuals and communities of faith move purposefully toward the light, the darkness is exposed and diminished. We are all called to be children of light and to let our lights shine so that all may see them and move toward their life-sustaining properties.

What the Bible Teaches Us about Good and Evil

What is the source of evil? Deutero-Isaiah says this:

> I am the LORD and there is none else, there is no God besides me: I girded thee, though thou hast not known me; that they may know from the rising of the sun, and from the west, that there is none besides me. I am the LORD, and there is none else. I form the light, and create darkness: I make peace, and create evil: I the LORD do all these things. (Isa 45:5–7 KJV)

I have wrestled with this text for decades. Why would God create evil? Why does God create light *and* darkness, peace *and* evil? It would have been better, I often think, if God had only created the light and peace. I choose to worship a God who is the God of all creation, the source of all wisdom, power, and love.

Since evil exists in our universe, is our God, the Creator and Sustainer of the entire universe, its source?

Since the time of Cain and Abel, human history has been written in blood and tears, and it continues to be so today. The sociologist John Searle once wrote, "I shall not attempt to write a history of mankind's inhumanity to man, for that would be to write a history of the world." The Bible is filled with stories of pain and suffering, of evil deeds and their consequences. In the Bible we read of wars and fighting, rapes and murders, violence performed in the name of God and violence performed for purely selfish purposes.

"'The only empirically verifiable doctrine of Christianity,' Reinhold Niebuhr noted on more than one occasion, 'is the doctrine of original sin.'"[45] The doctrine of original sin can be traced back to the Garden of Eden and Adam and Eve's decision to eat from the tree of good and evil, which God had commanded them to avoid. The truth of this story is evident if we search our own souls: had we been the ones placed in the garden and told not to eat the fruit from that one tree, we certainly would have taken and eaten. This is the truth of human nature. We are selfish creatures, capable of great harm.

A litany of the evil deeds committed in the Bible would be extensive. Shortly after the expulsion from the garden, Adam and Eve became parents to Abel and Cain. The murder of Abel by his brother Cain is the world's first recorded murder, and it took place when only four human beings existed!

The flood of Noah's time was caused because God saw that the world was filled with wickedness, corruption, and violence (Gen 6:5, 11). Following the flood, the tower of Babel was built, because the people wanted to, in their words, "build ourselves a city, and a tower with its top in the heavens, and let us make a name for ourselves" (Gen 11:4). In Genesis 19 the cities of Sodom and Gomorrah are razed. The biblical record, both the Old Testament and New Testament, is filled with stories of humanity's sinfulness. The "seven deadly sins"—pride, envy, gluttony, lust, anger, greed, and sloth—all take place within the pages of our sacred book.

But this is not the only story line in the Bible. Along with our ability to sin and fall short of the glory of God, we can also rise to astonishing heights, achieve remarkable results, and strive sacrificially and nobly to build God's kingdom. Stories of love and grace, mercy and love can be found throughout the Old and New Testaments. The story of many faithful men and women unfold within the pages of the Bible alongside the dark and evil stories, reminding us of the potential for good and evil within humanity.

---

[45] Quoted in Robert McAfee Brown, "Reinhold Niebuhr: His Theology in the 1980s", *Christian Century,* January 22, 1986, 66.

Noah faithfully builds the ark and saves himself, his family, and the animal world. A few chapters later, Abram pleads passionately on behalf of the citizens of Sodom and Gomorrah. Abram and Sarai become Abraham and Sarah and live faithful lives, passing on their beliefs, loyalty, and faithfulness to their children, grandchildren, and generations of Jewish, Christian, and Muslim followers. Joseph, despite his initial mean-spiritedness toward his long-lost siblings, becomes the instrument of salvation for the children of Israel because of his position within the Egyptian government. Many priests, leaders, kings, prophets, and ordinary citizens come and go across the biblical pages and are portrayed as children of light, persons dedicated to building God's kingdom on earth.

In addition to the Bible's detailing good and evil stories, we also read about the internal struggles of some key biblical characters. Not all characters are either good or evil. Many characters seem to live in the gray areas and move from good to evil, or evil to good. We see the development of good and evil in the hearts of biblical characters as they grow and develop. For example, characters who begin in the light but commit dark deeds include Aaron, Moses' brother, who leads the children of Israel in creating the golden calf in the wilderness *after* he witnesses the power of God in Egypt, the Red Sea, and Mount Sinai. King Saul starts his reign as a model sovereign but becomes troubled, depressed, and paranoid. Judas is called as one of Jesus' disciples, and even has the position of treasurer of the group, but is the person who betrays Jesus.

Meanwhile, other characters move from the darkness toward the light. Moses commits a murder as a young man in Egypt and is forced to flee to the wilderness. But at the burning bush, Moses turns around, repents, and becomes the greatest leader of Israel. King David commits adultery with Bathsheba and then orders her husband's death. David too repents, and is known in the tradition as the greatest of Israel's kings. The Pharisee Saul witnesses and approves of the slaying of Stephen, and even guards the coats of those involved in the execution. Indeed, he is a leading persecutor of the early church. But on the road to Damascus he is struck down and told to stop persecuting the Christian movement. He becomes one of the greatest theologians and evangelists of Christianity.

The Bible is a book that deals with real people with real-life issues; in reading the Bible, we read about both the good and the bad. Aaron, Saul, and Judas walked in the light but apparently were tempted and surrendered to their darker inclinations. On the other hand, Moses, David, and Saul, among many other characters, in moments of clarity were called out from the shadows of self to serve in God's light. They become role models for us because of their ability to respond and embrace the path that God set out for them—to be children of light.

Left to our own devices, we might choose to live according to our base nature and dwell in darkness. The stories of how biblical heroes overcame their dark natures and moved toward the light can give us the courage, hope, and inspiration to find a better way, a higher purpose, for our lives. God provides a path for us to walk on—a path of love, mercy, grace, and peace that leads us toward a fuller, more meaningful life.

Good and Evil Personalities throughout History

Some names can send shivers down our spines: Genghis Kahn, Ivan the Terrible, Adolf Hitler, Joseph Stalin, Pol Pot (Saloth Sar), Slobodan Milosevic, Saddam Hussein, and Osama bin Laden. These charismatic, dark leaders were able to rise to positions of authority by tapping into the evil side of our natures. They blamed and dehumanized large sections of their own and/or foreign populations, separated themselves from these "inferiors," then implemented campaigns of mass murder. They surrounded themselves with like-minded characters and seduced good people with the promise of economic prosperity. They became like Satan by offering the forbidden fruit to their desperate people.

Equally alarming is that not only were these and other individuals capable of committing acts of evil, but the leaders of other nations and their populations tended to turn away and allow these actions to take place. In 1915, Woodrow Wilson and the rest of the world turned a blind eye to the Armenian genocide. Franklin Roosevelt and other Allied leaders refused to bomb the rail lines leading to Auschwitz and the other concentration camps. In 1994, Bill Clinton and the United Nations turned away from the slaughter in Rwanda. And in 2004, George W. Bush and other world leaders chose to ignore the first mass genocide in the twenty-first century, which is still unfolding in Darfur, Sudan.

Edmund Burke (1729–1797) wrote, "All that is necessary for the forces of evil to win in the world is for enough good men to do nothing." To do nothing is to allow the forces of evil to succeed. On a daily basis we have the ability to resist evil, to choose good, to make conscious decisions to live our lives in a way that is pleasing to God. We can work to build a world of peace and reconciliation, or we can choose evil. These are the choices we are given as free people.

Just as history is filled with the names of evil individuals, so does it provide us with a roll call of saints. This past century saw three of the most loving, grace–filled, compassionate individuals who have ever lived: Mohandas Gandhi, Mother Teresa, and Martin Luther King Jr. These and other saints come and go across the world stage and show the rest of us a different way to live. Looking for guidance from God, they were able to place their own needs aside and hold God's light high. They walked paths of love and grace and peace. Rather than appealing to a small group of followers, they all of humanity as God's children and seek ways of reconciliation between conflicting groups.

Nelson Mandela, Bishop Desmond Tutu, Pope John Paul II, Bono—these and many more persons, some famous and some ordinary, simply use their faith in positive ways to serve humanity, to make the world a better place. We lift them up on pedestals and admire their work and lives, wishing there could be more people like them—wishing we could be more like them ourselves.

Conflict and Division in the Church

Everyone would love to believe that in walking through the doors of a church one leaves behind the world of evil and darkness and encounters only the children of light. But this is not so. Church consultants and researchers have long recognized the destructive role some church members have played in the life and work of the church. These persons operate by derailing, opposing, and otherwise creating conflict. Kenneth C. Haugk describes such persons:

> Antagonists are individuals who, on the basis of unsubstantiated evidence, go out of their way to make insatiable demands, usually attacking the person or performance of others. These attacks are selfish in nature, tearing down rather than building up, and are frequently directed against those in a leadership capacity. . . . For too long, congregations have been places where antagonists can operate with success. Their behavior is not as successful in other areas of life because in those areas it is simply not tolerated.[46]

I have often quoted a former district superintendent of the United Methodist Church, the Rev. Barber Waters, who used to say, tongue in cheek, "If you can be a Christian in the church, you can be a Christian anywhere." He knew that church members do not always treat others in the church in a manner that would make Jesus Christ proud.

---

[46] Kenneth C. Haugk, *Antagonists in the Church* (Minneapolis: Augsburg, 1988), 21–22, 39.

In his book *Sacred Cows Make Gourmet Burgers,*[47] Bill Easum describes the controlling, manipulative, mean-spirited individuals who keep local churches from fulfilling their missional purpose. Disputes over the location of the child care room, the manner and order in which worship is conducted, where the choir should stand for their anthems, where the church should invest its funds, who will be the liturgist on important weekends, and the color of the Sunday school classrooms all divert our attention from the primary message of the gospel. The sapping of the energy of good-willed Christians in petty, ant-like matters is a sign of evil's presence within the church.

Denominations spend a great deal of time and energy on matters that, when compared to the giant issues of our day, are inconsequential. Churches should be actively seeking solutions to the spread of HIV/AIDS, the arms race, the death of millions of persons each year from treatable diseases, universal health care, and quality education for all of God's children. Mainline denominations have spent more time, money, energy, and resources on the discussion of homosexuality in the past twenty years than on any other topic. Homosexuality, bringing prayer back to the public schools, ending abortion on demand, and how to teach science in the public schools are all important issues for the church to wrestle with. They are also issues that take our eyes off the billions of persons who are living in extreme poverty and the sinful wars that are consuming our limited resources. I have come to the conclusion that forces of darkness orchestrate these distractions and they prevent the church from taking its true place in society and the world. These diversions are often done so subtly, so smoothly, so carefully that we often fail to sense the demonic presence.

If the church is to reclaim its true character and mission, it must return to the sacrificial, giving, loving example Jesus set for us. The children of light need to develop an awareness of when they are being distracted, when they are being pulled off course from the primary purpose of the church. We must find ways to refocus the church around the teachings of Jesus. Jesus rebuked evil! Following the example set by Jesus means his church also must begin rebuking evil. We cannot let ourselves be sidetracked by these misguided individuals whose sole intent is to manipulate and control others. Being a faithful disciple of Jesus Christ means we must not allow the children of darkness to hijack his body.

Building a World of Peace and Justice

In Washington, DC, the embassies of virtually all the nations on the earth are

---

[47] Bill Easum, *Sacred Cows Make Gourmet Burgers* (Nashville: Abingdon, 1995).

located. The ambassadors of these foreign nations come to the United States to represent their countries and to actively pursue policies to promote their national interests. These embassies are actually extensions of the countries they represent; they are foreign islands surrounded by the waters of America. A visit inside these embassies transports you to those nations. You can literally visit scores of foreign nations within five miles in our national capital.

Paul tells us that we are ambassadors for Christ:

So if anyone is in Christ, there is a new creation: everything old has passed away; see, everything has become new! All this is from God, who reconciled us to himself through Christ, and has given us the ministry of reconciliation; that is, in Christ God was reconciling the world to himself, not counting their trespasses against them, and entrusting the message of reconciliation to us. So we are ambassadors for Christ, since God is making his appeal through us; we entreat you on behalf of Christ, be reconciled to God. (2 Cor 5:17–20)

Likewise, St. Augustine spoke of Christians as a "colony of heaven," set here on earth to represent heaven's policies and principles and to bring love, grace, mercy, and peace to the world.

How would you be judged as an ambassador of Christ? If you were placed on trial today, would there be enough evidence to convict you of being a disciple of Jesus Christ?

I have visited church members who own five or more sets of china— two everyday sets, two formal sets, and a set for special events such as Christmas. I know of families who replace an entire set of dishes when a small chip breaks off one piece. American Christians have fallen into the trap of consumerism and keeping up with the Joneses at levels that are frightening. For most Americans it is no longer a question of having or not having, but of having or having way too much.

How would your church be judged as an embassy of God? Is it an embassy that promotes the principles, morals, ethics, ideals, and actions of Jesus Christ?

I know of too many churches that are more interested in fund-raisers and social events than they are in building God's kingdom. Churches need to be disciple-making institutions. A subtitle for the church of Jesus Christ could be "Disciple University." The church's main concern must be to teach its members about the meaning of the cross. Sacrifice is where the disciple finds his or her life, and the rewards are there for all who seek this path.

What is necessary for the forces of evil to succeed in the world? As Edmund Burke said, the forces of evil will win if the forces of good do nothing. Perhaps we need to rephrase and update this expression: *All that is necessary for the forces of evil to win in the world is for enough good people to keep on buying things for themselves while ignoring the plight of 2.8 billion persons who live on less than two dollars per day.*

I believe that Nelson Mandela understood the difference between children of the light and children of darkness. Mandela spent twenty-seven years in prison in South Africa, much of it at Robben Island, off the coast of Cape Town. Mandela spoke these words in his inaugural speech as president of South Africa in 1994:

> Our deepest fear is not that we are inadequate. Our deepest fear is that we are powerful beyond measure. It is our light, not our darkness that most frightens us. We ask ourselves, "Who am I to be brilliant, gorgeous, talented, and famous?" Actually, who are you not to be? You are a child of God. Your playing small doesn't serve the world. There's nothing enlightening about shrinking so that other people won't feel insecure around you. We are born to make manifest the Glory of God that is within us. It is not just in some of us; it's in everyone. And as we let our own light shine, we unconsciously give other people permission to do the same. As we are liberated from our own fear, our presence automatically liberates others.

J. R. R. Tolkien created a fantasy world filled with characters who were predominantly good or evil. In the end, the good characters overcame evil and ushered in a new era of peace and justice. I wish we could incarnate the wizard Gandalf, the king Aragorn, the elf Legolas, the dwarf Gimli, the hobbits Frodo, Sam, Pippin, and Merry, and all of the other good characters of *The Lord of the Ring* and enlist their support in our struggle with dark and evil forces. But the world is not so simple, so black and white. We cannot incarnate a group of fictional characters, nor can we isolate and eradicate evil persons. The problems of the world and the individuals who live in it are far more complicated and shaded in tones of gray than those found in works of fiction or as described in sound bites from politicians.

To create a world of peace and justice, we will need to create and develop new means for dealing with the evil and darkness within each of us;

once we have learned to control our own darkness, we will be better prepared to strengthen our light. By embracing the light, we will have the opportunity to affect and influence others. It will become our task, then, to increase, enhance, and amplify the light.

The church needs more light. Our communities need more light. Our nation needs more light. The world needs more light. Let us then seek the light. When we find the light, we must reflect it to others with actions of love and peace, mercy and grace. Let us strive to become children of light, evangelists of light, and sources of light.

Chapter 7
Creating a Cultural Shift

Thinking of Peace Instead of War

Think of a Paradigm Shift as a change from one way of thinking to another. It's a revolution, a transformation, a sort of metamorphosis. It just does not happen, but rather it is driven by agents of change.

—Thomas Kuhn

We have grasped the mystery of the atom and rejected the Sermon on the Mount. Ours is a world of nuclear giants and ethical infants. We know more about war than we do about peace, more about killing than we do about living.

—General Omar Bradley

On January 20, 1969, Richard M. Nixon was inaugurated as the thirty-seventh president of the United States. His election was made possible by one of the most dramatic reversals of fortune in American politics. Nixon rose to the highest office in the United States following bitter defeats in the 1960 presidential election and the 1962 California gubernatorial race. Upon taking office he inherited the Vietnam War, a problem that he seemed unable to bring to a swift conclusion and that plagued his administration. He was forced to resign halfway through his second term due to the Watergate scandal. Although he is most remembered for his flawed Vietnam War policy and his resignation, it should never be forgotten that "only Nixon could go to China."

Born in California in 1913, Nixon came of age during the Great Depression and fought in the Pacific during World War II. On leaving the service he was elected to Congress from his home district, then was elected to the Senate in 1950. In 1952 Dwight Eisenhower selected the thirty-nine-year-old senator to be his running mate, and after Eisenhower won the election, Nixon served as vice president for eight years. In 1960 he won the Republican Party's nomination for president, but lost a closely contested race to John Kennedy. In 1962 Nixon ran for governor of California and again was defeated. Following this loss, Nixon resigned from public office and shared these memorable words with reporters: "You won't have Nixon to kick around anymore." But he did not quit entirely. He resurrected his image in the mid-1960s, captured the Republican Party's nomination again in 1968, and defeated Hubert Humphrey in a tumultuous election.

Richard Nixon was a man of contradictions. Although he was a member of the Society of Friends, a Christian denomination known for its pacifism and peace witness, he served in the navy during World War II, was an ardent Cold War hawk and lifetime anticommunist, and desperately sought a military solution to the war in Vietnam. But the same Richard Nixon spoke these words at his first inauguration: "The greatest honor history can bestow is the title of peacemaker. This honor now beckons America." His historic visit to China in 1972 opened that nation for the first time in over twenty years and led immediately to an improved relationship between the two countries. In addition, and perhaps of even greater importance, Nixon's trip to China led directly to improved relations between the United States and the Soviet Union, and served as one of the boldest initiatives ever undertaken by a president. It shocked our nation and the entire world.

Upon taking office, Nixon reportedly surveyed the world and saw the stalemated Cold War between the United States and the Soviet Union as the most pressing global issue of the time. Additionally, Nixon knew the giant nation of China, with a growing population of 850 million people, was an emerging world power. He understood the Vietnam War, the Korean War, and dozens of other small skirmishes in Africa, Asia, and Central and South America were the direct or indirect result of the Cold War. Determined to change the global political climate, he immediately encouraged his national security advisor, Henry Kissinger, to begin thinking of ways to approach the Chinese and Soviets in order to reduce the tensions among these three major nations.

Providentially, a border dispute broke out between the Soviet Union and China in 1969. In the subsequent months and years, the clash intensified, threatening to become a full-scale war. Nixon seized upon this event and secretly sent Kissinger (who was now secretary of state) to China to arrange for the president's visit. Kissinger's cloak and dagger visit reads like a spy novel and, with the help of leaders in Pakistan, paved the way for Nixon's trip. On February 21, 1972, Nixon shocked the world by arriving in Beijing.

With this visit, Nixon followed through on part of the pledge he had made at his inauguration to move the United States toward becoming a peacemaking country by ushering in an era of *détente*. His signing of the "Shanghai Communiqué" was a brilliant diplomatic triumph that brought China back onto the world stage. Within a few weeks of leaving China, Nixon was in Moscow to negotiate the first step in the Strategic Arms Limitation Treaty (SALT). Born in those few weeks was a search for accommodation among the world's most powerful nations of the United States, Soviet Union, and China. The first effort to reduce the threat from nuclear weapons had begun. Richard Nixon, a Cold War combatant, was able to see that unless the tensions were reduced between these three nations, a potentially cataclysmic nuclear war was just around the corner. *His hope was to allow for co-existence between the democratic and communist-led governments—a paradigm shift of revolutionary proportions.*

In hindsight, the wisdom of Nixon's trips to China and the Soviet Union look self-evident. It was foolish for the United States to remain enemies, in either a cold or active-conflict way, with the Soviet Union or China. These three nations ranked among the largest in the world in population and size and were enormously influential. Geographically, the Soviet Union was the largest nation in the world. At twenty-two million square kilometers, it was more than twice as big as the United States, and it had a population of almost 250 million people. At 850 million people, China had the world's largest population; its landmass was over nine million square kilometers.

But leaders do not have the wisdom of hindsight. What looks brilliant through the lens of history often appears idiotic and imprudent at the time.

Nixon's trip was unexpected; it made many in our country uncomfortable and fearful, worried about what might happen if we let down our guard, even for a moment, with these "evil, communist" nations. Even Nixon's own aides were bewildered with his intentions. After receiving his instructions from Nixon in 1969 to look for an opportunity to open the door to China, Kissinger spoke to the military advisor of his staff, General Alexander Haig, who recalled Kissinger remarking as he left the Oval Office: "Al, this fellow [Nixon] wants to open relations with China. I think he has lost control of his senses." If we are to build a world of peace and justice, we will need to learn how to become more comfortable being uncomfortable.

People yearn for peace and pray for peace all over the world. Politicians tell us their plans to bring peace and prosperity to their nations. Religions all are united in their proclamation that peace is the way to God. Yet, incredibly, we educate for war. We teach about past wars and lay the groundwork for future wars. If we are to make breakthroughs in the field of world peace, we will need to begin teaching about it and laying the groundwork for it. This will take a radical transformation, a paradigm shift running throughout all levels of our society in the way we think, teach, and reflect about war and peace.

Robert Fulghum seemed to understand this shift in values when he wrote his famous essay (it became the title of his first book of essays) "All I Really Need to Know I Learned in Kindergarten." Its simple message sums up this shift:

> All I really need to know about how to live and what to do and how to be I learned in kindergarten. Wisdom was not at the top of the graduate school mountain, but there in the sand pile at school.
>
> These are the things I learned:
>
> Share everything.
>
> Play fair.
>
> Don't hit people.
>
> Put things back where you found them.
>
> Clean up your own mess.
>
> Don't take things that aren't yours.
>
> Say you're sorry when you hurt somebody.
>
> Wash your hands before you eat.

Flush.

Warm cookies and cold milk are good for you. [48]

We teach these values to our young children, but we change this message as they grow. No longer do social skills comprise the primary message; as children mature they discover the world is not as snug and cozy as it was in kindergarten. They learn about competition, about coming in first, about how the winners receive and the losers go away empty handed. This education is part of growing up and learning the realities of the world, which are at odds with the simple, communal approach kindergarten fosters.

It would be nice to live in a world that matched our kindergarten experiences. It would be great if every child in the world had an opportunity to attend kindergarten, share toys, and eat warm cookies and drink cold milk each day. The reality is that many of the world's children will struggle even to live long enough to attend school, and for many who do live to school age, no schools are available.

A stumbling block to world peace is the way we approach the subject of history. We look at history through the lens of past wars and define our heroes by the military victories they achieved. We mark human history and define the past by learning the dates of wars and studying the strategies of successful generals and military leaders. We study the presidents of the United States who led our nation through times of war, but we neglect those who guided us in times of peace and prosperity. Our focus on war and the makers of war, and our general avoidance of periods of peace and individual peacemakers subtly and subliminally plants the seed in young people's minds that times of war are more interesting than times of peace. Further, children learn that resolving disputes through the use of military force is the way things have always been done and that this is a viable option for the future.

We must stop glorifying war and elevating its participants to the level of heroes. It is time to start teaching about the great peacemakers of history and the methods they employed in their lives and work, as well as developing a peace timeline that is taught as vigorously as the war timeline. Peace studies must be developed for our churches and schools, and we must shift the paradigm from glorifying the peacebreakers to praising the peacemakers.

I remember vividly my first encounter in Sunday school with the story of David and Goliath and recall the joy I felt in learning that God's chosen

---

[48] Robert Fulghum, *All I Really Need to Know I Learned in Kindergarten* (New York, Villard Books, 1989), 6–7.

child had conquered an evil giant. I learned David was a great warrior and had, in addition to slaying Goliath, captured Jerusalem and expanded Israel's borders by military conquests. King David, I learned, was a great biblical hero; in fact, so great was his influence that it was predicted that the Messiah would be a direct descendant of his.

I remember singing the words to "Joshua Fit the Battle of Jericho" and marching around the Sunday school classroom with the other students just as Joshua and the children of Israel had done around Jericho before defeating it. I remember how Pharaoh's army drowned crossing the Red Sea, and remember the feeling of justification knowing God had killed those bad people. We studied the actions of the judges, and I recall learning of Samson, Deborah, and Gideon and their military conquests. Even in church, war and fighting is in the curriculum, and we create heroes of those who fought.

In most American schools, it does not matter whether you study global, European, or American history—courses will devote most of their subject matter to the wars fought, the battles won, and the leading participants involved. In a typical American history curriculum, some background material is provided to learn of the Native Americans and the colonial period, but then comes the Revolutionary War, followed by the War of 1812, the Civil War, World War I, World War II, the Cold War, the Korean War, the Vietnam War, and the Gulf War. Approximately half of the class time and the textbooks are devoted to these wars, which cover a cumulative time span of thirty-three years our nation has been engaged in war, a total that represents only fifteen percent of the total length of time the United States has been a nation.[49]

The same exercise can be conducted for European or global history. We study the great generals and conquerors, from Alexander the Great to Julius Caesar, Attila the Hun, Charlemagne, William the Conqueror, Genghis Khan, Hernando Cortes, Napoleon Bonaparte, and Adolf Hitler. But we ignore the periods of time the world was at peace and we ignore the men and women responsible for these times of tranquility.

Our history and our identities are shaped in many ways by the wars our national and spiritual ancestors fought. We celebrate the victories achieved by these military figures, and we mourn their losses. Their victories and defeats become part of our makeup, a kind of DNA imprinted on our psyches by the cultural environment in which we live. This worldview is created and

---

[49] Thirty-three is a somewhat arbitrary number, because it is hard to define when some wars began, including the Revolutionary War (Bunker Hill? Declaration of Independence?) and the war in Vietnam. One could add to this total the forty-three years (1948–1991) that define the Cold War, a period that includes the Korean and Vietnam Wars. However, I believe thirty-three is a fair figure.

maintained in both our secular and religious environments, and it feeds a loyalty to our nation and faith that can be healthy when done in moderation, but dangerous when emphasized to the point of xenophobia.

War and military conquest are not just a part of our historic past, but of our everyday reality. When our nation is at war, its coverage dominates our news. We place our generals and military spokespersons on great pedestals and collectively unite to mourn our dead. When our nation is at peace, news from our soldiers, military personnel, military academies, and our ongoing military preparation are still reported extensively, as are wars other nations are engaged in. Chris Hedges writes powerfully about recent wars and the addictive power they have on individuals and nations:

> I learned early on that war forms its own culture. The rush of battle is a potent and often lethal addiction, for war is a drug, one I ingested for many years. It is peddled by mythmakers—historians, war correspondents, filmmakers, novelists, and the state—all of whom endow it with qualities it often does possess: excitement, exoticism, power, chances to rise above our small stations in life, and a bizarre and fantastic universe that has a grotesque and dark beauty. It dominates culture, distorts memory, corrupts language, and infects everything around it.[50]

Like all drug addicts, the making of war creates a constant longing, a craving appetite that needs a fix. Humanity's insatiable appetite for war is fed through the military-industrial complex that must create newer, faster, higher technological weapons, and then use them in battle to see that they work.

We become hooked as young people; war history is taught in schools and churches, heroes are made, and victories are cherished. But we devote far too little time and attention to the costs of war, of the lives destroyed, the hope crushed, the pain inflicted.

When I marched with my fellow students around the Sunday school classroom imitating Joshua and his army, I did not think of the men, women, and children who were slaughtered in the conquest, a total annihilation of every person who lived in Jericho.[51] When I learned of David's victory over Goliath, did I mourn? Did I think of the sadness King David inflicted when

---

[50] Chris Hedges, *War Is a Force That Gives Us Meaning* (New York: Public Affairs, 2002), 3.

[51] The lone exception was Rahab the harlot, who was spared along with her family because she had helped the Jewish spies gather intelligence about the city.

he captured Jerusalem and killed its former inhabitants? We read the praise of David recorded in the Bible, "Saul has killed his thousands, and David his ten thousands" (1 Sam 21:11), but do we ever think of those slain? Do we consider the grief those deaths created? The volume of tears that have been shed over the deaths of soldiers and civilians in war could fill an ocean.

The killing has not stopped; in fact, as we move further into the twenty-first century, my fear is that it is escalating. Once again Chris Hedges writes:

> Look just at the 1990s: 2 million dead in Afghanistan; 1.5 million dead in the Sudan; some 800,000 butchered in ninety days in Rwanda; a half-million dead in Angola; a quarter of a million dead in Bosnia; 200,000 dead in Guatemala; 150,000 dead in Liberia; a quarter of a million dead in Burundi; 75,000 dead in Algeria; and untold tens of thousands lost in the border conflict between Ethiopia and Eritrea, the fighting in Columbia, the Israeli-Palestinian conflict, Chechnya, Sri Lanka, southeastern Turkey, Sierra Leone, Northern Ireland, Kosovo, and the Persian Gulf War (where perhaps as many as 35,000 Iraqi citizens were killed). In the wars of the twentieth century not less than 62 million civilians have perished, nearly 20 million more than the 43 million military personnel killed.[52]

Only in the past few years have I realized our indoctrination toward seeing war in a positive way begins at a young age. Our playing field is clearly sloped toward war, and it is much easier to run downhill into war than fight our way uphill toward an alternative approach, toward building a world of peace and justice. Colman McCarthy writes about our education system as well, and how it favors a pathway that leads toward violence, from

> political leaders who fund wars and send the young to fight them, judges and juries who dispatch people to death row, filmmakers who script gunplay movies and cartoons, toy manufacturers marketing "action games," parents in war zone homes where verbal or physical abuse is common, high-school history texts that tell about Calamity Jane but not Jane Addams, Daniel Boone but not Daniel Berrigan.[53]

---

[52] Hedges, *War Is a Force,* 12–13.

[53] Colman McCarthy, *I'd Rather Teach Peace* (Maryknoll, NY: Orbis, 2002), xv.

He goes on to tell of an exercise he does in every class he teaches. He begins by pulling a $100 bill from his wallet and telling his students that whoever can identify the six persons whose names he will call out will win the money. He begins the quiz:

> Who is Robert E. Lee? All hands shoot up: the general who led the Confederate side in the Civil War. Everyone is one for one. Who is Ulysses S. Grant? All hands rise; the general who led the Union side. Who is Norman Schwarzkopf? The general who won the Persian Gulf War. Everyone is three for three and looking good.
>
> Who is Jeannette Rankin? No hands go up. Who is Dorothy Day? No one stirs. Who is Jody Williams? No one knows.
>
> I've done this one-hundred-dollar bill quiz hundreds of times, before students in classrooms, before students in large assemblies, and before large audiences of educators. It's safe money. It's safe, too, that everyone will know the first three but not the last three. They know the peacebreakers but not the peacemakers. They know the men who want to solve conflicts by killing but not the women who believe in loving.[54]

Our society's emphasis on war and peacebreakers is easily confirmed with a visit to a bookstore. Not long ago I visited a Barnes & Noble, a Borders, and a local, hometown bookstore. I was interested in how many books they sold under the category of war, and how many under the category of peace.

In all three stores I asked where I could find the "peace" section. Puzzled looks were followed at the chain stores with a quick computer search that eventually led me to the religion section. The response from the local bookstore was immediate: "We do not have a peace section." Although the religion sections in these large bookstores have expanded greatly in recent years, the books included there could hardly be categorized as "peace books." One finds in these sections Bibles and Bible commentaries, as well as books in subject areas such as meditation, atheism and agnosticism, Eastern religions, mysticism, and the largest section of all, Christian fiction.

To be fair, there is no "war" section in these bookstores either. However, if you visit the history section of any bookstore, you will find numerous books,

---

[54] McCarthy, *I'd Rather Teach Peace,* 15–16.

more books than you could read in a lifetime, on the various wars humans have fought. My unofficial tabulation of the books found in the history section from all three bookstores combined indicates approximately 75 percent are books in which some aspect of war is the dominant theme.

In one of the larger bookstores I discovered an entire bookshelf, eight feet high by six feet wide, filled with books on European wars. I counted three full rows with books devoted to warfare in the ancient world, two rows of books on the Napoleonic Wars, another two rows of books on World War I, and three and a half rows—146 books—documenting the events of World War II.

I turned the corner and came over to the U.S. history section. The dominant subsections here included books on the Revolutionary War, the Civil War, World War I, and World War II. Additionally, there were books on American naval history, on weapons and their use, and even more under a subsection called "military history." I found books on the War of 1812, the Spanish-American War, the Korean War, the Vietnam War, the Gulf War, and the War on Terror. I was disappointed, although not surprised, to find more books on the Civil War than there were Bible commentaries. In fact, the number of books on war, in one form or another, just from the American history section of the three bookstores exceeded the number of books in the entire religion section by nearly 3 to 1!

In chapter 1 I called for a massive "Marshall Plan" for the twenty-first century that reallocates our resources to provide the basic necessities of life missing in so many parts of the world. I will advocate here for a radical paradigm shift in our entire educational process, from preschool through college and graduate school. We need to begin teaching more about the peacemakers and less about the peacebreakers. We need to learn of the men and women who devoted their lives to finding and seeking nonviolent means of dealing with national and international conflict. We need to transform the way we think about war and peace and elevate the position peacemakers have in our collective psyches.

This movement has already begun in some progressive schools and colleges. Classes in peacemaking are now being taught in some high schools and colleges, and some colleges even offer a major in peace studies. But this trend is only in its infancy—and we have a long way to go. There are approximately 80,000 elementary schools in the United States, 30,000 high schools, and 3,000 colleges. Until every school in the United States offers as many peace studies courses as it does courses that focus on war, we will not change the paradigm that presents war as a viable option in the settling of international disputes. Pacifism, nonviolence, and active peacemaking are legitimate, effective schools of thought with a rich heritage of writings and ideals that need to be incorporated into the educational process.

Perhaps one day you will be sitting in a room with Colman McCarthy and he will promise one hundred dollars to anyone in the room who can identify the six people he names. Assuming that you already know enough about Robert E. Lee, Ulysses S. Grant, and Norman Schwarzkopf, let me help you claim his cash by providing you with the following peace history lesson.

Born on a ranch in rural Montana in 1880, Jeannette Rankin led a successful drive for the rights of women to vote in 1914, and in 1916 won election to the U.S. House of Representatives, four years before the passage of the Nineteenth Amendment to the Constitution giving women the right to vote. She was the first woman to serve in Congress and one of the first women to serve in any democratically elected position in the world. A lifelong pacifist, she voted against the entry of the United States into World War I. She chose to run for the Senate in 1918 but lost that election, partly as a result of her vote on the war. She did not run for anything again until 1940, when for a second time she won a term in the House of Representatives. Following the Japanese attack on Pearl Harbor in December 1941, a vote on going to war once again came before Congress. Again, Jeannette Rankin voted no. She is the only member of Congress to have voted no against U.S. involvement in World War I and World War II. John Kennedy later wrote of her, "Few members of Congress have ever stood more alone while being true to a higher honor and loyalty." She died in 1973 but was remembered by her home state of Montana, which placed a statute of her in the U.S. Capitol building in 1985.

Dorothy Day was born in 1897 and studied to become a journalist. Following a conversion experience, she became an activist and was well known for her campaigns in defense of the poor, the hungry, and the homeless. In 1933 she, along with Peter Maurin, founded the Catholic Worker newspaper to promote a neutral, pacifist position during the uneasy times of the 1930s. She later opened a "house of hospitality" in a New York City slum. A movement began and spread to other cities throughout the United States, Canada, and Great Britain. Today over a hundred Catholic Worker communities exist globally, including several in Australia, Germany, the Netherlands, Ireland, Mexico, New Zealand, and Sweden. Day chose to be a peacemaker by feeding the hungry, clothing the naked, and providing shelter to those in need. She wrote and spoke out against war and violence and was an ardent opponent of the Vietnam War. In 1978 she received the Pax Christi Teacher of Peace Award. She died in 1980. Following her death, Dorothy Day was declared a Servant of God, the first step toward sainthood, under the papacy of Pope John Paul II.

Jody Williams is the founding coordinator of the International Campaign to Ban Landmines (ICBL), which was officially launched in 1992 by six nongovernmental organizations. Born in 1950, Williams has overseen the growth of the ICBL to more than a thousand NGOs in more than sixty countries and has served as the chief strategist and spokesperson for the campaign. Working in an unprecedented cooperative effort with governments, UN bodies and the International Committee of the Red Cross, the ICBL achieved its goal of an international treaty banning antipersonnel landmines during the diplomatic conference held in Oslo in September 1997. She and her organization have saved thousands of lives through their activities and were awarded the Nobel Peace Prize in 1997.

The founder of the Nobel Prizes was Alfred Nobel (1833–1896), the man who invented dynamite. Nobel developed the process in which the volatile and unpredictable combination of chemicals called nitroglycerine could be mixed with silica and made into a safer, more reliable product. Nobel named this new material dynamite. But he wanted to be remembered for more than his invention. He established an endowment and structure to award prizes for achievements in economics, physics, chemistry, medicine, and peace.

At the age of 43, Nobel placed an ad in the newspaper seeking a "lady of mature age, versed in languages, as secretary and supervisor of household." He hired an Austrian woman, Countess Bertha Kinsky, who worked for him for a short time before returning to Austria to marry Count Arthur von Suttner. Nobel and Bertha remained close friends and wrote to each other for many years. Bertha von Suttner became very critical of the arms race developing between the leading nations of Europe toward the end of the nineteenth century and wrote a wonderful, simple book titled *Lay Down Your Arms.* She became a leading figure in the peace movement of the time. Undoubtedly, she helped Nobel's decision to establish a prize for persons or organizations that did the most to promote peace. In 1905, she herself was awarded the Nobel Peace Prize, a fitting choice given the work she did for peace.

It is hard to tell how history will judge Richard Nixon. During his presidency, the war in Vietnam was prolonged. He is the only president to have resigned; he left the office under great duress. Unlike presidents Theodore Roosevelt, Woodrow Wilson, and Jimmy Carter, Nixon never won the Nobel Peace Prize. But his words of wisdom continue to speak to us: "The greatest honor history can bestow is the title of peacemaker. This honor now beckons America." These words were incorporated into the heart of his first inauguration speech, delivered on January 20, 1969. Nixon's China and Soviet Union policies made many of those around him, and many of his fellow citizens, extremely uncomfortable. But these visits paved the way for détente and, eventually, the end of the Cold War.

The honor of being peacemakers is awaiting us. Jesus said, "Blessed are the peacemakers, for they will be called children of God" (Matt 5:9). Peacemaking is a sacred calling. It is also a task for those who are willing to forge their own pathway and break out of the box. The peacemakers who have won the Nobel Peace Prize are the men and women with the vision and passion to address the issues of their day with creative, innovative solutions. Many have lived in isolation and have earned the scorn and disdain of their contemporaries. Through their unconventional, often eccentric, thoughts and deeds, they have elicited paradigm shifts in the ways others have thought of war and peace. They have earned their honorary and revered title: peacemaker.

Many young athletes throughout the world train intensively to make their country's Olympic team and win a gold medal. They devote countless hours to conditioning and specific training for their particular event. The winners are placed on pedestals; some receive commercial endorsements, prizes, and professional contracts based on their accomplishments. We cheer with them in victory and agonize with them in defeat.

What a great day it will be when we hold the peacemakers in the same regard. But for this to become a reality, we must begin to make peace a priority. We must start teaching about peacemaking methods and learn about the great peacemakers in world history. We must learn the words of George Bernard Shaw, often quoted by Robert Kennedy: "Some look at the world and see how it is and ask 'Why?' I look upon the world as it could be and ask 'Why not?'"

In my mind, those who have received the Nobel Peace Prize stand at the summit of achievement. These are the most important men and women of the last hundred or so years. For their work and devotion in creating a world of peace and justice for all of God's children, I include their names here.

List of Nobel Peace Laureates

1901	Henry Dunant
	Frédéric Passy
1902	Élie Ducommun
	Albert Gobat
1903	Randal Cremer
1904	Institute of International Law
1905	Bertha von Suttner

1906	Theodore Roosevelt
1907	Ernesto Teodoro Moneta
	Louis Renault
1908	Klas Pontus Arnoldson
	Fredrik Bajer
1909	Auguste Beernaert
	Paul Henri d'Estournelles de Constant
1910	Permanent International Peace Bureau
1911	Tobias Asser
	Alfred Fried
1912	Elihu Root
1913	Henri La Fontaine
1917	International Committee of the Red Cross
1919	Woodrow Wilson
1920	Léon Bourgeois
1921	Hjalmar Branting
	Christian Lange
1922	Fridtjof Nansen
1925	Sir Austen Chamberlain
	Charles G. Dawes
1926	Aristide Briand
	Gustav Stresemann
1927	Ferdinand Buisson
	Ludwig Quidde
1929	Frank B. Kellogg
1930	Nathan Söderblom
1931	Jane Addams
	Nicholas Murray Butler
1933	Sir Norman Angell

1934	Arthur Henderson
1935	Carl von Ossietzky
1936	Carlos Saavedra Lamas
1937	Robert Cecil
1938	Nansen International Office for Refugees
1944	International Committee of the Red Cross
1945	Cordell Hull
1946	Emily Greene Balch
	John R. Mott
1947	Friends Service Council
	American Friends Service Committee
1949	Lord Boyd Orr
1950	Ralph Bunche
1951	Léon Jouhaux
1952	Albert Schweitzer
1953	George C. Marshall
1954	Office of the United Nations High Commissioner for Refugees
1957	Lester Bowles Pearson
1958	Georges Pire
1959	Philip Noel-Baker
1960	Albert Lutuli
1961	Dag Hammarskjöld
1962	Linus Pauling
1963	International Committee of the Red Cross, League of Red Cross Societies
1964	Martin Luther King Jr.
1965	United Nations Children's Fund
1968	René Cassin
1969	International Labour Organization

1970	Norman Borlaug
1971	Willy Brandt
1973	Le Duc Tho
	Henry Kissinger
1974	Seán MacBride
	Eisaku Sato
1975	Andrei Sakharov
1976	Mairead Corrigan
	Betty Williams
1977	Amnesty International
1978	Anwar al-Sadat
	Menachem Begin
1979	Mother Teresa
1980	Adolfo Pérez Esquivel
1981	Office of the United Nations High Commissioner for Refugees
1982	Alfonso García Robles
	Alva Myrdal
1983	Lech Walesa
1984	Desmond Tutu
1985	International Physicians for the Prevention of Nuclear War
1986	Elie Wiesel
1987	Oscar Arias Sánchez
1988	United Nations Peacekeeping Forces
1989	The 14th Dalai Lama
1990	Mikhail Gorbachev
1991	Aung San Suu Kyi
1992	Rigoberta Menchú Tum
1993	F. W. de Klerk
	Nelson Mandela

1994	Yasser Arafat
	Shimon Peres
	Yitzhak Rabin
1995	Pugwash Conferences on Science and World Affairs
	Joseph Rotblat
1996	Carlos Filipe Ximenes Belo
	José Ramos-Horta
1997	International Campaign to Ban Landmines
	Jody Williams
1998	John Hume
	David Trimble
1999	Médecins Sans Frontières
2000	Kim Dae-jung
2001	United Nations
	Kofi Annan
2002	Jimmy Carter
2003	Shirin Ebadi
2004	Wangari Maathai
2005	International Atomic Energy Agency (IAEA) and Director General Mohamed ElBaradei
2006	Muhammad Yunus and Grameen Bank

Chapter 8
The Realities of War

If Sherman Was Right and "War Is Hell," Why Do We Continue to Glorify It?

He who joyfully marches to music in rank and file has already earned my contempt. He has been given a large brain by mistake, since for him the spinal cord would fully suffice. . . . Heroism at command, senseless brutality, deplorable love-of-country stance—how violently I hate all this; how despicable and ignoble war is. . . . I would rather be torn to shreds than be part of so base an action. It is my conviction that killing under the cloak of war is nothing but an act of murder.

—Albert Einstein

One is called to live nonviolently, even if the change one works for seems impossible. . . . But one thing favors such an attempt: the total inability of violence to change anything for the better.

—Daniel Berrigan

The American Heritage Dictionary of the English Language's Fourth Edition (2000) defines a *Potemkin Village* as follows:

NOUN: Something that appears elaborate and impressive but in actual fact lacks substance: *the Potemkin village of this country's borrowed prosperity.*"

ETYMOLOGY: After Grigori Aleksandrovich <u>Potemkin</u>, who had elaborate fake villages constructed for Catherine the Great's tours of the Ukraine and the Crimea.

As a United Methodist pastor for over twenty years, I have officiated at hundreds of weddings and funerals. From time to time, those being married or those who died have been persons who have served or are currently serving in the military. I recall one wedding that included a groom, best man, and ushers who were actively serving in the Marines, and a bride and bridesmaids who were currently serving in the Navy. The dress uniform of the Marine men complemented the formal whites of the Navy women, providing a striking wedding party. I have done funerals for many veterans, and the military presence has ranged from a simple, flag-draped coffin to a full military burial, complete with a bugler, rifles, and horse-drawn caissons. At these worship services I have always been greatly impressed with the pageantry and display the military can provide. We honor our soldiers in notable and inspiring ways.

But the decorative uniforms and impressive rituals belie the reality of war. Like the fake village fronts Grigori Potemkin constructed in the eighteenth century to deceive Catherine II of Russia, the honor and glory we consign to warfare is elaborate and impressive but is in fact deceiving. We want to think of our soldiers as noble and gallant, dignified and righteous. We want to believe that our soldiers and our troops (no matter what nation we are from) are virtuous men and women whose actions are justified, no matter the particular situation. We glorify war and its soldiers, honoring their accomplishments and lamenting their defeats. And while it is true that many soldiers are brave and courageous, noble and righteous, we lose sight of their primary function: soldiers are sent to war zones to kill and to be killed. They train physically, emotionally, and intellectually to become superior to their enemies, so that they may be on the giving rather than receiving end of death. Sometimes those in power view soldiers as expendable commodities, to be used when diplomacy fails or when it seems that war will benefit the interests of the nation or its leader. The military may be filled with wonderful men and women, but their task is not glorious. The work of the soldier is savage, brutal, and vile. There is no glory in war.

The United States has the strongest, most dominant military in the history of the world. Our soldiers are better trained, better equipped, and better prepared than any other fighting force has ever been. No nation on the planet can approach our military strength, and none would be so foolish as to draw us onto the battlefield.

But to participate in the veneration of war, to elevate its place in human history, to idolize the glory of battle and exalt its warriors is to promote a false reality and to spread a lie. I have spoken to dozens of veterans who have shared with me their wartime experiences. These include veterans of World War II, the Korean War, the Vietnam War, the Gulf War of 1991 and the current wars in Iraq and Afghanistan. Far from glorifying war, these men and women speak of its terror—of the post-traumatic stress disorder they have experienced, of sleepless nights and, even worse, horrifying nightmares. Some peer into the shadows, expecting enemy combatants to appear at any moment. They show more sympathy for enemy soldiers than any other group I have known, because they know that all soldiers share the same situation—kill or be killed.

Who benefits from war? In the final analysis, perhaps no one really does. Those who have led great armies and conquered large territories have often watched these empires crumble during their lifetimes; in other cases, the empires collapsed soon after their deaths. Alexander the Great died at the age of 33, the severe wounds he suffered during his campaigns no doubt a contributing factor to his death. His empire was soon divided into four sections. The Roman Empire declined and fell; today we can visit the ruins, but the power of Rome is long gone. Charlemagne's empire dissolved soon after his death. The Crusaders held Jerusalem for less than a century until it was re-conquered by the Muslims. Saladin, the great Muslim liberator of Jerusalem, in turn died six months after he had recaptured the holy city. Genghis Khan died while leading his army to battle to secure one of his borders; his empire was divided between his sons, who could not control it. Napoleon raised one of the largest armies in world history and literally saw it dissolve before his eyes as men died from combat, hunger, disease, and exposure on their way to and retreat from Moscow. The German, Austro-Hungarian, Ottoman, and Russian thrones were all lost in World War I, a war that claimed 13.7 million soldiers but left the national boundaries essentially where they had been when the war began. Hitler's early gains were wiped out and the "thousand-year reign" of the Third Reich lasted merely twelve years.

Generals, kings, emperors, prime ministers, presidents, and popes have marched across the world scene, determined to write their names on history with military campaigns of victory and achievement—but they have left behind death and destruction, blood and tears, hatred and helplessness.

War is not glorious. The church's purpose is to partner with God in the building of the kingdom on earth; the reality is that war brings hell to earth. Christian leaders who use war as a means of foreign strategy pursue policies that are in contradiction to the life and teachings of Jesus Christ.

There is one group that does benefit from war. That group is the industrialists. Wars often have the effect of helping a nation's economy, and the producers of military products usually see rising profits during wartime. In his book *Wealth and Democracy,* historian Kevin Phillips documents the politics of the rich and poor and traces the former's increase in wealth all the way back to the Revolutionary War and the profits made during times of war.[55] In 1963 a young Bob Dylan wrote "Masters of War," a song never as popular as some of his other hits, but as prophetically powerful as "Blowin' in the Wind." Here is one verse of that song:

You fasten the triggers

For the others to fire

Then you set back and watch

When the death count gets higher

You hide in your mansion

As young people's blood

Flows out of their bodies

And is buried in the mud

The defense industry is a multi-billion-dollar enterprise that produces wealth for its executives and stockholders at rates that boggle the mind. Corporations such as Halliburton and Bechtel have profited enormously from the wars in Afghanistan and Iraq, and their CEOs have received salaries and stock options worth hundreds of millions of dollars. Dylan continues:

But there's one thing I know

Though I'm younger than you

Even Jesus would never

Forgive what you do

---

[55] Kevin Phillips, *Wealth and Democracy* (New York: Random House, 2002).

The Myth of War

The myth that wars are glorious and magnificent and that soldiers are true and just goes back to the beginning of human history. Prostitution has often been called the world's oldest profession, but I wonder if soldiering predates prostitution. The earliest writings we have speak of war and armies and combat—and use words such as *duty, valor, noble, glory, honor, and merit* to describe the qualities of their soldiers.

Young soldiers do not give their lives for their countries—national leaders steal the lives of their young people in order to cover up for their unwillingness and/or inability to find peaceful solutions to conflicts. Too many politicians lack the skills and training necessary to negotiate effectively with others; instead, they turn too quickly to a knee-jerk, learned pathway that leads to violence. Since the beginning of time, might has determined right—that is, whoever has had the strongest army has been able to control their destiny and be in command of international relationships. We need to turn this phrase around, as Abraham Lincoln did in his Cooper Union Address: "Let us have faith that right makes might, and in that faith, let us, to the end, dare to do our duty as we understand it."[56]

Perhaps the greatest contributing factor to the esteemed place we give to members of the military is patriotism. Americans love their country. We believe the United States it is the greatest nation in the history of the world. We are convinced of the special place our nation holds in the world; therefore, the actions our nation undertakes and the policies it implements must represent the right things to do. Blindly, we accept the words and ideas of our leaders and follow them to wherever they may lead, including war.

Nations have long rallied around leaders who call their people to wage war on "the enemy," even if this enemy has to be fabricated. It seems rather easy to rally people to war, and this has been documented back to the time of the ancient Greeks, who under the leadership of Pericles went to battle during the Peloponnesian War. While Pericles is known as one of the great orators of human history, he gave more credit and power to his colleague Demosthenes: "When Pericles speaks, the people say, 'How well he speaks.' But when Demosthenes speaks, the people say, 'Let us march!'"[57]

In the more than two thousand years since Pericles and Demosthenes have we come no further along than this? How do eloquent, charismatic

---

[56] *The Collected Works of Abraham Lincoln,* ed. by Roy Basler (New Brunswick, NJ: Rutgers University Press, 1953), vol. 3, 550.

[57] *Lend Me Your Ears: Great Speeches in History,* selected and introduced by William Safire (New York: Norton, 1992), 25.

speakers articulate persuasive arguments, effectively sending men and women off to their deaths to fight and die for their countries? Consider these sobering words, spoken by the Nazi leader Hermann Goering during the Nuremberg Trials following World War II:

> Why, of course the people don't want war. Why should some poor slob on a farm want to risk his life in a war when the best he can get out of it is to come back to his farm in one piece? Naturally, the common people don't want war: neither in Russia, nor in England, nor for that matter in Germany. That is understood. But after all it is the leaders of the country who determine the policy, and it is always a simple matter to drag the people along, whether it is a democracy, or a fascist dictatorship, or a parliament, or a communist dictatorship. . . . Voice or no voice, the people can always be brought to the bidding of the leaders. That is easy. All you have to do is to tell them they are being attacked, and denounce the pacifists for lack of patriotism and exposing the country to danger.[58]

Goering's cynical prediction of how simple it is to manipulate public opinion was in evidence in the United States in the 1960s. As the war in Vietnam escalated, claiming more and more American and Vietnamese lives, Eugene McCarthy in 1968 boldly threw his hat into the ring as a presidential contender, challenging the incumbent president of his own party, Lyndon Johnson. Years later McCarthy recalled:

> As [the war] continued to go badly, its advocates became more defensive. The motives of those who spoke out against the war were questioned, as was their patriotism, and in the case of the Democrats, their loyalty to the party. Critics were called "nervous Nellies" and "special pleaders," and, in the language of cattle handlers, as ready to "cut and run."[59]

---

[58] This quote does not appear in the transcripts of the Nuremberg Trials, because Goering did not speak them at his trial but privately to a German-speaking intelligence officer and psychologist named Gustave Gilbert. Gilbert kept a journal and later printed it under the title *Nuremberg Diary*. This quote was part of a conversation Gilbert had with Goering on April 18, 1946.

[59] Bob Herbert, "The Man Who Said No to War," *New York Times,* December 15, 2005, op ed page.

William Sloane Coffin says it simply and powerfully: "All nations make decisions based on self–interest and then defend them in the name of morality."[60]

Pride, Patriotism, and the Dehumanization of the Enemy

Pride is the first of the seven deadly sins. Each of us must find a balance between excessive pride and excessive humility. Persons with severely low self-esteem run the risk of not loving and caring for themselves. They may fear that others will not listen to them, and so they remain silent. Persons with large egos are often self-absorbed and narcissistic. They risk being loud, obnoxious, and overbearing. It is difficult being with someone with an over-inflated ego; their pride often prevents them from seeing the world around them as it truly is. When one's self-image grows too large, pride moves in and is manifested in arrogance, conceit, and smugness. Pride deserves its place as the first of the seven deadly sins.[61]

Patriotism is a form of pride on a national scale. Once again, a balance needs to be struck between too little and too much. Persons who hate their country may be led toward revolutionary activities, or they may choose to leave their country altogether in a search for a new national identity. Overly enthusiastic patriotism can lead to jingoism (zealous patriotism expressing itself especially in hostility toward other countries) and xenophobia (an intense fear or dislike of foreign people, their customs and culture, or foreign things).

Although we find pride on an individual scale to be sinful, excessive patriotism is often applauded and celebrated. But fervent patriotism can become sinful when we blindly believe what our leaders say simply because they are from our country, and disbelieve what foreign leaders say simply because they are from other countries. The phrase "My country, right or wrong" is a dangerous slogan. We may love our country even if we understand that it is not perfect, but we must strive to correct its faults and weaknesses. When we love our country and continue to support programs and policies that we know are immoral, we participate in immorality ourselves.

Chris Hedges, whom I quoted in the last chapter for his comments regarding the addictive nature of war, also writes powerfully about patriotism and how our love of country drives us toward war:

---

[60] William Sloane Coffin, *Credo* (Louisville, KY: Westminster John Knox, 2004), 80.

[61] The other sins are greed, lust, envy, gluttony, wrath, and sloth.

It is part of war's perversity that we lionize those who make great warriors and excuse their excesses in the name of self-defense. . . . We call on the warrior to exemplify the qualities necessary to prosecute war—courage, loyalty, and self-sacrifice. The soldier, neglected and even shunned during peacetime, is suddenly held up as the exemplar of our highest ideals, the savior of the state. The soldier is often whom we want to become, although secretly many of us, including most soldiers, know that we can never match the ideal held out before us. And we all become like Nestor in *The Illiad,* reciting the litany of fallen heroes that went before to spur on a new generation.

A few pages later, Hedges continues:

While we venerate and mourn our own dead we are curiously indifferent about those we kill. Thus killing is done in our name, killing that concerns us little, while those who kill our own are seen as having crawled out of the deepest recesses of the earth, lacking our own humanity and goodness. Our dead. Their dead. They are not the same. Our dead matter, theirs do not. Many Israelis defend the killing of Palestinian children whose only crime was to throw rocks at armored patrols, while many Palestinians applaud the murder of Israeli children by suicide bombers.[62]

War through the Ages

Although war is glorified in some journalistic and literary circles, many other great writers have addressed the subject of war in more honest terms. Far from lifting war up as a grand enterprise to be praised, they write of its destructive power, the terrible toll it takes on soldiers and civilians alike. Throughout history great writers have captured the corruption and folly, madness and waste of war. In the following pages, I have collected a handful of accounts of battles and war scenes from some of the greatest writers in history. The purpose is to help us come to grips with the reality that *war should be avoided at all costs,* and not considered as a viable solution to any situation.

---

[62] Chris Hedges, *War Is a Force That Gives Us Meaning* (New York: Public Affairs, 2002), 8, 11, 13–14.

To the ancient Greeks, the model soldier was Achilles, whose exploits from the mythic battle of Troy earned him great fame. But Homer, the author of The Illiad, was realistic in his depiction of warfare:

> And next Achilles lunged
>
> at Demoleon, son of Antenor, a tough defensive fighter—
>
> he stabbed his temple and cleft his helmet's cheekpiece.
>
> None of the bronze plate could hold it—boring through
>
> the metal and skull the bronze spearpoint pounded.
>
> Demoleon's brains spattered all inside his casque,
>
> the Trojan beaten down in his fury. Hippodamas next,
>
> he leapt from his chariot fleeing before Achilles—
>
> Achilles's spearshaft rammed him through the back
>
> and he gasped his life away, bellowing like some bull
>
> that chokes and grunts when the young boys drag him round.[63]

Alexander the Great considered himself the living embodiment of Achilles, destined to unite the Greeks and spread their culture throughout the known world. He secured his position as the head of a united Greece by first crushing and obliterating Thebes, the one city-state that held out against him. Alexander butchered more than six thousand Theban men, women, and children—erasing from the collective memory of Greece an entire city in the world's first known act of genocide. So began his decade-long swath of conquest and barbarism on an unprecedented scale. Far from glorious, historian Victor Davis Hanson writes that

> in general, Alexander's murdering falls into five categories: the sheer carnage he wrought on the battlefield in a constant and unnecessary war of aggrandizement; the routine murder of defenders and civilians in sieges; the slaughtering of tribes and villagers during years of policing and guerrilla warfare; the oft-forgotten human costs of his megalomaniacal, unnecessary and often crazed adventures; and the more mundane casual

---

[63] Homer, *The Illiad,* trans. Robert Fagles (New York: Viking, 1996), book 20, lines 449–58.

extermination of rivals, friends, family and strangers. . . . I would think it a very conservative estimate to assume a quarter million town and city residents were slaughtered between 334 and 324 BCE, most of them civilian defenders who unfortunately lived in the path of Alexander's trek east.[64]

Roman Rule

The *Pax Romana,* the "Peace of Rome," was established at the point of the sword. Rome conquered the area surrounding the Mediterranean Sea through military campaigns. To read of Caesar's battles through Gaul is to understand the savagery of war and the total destruction of the enemy necessary for victory. Roman historians write of the rivers of blood that flowed through the valleys where his army fought. By the end of the Gallic Wars, the campaign had resulted in eight hundred conquered cities, three hundred subdued tribes, one million men sold into slavery, and another *three million dead* on the battlefields.

Roman rule extended throughout the Holy Land; Christians know well the story of Jesus' life and death under the sovereignty of Rome. Growing anger against Roman suppression of Jewish life resulted in sporadic violence that escalated into a full-scale revolt in 66 CE. Superior Roman forces led by Titus were finally victorious, razing Jerusalem to the ground in 70 and defeating the last Jewish outpost at Masada three years later.

The destruction of Jerusalem and the temple was catastrophic for the Jewish people. According to historian Josephus Flavius, hundreds of thousands of Jews perished in the siege of Jerusalem and elsewhere in the country, and many thousands more were sold into slavery. A last, brief period of Jewish sovereignty in ancient times followed the revolt of Shimon Bar Kokhba (132 CE), during which Jerusalem and Judea were regained. However, given the overwhelming power of the Romans, the outcome was inevitable. Three years later, in conformity with Roman custom, Jerusalem was "plowed up with a yoke of oxen," Judea was renamed "Palaestinia" and Jerusalem "Aelia Capitolina."

The Romans celebrated their conquering armies with victory columns and arches through which the triumphant commanders and armies marched, displaying the spoils of war along with captured slaves—all to wildly cheering crowds. Visitors to Rome today will find many arches and victory columns throughout the city that herald victorious generals and armies from centuries

---

[64] Victor Davis Hanson, "Alexander the Killer," in *Great Commanders,* ed. by John Guttman, Leesburg,VA, Primedia, 2005, 56–57.

ago—past evidence of the rituals used to glamorize the soldiers and showcase their savage victories.

The Church Blesses Charlemagne

In the year 800, on Christmas Day, Pope Leo III placed a crown on the head of Charlemagne, aka Charles the Great. Charlemagne was fifty-eight years old and near the height of his power; he would live and reign another fourteen years. Although he never used the title officially, he became the first ruler of the Holy Roman Empire, a so-called kingdom described by wits as neither holy, Roman, nor an empire.

Charlemagne was sixteen years old when his father died, and he and his brother each inherited half of their father's kingdom. He soon began a series of military campaigns designed to increase his empire by conquering Bavaria and Saxony, destroying the troublesome Avars, shielding Italy from the raiding Saracens, and strengthening the defenses of Francia against the expanding Moors of Spain. The Saxons on his eastern frontier were pagans; they had burned down a Christian church and made occasional incursions into Gaul. These were sufficient reasons for Charlemagne to engage in eighteen campaigns (772–804), waged with untiring ferocity on both sides. Charlemagne gave the conquered Saxons a choice between baptism and death, and had 4,500 Saxon rebels who chose death beheaded in one day. It is said that Charlemagne participated in the decapitations himself. Following the execution of the final captured Saxon, Charlemagne proceeded to the town of Thionville to celebrate the nativity of Christ.

"By sword and the cross," Charlemagne became the conqueror of Western Europe. His military campaigns were vicious and brutal, and he was responsible for more violence and bloodshed during his time than any other person. Despite this, the church officially recognized him with the placing of a crown on his head, anointing of oil, and adoration in Rome under Pope Leo III on the birthday of the Prince of Peace.

The Crusades

Most Christians know little of the Crusades, the attempts by Western Europeans to take back the Holy Land from the Muslims and establish a Christian kingdom there. In the year 1095 Pope Urban II personally promoted a holy crusade to reclaim the Holy Land from the Turks. The First Crusade was launched in 1096 and led to the capturing of the holy city of Jerusalem in 1099. What follows is a description of the activities of the Christian crusaders after the Muslim defenders of the city surrendered:

There the orgy of slaughter began. For two whole days these Christian soldiers massacred every living creature that was not of their own kind. At the Temple Mount alone it was said that ten thousand were killed. According to the Fulcher of Chartres, some of these had their bodies ripped open, because it was rumored that Muslims were swallowing gold bezants in desperation. For the whole city the estimate of the slain was forty thousand Muslims—men, women, and children. The Church of the Holy Sepulcher, the holiest church in Christendom, the site of Calvary, was a pool of blood. They found the Jews of Jerusalem huddled in their synagogue, ready for martyrdom. And they burned the prayer place down, dancing around the burning pyre and singing the Te Deum. "In the Temple and the porch of Solomon, men rode in blood up to their knees and bridle reins," wrote one expansive participant, Raymond of Aquilers. "Indeed, it was a just and splendid judgment of God that this place should be filled with the blood of unbelievers since it has suffered so long from their blasphemies."[65]

The Napoleonic Wars

After gaining control of the French army and government in the wake of the French Revolution and subsequent Reign of Terror, Napoleon organized his "Grand Army" and set off to conquer the European continent. After defeat at the hands of Admiral Nelson and the British navy, Napoleon turned his army eastward and took on the Austrian Empire. In 1812, at the height of his powers, he entered and attacked Russia. He led an army estimated at 750,000 men, one of the largest armies ever assembled.

The Russians, fearful of the approaching army, pursued a scorched-earth policy, retreating and destroying everything in their path so the French could not benefit from it. There was only one major battle during the invasion. On the outskirts of Moscow the Russians dug in, and on September 7, 1812, the Battle of Borodino was fought. It has been described as the largest and bloodiest single-day battle of the Napoleonic Wars, and perhaps the deadliest day of fighting ever. Historians estimate between 28,000 and 50,000 French soldiers were killed, with estimates of Russian dead ranging from 38,500 to 58,000. Following the battle, the Russians retreated, giving Napoleon the prize he sought—Moscow.

---

[65] James Reston Jr. *Warriors of God* (New York: Doubleday, 2001), 71–73.

But the French were unprepared for the severe Russian winter, which set in with unusual harshness that year. Soon after arriving, Napoleon himself retreated from Russia, with his army shrinking by the day. Less than 22,000 French troops survived and made it back to Paris. In total, an estimated one million persons from the French and Russian armies, died as a result of Napoleon's vanity. And Napoleon, who had been acclaimed many times over in the streets of Paris, had no "arc de defeat" built after this disaster.

The United States and Native Americans

The history of the United States' dealing with the Native Americans is a history of shame and disgrace—perhaps America's darkest moment. Many European-Americans considered the Native Americans to be subhuman; they were relentlessly driven from their land, forced into slavery, and brutally exterminated. In haunting words that cut through my soul 125 years after they were spoken, Chief Joseph of the Nez Perce shared these words on the depths of defeat:

> Tell General Howard I know his heart. What he told me before, I have it in my heart. I am tired of fighting. Our chiefs are killed. Looking-Glass is dead, Ta-Hool-Hool-Shute is dead. The old men are all dead. It is the young men who say yes or no. He who led on the young men is dead. It is cold, and we have no blankets; the little children are freezing to death. My people, some of them, have run away to the hills, and have no blankets, no food. No one knows where they are—perhaps freezing to death. I want to have time to look for my children, and see how many of them I can find. Maybe I shall find them among the dead. Hear me, my chiefs! I am tired: my heart is sick and sad. From where the sun now stands I will fight no more forever.[66]

Modern Warfare

For most of human history, technological advances in warfare have been slight. Most warfare has primarily been a hand-to-hand enterprise. The same techniques that Alexander the Great used in the fourth century BCE were similar to those used by William the Conqueror in 1066. The discovery and application of dynamite and gunpowder, however, radically changed the face

---

[66] *Lend Me Your Ears*, 108.

of war in the eighteenth century. As the Industrial Revolution advanced, the technology used to wage war also advanced.

Although rifles and other guns were used in the Napoleonic Wars and the American Revolutionary War, their restricted ability to shoot for distance and accuracy limited their impact. By the time of the American Civil War, however, both the distance and accuracy of guns had increased significantly. These changes continued into World War I, where the machine gun, poisonous gas, the tank, and early airplanes made dramatic appearances. World War II saw these technological advances continue as the battle for the skies became as important as those taking place on land. The introduction of the atomic bomb at the end of World War II ushered in a whole new awareness of and horror at what human knowledge is capable of producing.

Recent advances in military technology include satellite-, laser-, and drone-guided missiles, "smart bombs," night vision goggles, and computer guidance systems. Warfare today can be like playing sophisticated video games, with enemy causalities counted from a distance and face-to-face fighting avoided when possible.

Although literature continued to express the pain and futility of war (see *All Quiet on the Western Front* by Erich Maria Remarque, *A Farewell to Arms* by Ernest Hemingway, and *Slaughterhouse Five* by Kurt Vonnegut), photos and film brought a new dimension of war back from the front to our communities and homes. Photography was still in its infancy as the Civil War was fought, but thousands of pictures were taken of battlefields strewn with the dead and wounded. Likewise, the motion picture industry had just been born when World War I was fought, and primitive footage of that war is available. By World War II the motion pictures were well advanced, and audiences could see footage of the war (as permitted by our military censors) at theaters around the country.

Television brought the Vietnam War into our living rooms, making that conflict the first war to be "watched" by millions of Americans. During the Gulf War, press conferences with telegenic military leaders included video footage of sophisticated air strikes as seen from above. During the initial operations of the Iraq War, television crews were "embedded" in military units, and their reports from the front spoke of the adrenalin rush the soldiers (and reporters) experienced as they advanced into Iraq.

In the past few decades many movies have contributed to our understanding of war. Movies such as *Platoon, Saving Private Ryan, Born on the Fourth of July, Good Morning Vietnam, Apocalypse Now, Forrest Gump,* and *Black Hawk Down* dramatically illustrate the truth of the wars they depict. These wars did not benefit the soldiers but showed us how the men and women, some brave and courageous, others cowardly and weak, were used as pawns in a giant chess game, sacrificed in the name of nationalism and pride. Wars today, by and large, are fought by the underprivileged, by the lower economic classes of our and other nations' populations.

The great war movies, like the great war literature, help show us the sanctity of human life and its utter waste in the futility of war. Far from lifting up war as glorious, they bring us to the front with all of its realism, horror, and violence. They help us question those in authority and demand that we seek real ways to solve conflict, remembering the words of the Roman writer Cicero: "A bad peace is better than a good war."

Americans have a special place in our hearts for Franklin Delano Roosevelt, who led the United States through the Great Depression and World War II. But Roosevelt was no fan of war:

> I have seen war. I have seen war on land and sea. I have seen blood running from the wounded. . . . I have seen the dead in the mud. I have seen cities destroyed. . . . I have seen children starving. I have seen the agony of mothers and wives. I hate war.

I came of age during the late 1960s and early to mid-1970s, when the United States was involved in the war in Vietnam. It was a time for soul searching, and discussion and debate over that war led to splits in families and between neighbors, church members, and friends. Over 58,000 American soldiers were killed in the Vietnam War, as well as an estimated one to two million Vietnamese. Reflecting back on that war some thirty years later, we are still wondering what that war was all about and how history could have led us down a different path. Today Vietnam is an emerging nation—flourishing, by many reports, with a rapidly growing economy and peaceful, industrious citizens. Did the war in Vietnam do anything other than lead to so many deaths and so much destruction?

I remember seeing a poster during the Vietnam War of a young soldier who had been wounded in the field and was being provided aid by a medic. Under the picture was the caption "Whose Blood Will Save This Man?" Below the caption, in handwritten ink, were the time, date, and place for a blood drive. It was an effective call to donate blood.

As a Christian, it seems to me that the one whose blood saved that young soldier was Jesus Christ. He chose the cross, the greatest example of God's love overcoming evil the world has ever witnessed. He taught us to love our enemies, to pray for those who persecute us, to turn the other cheek, to walk the extra mile, and to offer our cloaks as well as our coats. He did not advocate violence or warfare. He chose another pathway.

War is violent, ugly, and unnecessary. I look at my country's soldiers as victims of humanity's inability to live in peace and of our rush to solve issues through violence. Our soldiers are noble people. Our troops are made up of thousands of men and women wanting to do "the right thing," wanting to demonstrate their commitment to their country and communities. Our troops engage enemy troops who also want to do the right thing, who want to demonstrate the commitment they have to *their* country and communities.

Through my years in ministry I have prayed with and for hundreds of young men and women I have known who have been or are currently in the armed services. And I have remembered the words of Jesus and have prayed for my enemies as well, remembering that they are equally victims of their patriotism and nationalism.

All soldiers, even those who return from war, are causalities of the conflicts in which they participate. Some soldiers lose their lives or limbs, while others lose or damage their souls. Healing may take years. My uncle, a World War II veteran, only in last past decade of his life begun to deal with the trauma he experienced while fighting in the South Pacific fifty years earlier. My brother-in-law is a disabled Vietnam War veteran who was declared psychologically unable to work fifteen years after the war ended. When he gathers with his platoon buddies for a weekend, they still post a guard and take overnight shifts to protect each other.

War is not glorious. Those who make this claim do not know what they are talking about. The greatest gift a national leader can give to his or her people is the gift of peace. Peace leads to life-sustaining activities and prosperity. A leader who creates an environment and conditions for war builds a Potemkin village, an illusion that all will be better once the war is completed. This information is false, and must be exposed for the charade it constructs.

As followers of the Prince of Peace, we must help all soldiers avoid having to commit violence, to kill for their countries, and to put their lives at risk. We honor the men and women who are willing to give their lives for our country by working to create a world of peace and justice for all of God's people.

Chapter 9

The Economic and Social Costs of War

Every gun that is made, every warship launched, every rocket fired signifies, in the final sense, a theft from those who hunger and are not fed, those who are cold and are not clothed. This world in arms is not spending money alone. It is spending the sweat of its laborers, the genius of its scientists, the hopes of its children.

—Dwight Eisenhower

When someone steals another's clothes, we call them a thief. Should we not give the same name to one who could clothe the naked and does not? The bread in your cupboard belongs to the hungry; the coat unused in your closet belongs to the one who needs it; the shoes rotting in your closet belong to the one who has no shoes; the money which you hoard up belongs to the poor.

—Basil the Great

I have served as pastor to three United Methodist Churches in Connecticut. In each of these congregations, the financial situation was always tenuous. We were able to balance the budget and pay our expenses, but it was often close, and the margin of error was slim. Too often, we depended upon a great Christmas offering to make the budget and get the final denominational obligation check in the mail in time to keep the church's bureaucratic representatives away.

But during the year, we would often fall behind. This would happen at the beginning of the year and again in August. In January, our cash flow issues developed as the winter weather took its toll on attendance (and thus income) and as the expenses rose—elevated utility bills, snow plowing, and the annual insurance bill that always came due mid-January. In August, our financial struggles would again be caused by lower attendance, a factor throughout New England where, for some reason, many Christians take the summer off from worship.

During these times our church treasurers had to be creative. Juggling bills and trying to keep the church's checking account in the black demanded patience, courage and, in some cases, the slight of hand transfer of funds from one account into another to cover a potential deficit. This was always done with the knowledge and support of the church's leaders, and it was documented. Funds were placed into the proper accounts when the cash flow issues righted themselves, usually in the spring during Lent, and in mid-autumn after church members returned from their summer sabbaticals.

We jokingly called this practice "robbing Peter to pay Paul." Although the origins of this phrase are obscure, Robert Hendrickson has uncovered the following: "The expression, 'rob Peter to pay Paul' goes back at least to John Wycliffe's 'Select English Works,' written in about 1380. Equally old in French, the saying may derive from a 12th-century Latin expression referring to the Apostles: 'As it were that one would crucify Paul in order to redeem Peter.' The words usually mean to take money for one thing and use it for another, especially in paying off debts."[67] I think of this phrase when contemplating the economic costs of war. In a word: nations with high military expenses rob their populations and the poor of the world to pay their military bills.

The headline for the lead editorial in the *New York Times* on February 27, 2005, was "Thousands Died in Africa Yesterday." The editorial compared the tragic deaths of 225,000 persons from the devastating tsunami of December 26, 2004, with the current, ongoing crisis of poverty facing so many nations in Africa. The editorial concluded with the following:

---

[67] Robert Hendrickson, *Encyclopedia of Word and Phrase Origins* (New York: Facts on File, 1997).

One hundred years ago, before we had the medical know-how to eradicate these illnesses, this might have been acceptable. But we are the first generation able to afford to end poverty and the diseases it spawns. It's past time we step up to the plate. We are all responsible for choosing to view the tsunami victims in Southeastern Asia as more deserving of our help than the malaria victims in Africa. Jeffrey Sachs, the economist who heads the United Nation's Millennium Development Project to end global poverty, rightly takes issue with the press in his book, *The End of Poverty*. "Every morning," Mr. Sachs writes, "our newspapers could report, 'More than 20,000 people perished yesterday of extreme poverty.'"

So, on this page, we'd like to make a first step.

Yesterday, more than 20,000 people perished of extreme poverty.

Developing World Realities

Having been to one of the world's poorest nations, Mozambique, three times in the past decade (1998, 2002, and 2006), I have seen the devastating effects of poverty firsthand. During my first trip, it was estimated that 100,000 homeless children were living on the streets of Maputo, the capital city, struggling daily to survive. Most of those children have died. They have been replaced by a new generation of children who rummage the same dumps and beg in the same locations as their predecessors. The sight of children taking care of other children while living on the streets is a common sight in developing nations across the world.

The AIDS virus is spreading rapidly in the urban areas of Africa, with an estimated 30-40 percent of city populations already infected, and it is making inroads into rural areas as well. In fact, it is estimated that up to 40 percent of the sub-Saharan African population will die in the first decade of the twenty-first century from AIDS and other treatable diseases. Already, 10-20 percent of the population has died, and most of those currently infected will also soon die. The total population of sub-Saharan Africa is approximately 650 million; therefore, some 300 million people will die in this ten-year period in the greatest plague in human history. What is making the situation even worse is that AIDS is killing the strongest members of African society, that is, those who are sexually active, the men and women aged roughly 16-45. Entire villages are being reduced to populations of the very old and the very young, with no one to carry on the tasks of daily existence. Slogans such as "no child left behind" do not work in these nations; few children receive the resources they need to thrive.

In addition to the AIDS pandemic throughout much of the Third World, approximately half a million children die of preventable and treatable diseases, as well as other symptoms of poverty, each month, according to Oxfam International. This is the equivalent of two massive tsunamis per month, year in and year out. The tsunami of December 26, 2004, provided stunning photographic and video footage; the children who die month after month do so away from the cameras in isolated villages and towns, in cities such as Maputo, Mozambique, and Soweto, South Africa, and Kampala, Uganda. Out of sight, out of mind, out of thought, these poor children are the victims of misplaced spending habits by the citizens and governments of the developed nations. In a world of growing wealth and prosperity in the industrialized nations, hundreds of millions of children are being left behind.

As individuals we make choices about how we spend our personal income, but we are also citizens of sovereign nations that make decisions on how to use governmental resources and revenues. At the UN Millennium Development Summit in 2000, the richest nations in the world agreed to spend 0.7 percent of GDP (Gross Domestic Product) on aid to the poor countries. Adrian Lovett, campaign director of Oxfam International, said:

> Our position is that those who have the ability to help the poorest would do so. You wouldn't hear much of the electorate arguing against that. And, even if every nation hit this target, we are only talking about 70 cents in every $100.[68]

Yet even this modest target seems unattainable to the richest nations. On average, rich countries give only 0.25 percent of their GDP in aid and assistance to developing nations; the contribution of United States is under 0.2 percent. The following chart shows the United States dead last among the Western developed nations in terms of the percentage of our GDP given for aid in poor nations.

---

[68] Quoted in Mark Rice-Oxley, "Forgive Us Our Debts? Obstacles Lie Ahead," *Christian Science Monitor,* February 9, 2005.

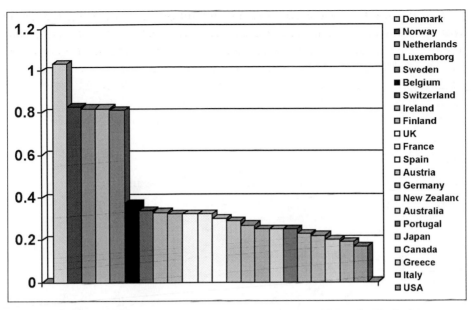

□ Denmark	
■ Norway	
▨ Netherlands	
▨ Luxemborg	
▨ Sweden	
■ Belgium	
▨ Switzerland	
▨ Ireland	
▨ Finland	
□ UK	
□ France	
□ Spain	
▨ Austria	
▨ Germany	
▨ New Zealanc	
▨ Australia	
▨ Portugal	
▨ Japan	
▨ Canada	
▨ Greece	
▨ Italy	
▨ USA	

Percentage of Gross Domestic Product Given in Relief to
Third World Nations

Why is the United States at the bottom of the list? To answer this we must also answer other fundamental questions about how the United States sees itself in the world and the direction we as a nation are moving toward.

- Are we still the nation of the Marshall Plan that offered food and assistance to those in Europe in the time of their greatest need?
- Are we a light to the nations, a beacon of hope, freedom, and democracy?
- Are we the nation our founding fathers conceived two hundred years ago, the nation Emma Lazarus wrote about in "The New Colossus," her famous poem for the Statue of Liberty? "Give me your tired, your poor, your huddled masses yearning to breathe free, the wretched refuse of your teeming shore. Send these, the homeless, tempest tossed to me, I lift my lamp beside the golden door!"
- Are we a nation doing all we can to build a world of peace and justice for all of God's people, reflecting our Judeo-Christian heritage?

For over fifty years the Cold War was played out between the United States and the Soviet Union in part through a series of proxy wars, but primarily through the proliferation of nuclear weapons in a defense strategy based on mutual annihilation. The theory behind this policy reasoned that both the United States and Soviet Union had enough weapons to destroy the world hundreds of times over; therefore, neither would move to use nuclear weapons because each would know a retaliatory attack could lead to its own destruction.

One of the primary weaknesses of this argument (beyond its obvious insanity) is that it ignored the tremendous amounts of money invested into the nuclear weapons program from both nations. The nuclear arms race demanded a huge share of the national income of both the United States and Soviet Union, thus diverting valuable funding for programs such as health care and education, food and clothing, medicines and emergency relief funds. The arms race was undertaken at a huge cost to the people of both nations. I am convinced that the billions of dollars spent on researching, developing, building, housing, and maintaining these nuclear weapons—which, in theory, were never to be used—was one of the greatest wastes of resources in world history.

When the Soviet Union collapsed in 1991, it left the United States as the world's sole superpower. During the ensuing decade, military spending leveled off. Politicians spoke of a peace dividend to describe the economic benefit a decrease in military spending would yield. Although the military budget of the United States was not reduced, it did not grow at the same rate it had in the 1980s. The national debt became a focus of real concern, and the budget deficit was transformed into a budget surplus. In addition, spending for social programs such as education, health care, and housing were maintained, and the economy grew at a steady rate. Inflation remained low, and workers across the economic spectrum benefited from higher salaries and benefits.

Since the advent of the War on Terror in 2001, the defense budget of the United States has grown at a rate of 12-15 percent per year. In 2007, the military expenditures of the United States will exceed the military budgets of all of the other nations of the world combined! The following chart shows the military budgets of the thirteen nations who have the highest defense spending:

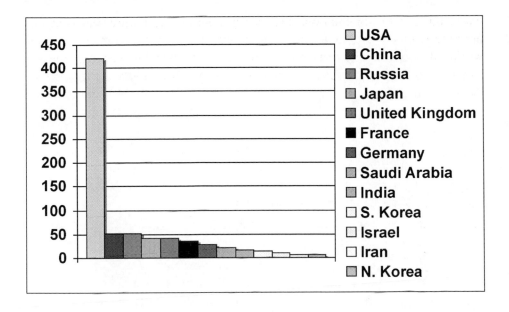

450
400
350
300
250
200
150
100
50
0

☐ USA
■ China
▨ Russia
☐ Japan
▨ United Kingdom
■ France
▨ Germany
▨ Saudi Arabia
☐ India
☐ S. Korea
☐ Israel
☐ Iran
▨ N. Korea

World Military Spending, 2004 (in Billions of Dollars)

The military budget for the United States in 2007 is approximately $520 billion; this figure does not include the ongoing costs of the wars in Iraq and Afghanistan (which as of April 1, 2007, has exceeded $400 billion). Additionally, according to economist Jürgen Brauer, in tracking U.S. military expenditures by the more comprehensive National Income and Product Accounts (NIPA), a more accurate figure for what the United States spends on the military emerges. For example, in 2003, the NIPA showed military expenditures that exceeded by $100 billion Department of Defense figures. Including military-related costs that are located in other federal budget line items, Brauer estimates that the real costs of our commitment to war are at least 25-33 percent higher than the official line item for "defense" in the annual budget.[69] Therefore, when we add expenses from our total national budget, the resources we will devote to the military in 2007 are more accurately in the $725 billion range ($500 billion defense budget, plus $125 billion that Jürgen Brauer indicates is the minimum amount of military spending hidden in other federal budgets, plus $100 billion for our ongoing military actions in Iraq and Afghanistan).

---

[69] This paragraph is based on a speech Brauer delivered in June 2004. The full speech and an article about this subject can be found at http://www.aug.edu/~sbajmb/paper-Brunswick.pdf.

Theoretically, the money we are spending on the military is designed to make us safer, to defend our nation, and to promote peace throughout the world. However, many military experts are now claiming that our military action in Iraq is putting our soldiers and nation at a higher level of risk. We are creating more terrorists, more hatred, and more desperation. Our commitment to solving world conflicts through a policy of preemptive military force rather than through diplomacy, peacekeeping and development aid is making both the United States and the world a much more dangerous place. Military expenditures keep us from addressing the issues of poverty that lead to hopelessness, despair and, eventually, violence. Our military siphons funds and brainpower away from core human needs.

Tragically, the military budget of the United States for just the year 2007 ($520 billion) is almost equal to the United Nations' Millennium Development goals for all of the countries involved for a *ten-year period* ($547 billion). The United Nations' Millennium Development Fund was developed to eradicate extreme poverty in Third World nations, the kind of poverty that helps fuel the growth of hatred and violence. Averaging just under $55 billion per year, this amount is to be raised by the industrialized nations of the world.

A Change of Priorities

Currently, the United States has approximately 500,000 active military personnel deployed in the United States and throughout the world. We have 725 bases scattered throughout three-quarters of the world's nations.

Contrast that number with the number of persons currently serving in the Peace Corps. Begun by President John F. Kennedy in 1961, a total of 700,000 persons have served in the Peace Corps through these four decades, and they have been deployed in 138 different nations. There are currently 7,000 men and women serving in the Peace Corps, approximately one-seventieth of the amount of American men and women serving in the armed forces.

Peace Corps workers struggle to find enough money to purchase new seeds to plant a field with peanuts, corn, tomatoes, or cucumbers. Once planted, the fields become renewable as seeds from each harvest are used for future plantings. Many Peace Corps workers are continually short of the funds necessary for medical supplies, books for teaching, tools for farming, and materials for constructing safe, decent places for God's children to live.

Conversely, our military is generally supplied with the newest, most sophisticated equipment in the world. We are constantly funding newer, faster, bigger, stronger, and more powerful helicopters, planes, tanks, and jets. Our military hardware is several generations beyond what other nations can put on the battlefield. We have more accurate missiles, bombs, and guidance systems than the world has ever seen. We are determined to intimidate our enemies with the overwhelming superiority of our equipment and technology—"shock and awe," to use former Defense Secretary Donald Rumsfeld's phrase—with the goal of quick surrender and acceptance of "peace" on our terms.

Moving toward a policy of peace and justice for all of God's people will require a dramatic paradigm shift that will redirect the use of our resources and capital. Fifty years ago Albert Einstein, Bertrand Russell and eight other prominent scientists signed a manifesto warning of the dire consequences of a nuclear war. This statement, the Russell-Einstein Manifesto, was Einstein's final public act, and he died shortly after signing it. I believe its words are as important today as they were then in helping us develop a vision of where we are headed. They included these words:

> We have to learn to think in a new way. We have to learn to ask ourselves, not what steps can be taken to give military victory to whatever group we prefer, for there no longer are such steps; the question we have to ask ourselves is: what steps can be taken to prevent a military contest of which the issue must be disastrous to all parties?

The United States has the technical ability to solve many of the world's severest problems. That it has not done so reveals where its desires and priorities lie. I would submit that the real issue is not the age-old dilemma of the "haves" and "have-nots"; it is now an issue of the "haves" not wanting the "have-nots" to share in our material prosperity and abundance.

This change in attitudes and spending habits will not be easy and will not take place without some level of discomfort and sacrifice. Any announcement by the Pentagon to close military bases in the United States or around the world sends chills throughout communities that are dependent on the flow of dollars through these bases. But the alternative, economically as well as morally, of maintaining the military-industrial status quo is even more unacceptable. To beat our swords into plowshares will take a commitment of time. It will not take place overnight, but it must be started now. To beat our spears into pruning hooks will take the commitment of all of us; it is a vision of God's plan for peace and justice for all of God's children.

Pioneers

Hats off to Bill and Melinda Gates and Bono, together named *Time* magazine's Persons of the Year in 2006 for their humanitarian work. *Time* named them, simply and powerfully, "The Good Samaritans." Bill Gates, the world's richest man, is putting his money where his heart is. Founded in January 2000, the Gates Foundation is committed to promoting greater equity in global health, education, and the building of public libraries. Additionally, the Gates Foundation supports at-risk families in Washington State and the greater Portland area. Currently the endowment of the Gates Foundation stands at $33.7 billion, and it has awarded over $9 billion in grants since its inception.[70]

In 2003, Bill Gates challenged the scientists of the world in a speech titled "Grand Challenges in Global Health." Delivered in Davos, Switzerland, the speech laid out before the world's scientists the greatest health obstacles facing doctors in tropical, developing nations. He outlined the fact that in these areas laboratories and doctors are few and far between, vaccines spoil without refrigeration and require syringes which, when reused, can transmit AIDS. Further, mosquitoes have developed resistance to insecticides. Crops growing in these regions offer limited nutritional value. Men, women and children continue to die from diseases we have long had the cures for. Gates asked the scientists to consider experiments and research to present solutions to these age-old, contemporary problems. He set aside $200 million from the Gates Foundation to be awarded to scientists and laboratories that presented proposals to deal with these problems.

In late 2005 the Gates Foundation awarded $450 million, over twice what Gates had originally offered, to forty-three (out of 1,600 proposals presented) winning teams. Although he hopes all of these projects will prove beneficial and show promising results, Gates is brutally realistic about their chances for success: "Eighty percent of these are likely to be dead ends. But even if we have a 10 percent hit rate, it will all have been worthwhile."[71] Winning projects included plans to develop bananas and sorghum that make their own vitamin A, chemicals that render mosquitoes unable to smell humans, drugs that kill tuberculosis germs in people who do not even know they are infected, and vaccines that are mixed into spores, plastics, or sugars that can be delivered in glasses of orange juice.

---

[70] On June 25, 2006 Warren Buffett announced his intention of donating ten million shares of Berkshire Hathway shares worth an estimated $30.7 billion, thus doubling the Bill and Melinda Gates Foundation. Buffett's shares will be given over a ten year period.

[71] Donald G. McNeil, "Better Bananas, Nicer Mosquitos," *New York Times* December 6, 2005.

Bono, the Irish rock star from the band U2, was recognized along with the Gateses for his role in helping developed nations see and understand how millions of lives are affected by their decisions. He has played a significant role in the G8 summits and was a powerful force in persuading the wealthiest nations to forgive many of the debts Third World nations had accumulated. In 2002 he founded the organization DATA (the letters have a dual meaning: Debt, Aids, Trade, and Africa; and Democracy, Accountability, Transparency in Africa), which calls on the governments of the world's wealthiest nations to provide more resources for Africa and to adopt policies to help rather than hinder Africa's achieving long-term prosperity. At the core of DATA's mission is the understanding that these issues are not about charity but about equality and justice.

Bill and Melinda Gates and Bono are examples of the very rich committing their time, energy, and resources to making the world a better place. They are good neighbors, showing mercy to the least, the last, and the lost. They are showing the way to invest in social programs and are active peacemakers in the world today.

A Case Study of War and Peace: Mozambique

During a trip to Mozambique in 2006, I had the opportunity to sit down with a group of students who were enrolled in the Cambine Bible School, located just out of the town of Maxixe in Inhambane Province. The students ranged in age from 19 to 50 and were studying to become United Methodist pastors. Knowing that Mozambique had been at war for thirty years, I was interested in their thoughts on war and peace.[72]

Of the thirty students who gathered, twenty-two knew someone personally who had been killed in war. Many described the deaths of their relatives or friends with great sadness and heavy hearts. Miquel Sanchez seemed to sum up what his colleagues were saying on the economic cost of the war:

> I lived during the war. It was terrible. Many people I knew were
> captured; others were killed. They destroyed our fields and took
> our animals. We were hungry for many years and could not go to

---

[72] Mozambique's war of independence from Portugal took place from 1964 to 1974 and was immediately followed by a "civil war," in reality a proxy war between forces supported by Western powers (RENAMO) and forces supported by Eastern powers (FRELIMO) that was waged from 1974 to 1992.

school because there were no teachers. Our economy was set back and is only now beginning to return to the level it was at before the war. People who have seen war and the blood it produces will never be in favor of making more war.

We also spoke about peace and the advantages and benefits their nation had enjoyed since a treaty was drawn up and signed by the members of RENAMO and FRELIMO in 1992. Although Mozambique has suffered from devastating floods (1999) and endured terrible droughts (2001–2003), all of the students pointed to the economic benefits made possible because of the peace treaty. Homes are being built, crops and fields planted, domestic animals are being raised again, schools have opened, and foreign investors have returned. The nation is also experiencing the growth of small businesses, and roads destroyed during the war have been rebuilt. In general, Mozambique is on the rebound from its position as the poorest nation in the world.[73]

On the Home Front

In the same way our elephant-like military budget siphons funds away from possible international development projects, it also diverts resources from potential domestic plans. By nearly any measure, the United States ranks as one of the richest nations in the history of the world. The World Bank and International Monetary Fund list national wealth several ways, including per capita income and personal purchasing power. Per capita income measures the income level of every person in a society; personal purchasing power measures income and other financial assets members of a nation have access to. The United States ranks eighth on the per capita spending chart and third on the personal purchasing power chart.[74]

With such wealth, it would follow that the United States would use its resources to develop and maintain a high standard of living, and many Americans do enjoy a high standard of living. But this wealthy nation also has pockets of shameful poverty. Roughly 13 percent of the American population falls under the poverty line, including almost 15 percent of children under the age of 18. A UNICEF study released in 2007 of children's well-being in the

---

[73] In 1994 the United Nations listed Mozambique as the poorest nation in the world as measured by its per capita income. By 2004 Mozambique had climbed thirty spaces on that list and had passed the war-torn nations of Iraq and Afghanistan, among others, on the national wealth list.

[74] International Monetary Fund, "World Economic Outlook Database," September 2006, http://www.imf.org/external/pubs/ft/weo/2006/02/data/weorept.aspx.

---

richest eighteen nations in the world ranks the United States as seventeenth, just ahead of our ally in the War on Terror, Great Britain.[75] Speaking at a press conference in London, Jonathan Bradshaw, a professor at the University of York, stated, "For the last two decades, we have failed to invest in children. It's a pretty bleak picture."[76]

Dimensions of child well-being	Average ranking position (for all 6 dimensions)	Dimension 1 Material well-being	Dimension 2 Health and safety	Dimension 3 Educational well-being	Dimension 4 Family and peer relationships	Dimension 5 Behaviours and risks	Dimension 6 Subjective well-being
Netherlands	4.2	10	2	6	3	3	1
Sweden	5.0	1	1	5	15	1	7
Denmark	7.2	4	4	8	9	6	12
Finland	7.5	3	3	4	17	7	11
Spain	8.0	12	6	15	8	5	2
Switzerland	8.3	5	9	14	4	12	6
Norway	8.7	2	8	11	10	13	8
Italy	10.0	14	5	20	1	10	10
Ireland	10.2	19	19	7	7	4	5
Belgium	10.7	7	16	1	5	19	16
Germany	11.2	13	11	10	13	11	9
Canada	11.8	6	13	2	18	17	15
Greece	11.8	15	18	16	11	8	3
Poland	12.3	21	15	3	14	2	19
Czech Republic	12.5	11	10	9	19	9	17
France	13.0	9	7	18	12	14	18
Portugal	13.7	16	14	21	2	15	14
Austria	13.8	8	20	19	16	16	4
Hungary	14.5	20	17	13	6	18	13
United States	18.0	17	21	12	20	20	–
United Kingdom	18.2	18	12	17	21	21	20

Child Well-Being in Rich Countries:
A Summary Table

On the other end of the spectrum, the life expectancy of citizens living in the United States is now just under seventy-eight years; this places us twenty-ninth on the global list of national life expectancies, behind such nations as Japan, Australia, Switzerland, Sweden, Canada, Italy, France, Liechtenstein, Spain, Norway, Greece, Austria, the Netherlands, New Zealand, and fifteen other nations.[77] These and other nations have relatively small military budgets and spend a higher proportion of their federal budgets on social programs.

---

[75] UNICEF, *Child Poverty in Perspective: An Overview of Child Well-Being in Rich Countries*, 2007, http://www.unicef.org/media/files/ChildPovertyReport.pdf

[76] "UK, US worst places for child well-being, UN report Says," BBJ, Feb 14,2007.

[77] This list of countries is based on the CIA's *World Factbook* 2006 estimates, found online at https://www.cia.gov/cia/publications/factbook/rankorder/2102rank.html.

While it is true that diet, exercise, and other factors contribute to life expectancy, the point is this: in one of the richest nations in the history of the world, we could be doing much better in educating our children and caring for our seniors. We could eliminate poverty within our country if we used a portion of the military budget to invest in our own people. Numerous persons died in New Orleans in the aftermath of Hurricane Katrina who could have been rescued if a large percentage of the Mississippi and Louisiana National Guard had been stationed at home and not in Iraq and Afghanistan. Helicopters that could have been used to save lives here were deployed overseas in war zones. The $15 billion it would cost to build levees that could withstand a future Category 5 hurricane in New Orleans pales in comparison to what we spend on our military.

How did the military budget of the United States grow to such an astonishing amount? Who chose the United States to become the world's power broker, supporting dictators or democracies when their actions enhanced American interests, and blocking or overthrowing other governments when they chose pathways that did not further our interests? How did we get to the point where the federal government spends $500 billion on military expenses and only $16 billion on helping those who have nothing?

When the churches I served "robbed Peter to pay Paul" we were, in essence, borrowing from one area of the budget to pay bills in another. In nearly every circumstance, however, we were able to repay the borrowed money by the end of the calendar year. No one was hurt by our creative shell game, and all was sorted out in the end. We were able to balance our books and even the score.

When the citizens of the United States, individually and on a national scale, rob Peter (global health initiatives, aid to developing nations, food to the hungry, clothing to the naked, housing to the homeless) to pay Paul (incessant defense spending, excessive personal consumption), people die. When we choose guns over butter, we choose death over life. While the majority of residents in the United States live comfortably, enjoying material resources undreamed of just fifty years ago, a child dies every three seconds somewhere around the world from a treatable disease. The greedy, insatiable demands of our military-industrial system devour billions of dollars that could be used for the poor. It is said that Nero fiddled while Rome burned; likewise, we Americans are apathetic toward our nation's colossal military spending and are busy consuming while billions struggle daily simply to stay alive. We are being poor stewards of the resources God has provided to us, continuing to place our confidence in weapons of war (nationally) and taking solace in our comfortable lives (personally) rather than being good neighbors to the world's poor and suffering.

I am convinced this generation of Americans would like to be remembered as the generation that created a world of peace and justice. I am convinced this generation of Americans would like to be remembered as the generation that created hope in desperate areas of the world, that chose to build schools and hospitals rather than guns, bullets, and bombs. This is the generation that can choose to stop robbing Peter to pay Paul; this is the generation that can choose butter over guns. We have the technology, we have the resources, we have the wisdom, and we have the moral obligation. Do we have the desire?

Chapter 10

Equipping the Saints for the Work of Ministry and Peace

The gifts he gave were that some would be apostles, some prophets, some evangelists, some pastors and teachers, to equip the saints for the work of ministry, for building up the body of Christ, until all of us come to the unity of the faith and of the knowledge of the Son of God, to maturity, to the measure of the full stature of Christ. We must no longer be children, tossed to and fro and blown about by every wind of doctrine, by people's trickery, by their craftiness in deceitful scheming. But speaking the truth in love, we must grow up in every way into him who is the head, into Christ, from whom the whole body, joined and knit together by every ligament with which it is equipped, as each part is working properly, promotes the body's growth in building itself up in love.   —Ephesians 4:11–16

Sometime we must interfere. When human lives are endangered, when human dignity is in jeopardy, national borders and sensitivities become irrelevant. Wherever men or women are persecuted because of their race, religion, or political views, that place must – at that moment – become the center of the universe.   —Elie Wiesel

All around the world, from the beginning of time, men, women, and children have gazed upon the stars and pondered their existence. Different cultures and different peoples developed separate myths and legends about what they saw in the stars, with constellations created to communicate important social, tribal, cultural, and national information. Simple (the Big Dipper) and complex (Scorpio, Tarsus) patterns were identified, which were passed down from generation to generation as a way to record the seasonal cycles of life and death that could be observed, documented, and noted. Astrology was an accepted "science" that not only helped tell the story of humanity's past but helped foretell current and future events as well.

Although different societies and cultures developed different myths, legends, and stories about the stars and constellations they observed, they had in common the belief the earth was at the center of the universe. They believed the sun and other celestial bodies (the moon, stars, planets, comets) circled the earth. So certain were these civilizations the earth was the center of the universe that conflicting theories and hypotheses were vehemently challenged and rejected. Hence, men such as Galileo were persecuted and ostracized despite the overwhelming verifiable data confirming their conclusion that the earth was not at the center of our solar system, much less at the center of the universe. For countless theologians, astrologers, sorcerers, and stargazers, belief in the earth as the center of the universe established the central place humanity has in the heart of God.

Of course, we now know the earth is not the center of the universe. The earth circles the sun, one of eight planets that do.[78] Our sun is one of two hundred billion stars that make up the Milky Way, a spiral galaxy in which our solar system is located. Our galaxy is simply one of hundreds of thousands of other galaxies that make up the known universe. Creation is larger than anyone can fully understand, with the cosmos extending billions of light years in every direction. Each new discovery by the Hubble Telescope or ground-based radar systems that teaches us about the physical realities of the heavens helps us come to a greater appreciation of the magnificent hymn "How Great Thou Art":

O Lord my God! when I in awesome wonder

consider all the worlds thy hands have made,

I see the stars, I hear the rolling thunder

thy power throughout the universe displayed.

---

[78] Astronomers have recently decided that Pluto is not a planet but belongs to the class of "dwarf planets."

Then sings my soul, my Savior God to thee;

how great thou art, how great thou art!

Then sings my soul, my Savior God to thee;

how great thou art, how great thou art!

Humanity's ongoing quest to understand the universe can serve as a metaphor for our individual spiritual development. Like the early astronomers who thought the earth was located at the center of the universe, we all begin life believing and behaving as though, as individuals, we are at the center of the universe. Human infants are completely incapable of independent survival, and their needs are taken care of by parents, extended family members, or guardians. Infants need to be changed, fed, held, cared for, and loved. Indeed, anyone who has parented children knows these newborns do indeed become the central focus of the household as plans and activities are scheduled around the baby's needs.

As babies grow from infants to toddlers, they gradually become aware of the existence of others whose orbits cross theirs from time to time—parents, siblings, grandparents, cousins, neighbors, and playmates. Children are, by nature, self-centered, often refusing to share and sometimes aggressively taking toys or objects from other children. They have yet to develop the qualities of sympathy and empathy, and their personal needs dominate their lives. They quickly learn words such as "me," "mine," and "I want."

One of the most important lessons parents teach their children is to share, to relinquish their need to possess everything, to help them understand they are not the center of the universe. For some children and individuals, this process is relatively simple; others never seem to learn this basic lesson. But for everyone, this is an ongoing process. It is not only supermodels, athletes, or actors who play the role of prima donnas. We all, from time to time, forget our place in the cosmos as one of billions of individuals living on a small planet. We are all guilty of reverting back to an "I want" mode of existence. The struggle to overcome this self-centered view of the universe is the call of the divine, working through grace, to be better individuals than we currently are.

The process of understanding we are not at the center of the universe develops in stages. We grow in our knowledge of the world around us as our understanding expands, like concentric ripples in a pond spreading out from a thrown rock. Our orientation moves from self, to family, to clan, to tribe, and then to nation. Our maturity is not complete, however, until we reach the last ripple, which includes our being citizens of Planet Earth.

One of the most important missions of a church is to help its members mature spiritually—to help them discover, for themselves, they are not the center of the universe and the more they give of themselves, the more they will receive. Mature Christians move from "me" to "your"; we grow from "mine" to "yours," and "I want" becomes "you need." As Jesus said, "If any want to become my followers, let them deny themselves and take up their cross and follow me. For those who want to save their life will lose it, and those who lose their life for my sake, and for the sake of the gospel, will save it" (Mark 8:34–35).

To create a world of peace and justice, the church of Jesus Christ will need to be one of the institutions to lead the way. With approximately two billion Christians in the world comprising nearly 40 percent of the earth's population, the church is by far the largest faith community on the planet. Knowing that Jesus taught and lived a life of peace and justice, it seems a given that his church needs to follow in his footsteps. Unfortunately, living as Christ's body and being faithful to Jesus' vision has not always been the clear goal or objective of individual Christians, local congregations, denominations, or the universal church. To lead the world toward peace, the church will need to make a concentrated decision to make this a priority.

Throughout my ministry I have been disappointed that the real purpose of the church is so often overlooked. We accept the superficialities of our faith but miss the deeper, truer spiritual heights accessible to anyone who has the desire and patience to find them. Ignoring the spiritual depths, we also neglect and disregard the gospel demands to take our faith out into the world through mission and outreach.

Too many pastors and too many church members believe the purpose of the church is to get newcomers to join their congregation and then to get these new members, along with those who are already members, to "serve" on one or more committees. This is not the purpose of the church! The purpose of the church is to make disciples of Jesus Christ. The purpose of the church is to be the body of Christ. The purpose of the church is to encourage, assist, and inspire individuals to move further along their faith pathway through worship, education, spiritual growth, evangelism, and mission work in order to build God's kingdom on earth. The purpose of the church is to build a community of Christ-like people! We know Christ did not sit on committees. We know Christ did not organize bake sales. We know Christ did not die on the cross so that his followers could organize bingo nights in church basements and Victorian teas in fellowship halls. He called his followers to a life of discipleship. He wanted us to be his body.

The responsibility for church members' thinking their role in a local congregation simply equates to serving on committees, staffing fund-raisers, and attending social events lies on the shoulders of clergy and church leaders who have stressed these activities for decades. For years mainline churches in the United States have been offering a watered-down, milquetoast version of Christianity that more accurately can be described as "gospel light." Having taught, preached, and modeled that discipleship is compatible with the American Dream, it is no wonder many contemporary church members know so little about the demands of the cross.

Of course, it has never been easy to be a disciple of Jesus Christ. The world and its values call us, tempt us, and lure us. These temptations, in essence, are the voice inside each of us telling us we are the center of the universe—that we need a new car, a larger home, two-week vacations to exotic locations, new shoes, and fancy clothing. We live in a consumer-driven society where the truth of the gospel is clearly countercultural.

Those of us living at the beginning of the twenty-first century find ourselves in company with those who through the centuries have also struggled to be faithful disciples of Jesus Christ. There are few church members who want their pastor to take stands on issues of social justice, or oppose any wars or military actions initiated by their government. Still fewer who attend worship regularly are prepared to sell all they have to feed the poor and clothe the naked. Many church members have their needs met through a pleasing worship service complete with a nice choir anthem and music, a sermon to give them something to think about for the coming week, competent childcare, well-organized Sunday school classes, and an active youth program. Having an institution where their children can be baptized, raised, and married, and where they can have their funerals, is all it often takes to provide a comfortable setting for many modern church members.

One of the problems congregations face is many people join churches in order to be helped and to be served, rather than to be challenged to help and serve others. The "comfortable pew," the place where most of the Christians in the United States sit for worship, has become the place where H. Richard Niebuhr's famous aphorism, "To comfort the afflicted and afflict the comfortable," has mutated into "To pamper the comfortable while neglecting the afflicted." When the church itself has lost its voice, its purpose, and its mission, how much harder will it be for church members to find their way to a life of radical discipleship?

Churches are to help their members grow in faith and spirit so we are prepared to take up our crosses and follow Jesus. To do so requires a direction and purpose that is often at odds with those who are more devoted to the church as an institution than to the church as the body of Christ. Many pastors and church members are guilty of making their local congregation the center of the universe, modifying Wesley's well-known phrase "I see the whole world as my parish" into the more self-serving expression "I see the parish as my whole world." Many of us confuse serving the church with serving God. Unfortunately, they are not always the same thing.

To be disciples of Jesus Christ, individuals must first make a commitment within. It is the responsibility of the churches, then, to take these seekers, the "raw material," and help shape them in the shadow of the cross. Anything less will be a distortion and watering down of the gospel message.

The Body of Christ

If the church is to be the body of Christ, then let us look at the various body parts and see how they fit together. Symbolically speaking, the following functions of the human body correspond to parts of the body of Christ:

Body Part	Ministry
Heart	Worship
Brain	Christian education
Soul	Spiritual growth
Voice	Evangelism
Muscles	Mission and outreach
Skeleton	Committee work
Fat	Social and fund-raising events

Worship: The Heart of the Church

Worship is at the center of the life and purpose of the church; it is the heartbeat of the congregation. Weekly services, combined with special seasonal services, weddings, and funerals, define who we are and whose we are. Worship brings the faith community together for thanksgiving and praise. In worship we sing the songs of the faith, hear the Scriptures read and the Word proclaimed, pray for those in need, celebrate baptisms and share the Eucharist. But worship also serves as an opportunity to inspire and instruct church members. Worship pumps the life-giving force of the Holy Spirit into and through the body of Christ. True worship helps transform individuals into disciples of Jesus Christ.

The Christian church is only as vibrant as its worship services. I have been to churches where the worship leaders conduct the morning liturgies as though they were a heavy burden or a tremendous inconvenience. I have heard sermons during which I thought the preacher was about to fall asleep. I have heard choir anthems that sounded like dirges, and seen ushers scold wiggly children, latecomers, and couples who wished to hold hands.

Traditional or contemporary, morning or evening, Sundays or weekdays, in beautiful cathedrals or simple spaces, worship needs to connect the community of faith with Almighty God, the Creator and Sustainer of the universe and the source of all wisdom, power, and love. Worship needs to bring the community of faith to a higher place. We are to *celebrate* worship, not endure it. When worship is heartfelt and beautiful, it is pleasing to God and participants feel the presence of the Holy Spirit. Worship serves to motivate and move its members to a deeper level of commitment and active service in God's name. It is the heartbeat of the church from which all programs and activities begin.

Christian Education: The Brain of the Church

Jesus' disciples, friends, and enemies called him "Rabbi." The word *rabbi* means "teacher," in general, or can be more accurately translated as "my teacher." Jesus was, first and foremost, a teacher. When the church seeks to be the body of Christ, we must be a teaching church. Jesus taught through his words and actions wherever he was. He taught on the streets, in the synagogues, at the temple in Jerusalem, and in private discussions with his disciples. He used stories and parables to convey God's eternal truths to all of his followers.

The church of Jesus Christ needs to teach its members the eternal truths of the gospel—his values, morals, and principles, which are often countercultural. We need to teach his grace and forgiveness, his love and mercy, his thirst for peace and justice. The ability to quote Scripture is meaningless unless there is the wisdom to integrate Scripture into our lives. It is the responsibility of the church to link the knowledge of our faith with the world around us.

Spiritual Growth: The Soul of the Church

There are some who confuse Christian education with spiritual growth. Although the two are related and often overlap, there is a distinction. There are those whose knowledge is great, who can read the Bible in Greek and/or Hebrew and can quote Scripture with ease. There are those who know church history backwards and forwards or can recite the creeds of the church from memory. There are denominations with fantastic libraries and archives that document their impressive past. But sometimes these individuals and churches lack spirituality. Knowledge is not to be confused with faith; book smarts do not equal spirituality.

We are all on spiritual journeys, traveling, hopefully, in the footsteps of Jesus. Our spirituality, symbolically represented as the soul of the body of Christ, needs to keep growing and maturing as we move deeper into our faith. The Wesleyan ordination question applies to all Christians equally: "Are you going on to perfection?" I rephrase his question as follows: "Is there evidence of your spiritual growth?"

I recall fondly the first day of kindergarten for my oldest son, Aaron. As he came off the bus, I greeted him enthusiastically and asked him how his day had gone. He told me that he had had a wonderful day but he had not learned how to read. It took me a moment to understand what he was saying. We had been telling Aaron for months he would learn to read when he went to school. In his unique, five-year-old mind, he had assumed he would learn to read the first day of school.

In the same way, when confirmation class students or other persons are accepted into the membership of a local church, they sometimes mistakenly believe they have arrived, that their journey into Christianity is now concluded. But being members of the body of Christ and faithfully living as disciples of Jesus Christ require an ongoing journey that includes the use of the spiritual disciplines as we move deeper in our faith.

The spiritual disciplines are tools of the church to help us deepen our faith and relationship to God through Jesus Christ. Also known as the "means of grace," they serve to remind us of our place in the universe and help us understand our own personal desires in relationship to the great needs of the world. Available to every Christian, they remind us to be disciples of Jesus Christ we must do more than attend an hour of worship each week.

The Spiritual Disciplines

Prayer

Reading Scripture

Meditation

Fasting and feasting

Serving others

Worship and sacraments

Holy reading

Sabbath rest

As individual Christians we must accept we are a piece of the universe and not its center. This awareness comes as we develop a sense of humility and meekness. There is no true spiritual growth without insight into ourselves. The spiritual disciplines help to remind us of whose we are. They serve as constant reminders we are not to be self-absorbed individuals, seeking to have our own needs met—participants in an ongoing, relentless struggle to accumulate more "toys." There is an ongoing struggle between the material and spiritual worlds. True spiritual development links us with the mind and will of Jesus Christ, providing us with inner peace, joy, and righteousness. We are then ready and prepared to move into the world as agents of change, determined to serve the least, the last, and the lost.

Mission and Outreach: The Muscles of Christ

Christianity is not an inactive religion; ours is not a spectator faith. I often told the congregations where I served that they were not called to be passive pew potatoes. Although we are saved by grace through faith, this faith must be expressed in our actions of mercy in building God's kingdom on earth. As the Letter of James says, "Just as the body without the spirit is dead, so faith without works is also dead" (Jas 2:26). Speaking more on the same topic, James writes:

> If any think they are religious, and do not bridle their tongues but deceive their hearts, their religion is worthless. Religion that is pure and undefiled before God, the Father, is this: to care for orphans and widows in their distress, and to keep oneself unstained by the world. (1:26–27)

Churches need to become training grounds for mission workers, the "laborers in the vineyard" (Matt 20:1–16). In addition to attending worship, engaging in the spiritual disciplines, and being active in Christian education classes, the disciple of Jesus Christ must become active in the world through mission programs and projects. Christian mission work is more than a check-writing exercise! A hands-on experience helps the giver as much as the receiver in that we are able to meet Jesus Christ face to face in those we serve. To be disciples of Jesus Christ, persons must find their mission project and then apply themselves with as much passion and energy as possible. There are countless mission opportunities:

- Thousands of shelters and soup kitchens spread across the United States in every city and state are desperately short of volunteers.

Churches could staff every one of these operations with volunteers to spare if we were to make this a priority.

- Programs such as the Appalachian Service Project and the Sierra Service Project offer youth the opportunity of serving Christ by volunteering in Appalachia or the Sierra foothills.
- Habitat for Humanity, founded in 1976 by Millard and Linda Fuller, is a nonprofit, ecumenical Christian housing ministry that seeks to eliminate poverty housing from the world. An international organization, Habitat has built more than two hundred thousand houses around the world, providing more than a million people in more than three thousand communities with safe, decent, affordable shelter. They are always looking for volunteers and assistance.
- Volunteers in Mission (VIM) is a relatively new field in mission work. VIM teams travel inside or outside of the United States to participate in specific projects as needed, such as disaster relief or building and educational projects.

The list is, of course, endless and extends to mentoring programs, tutoring at a local school, Meals on Wheels, nursing home and hospital visitation, and refugee resettlement programs. As the body of Christ we are called to serve, and in service we are blessed.

Evangelism: The Voice of the Church

Evangelism represents the voice of the body of Christ, the means through which the good news of Jesus Christ is conveyed to the world. This voice appears in a great variety of ways—from worship service broadcasts, talk shows, and commercials on radio and television, to articles, letters to the editor, opinion pieces, advertisements in local newspapers and telephone books, and to signs in front of the church and throughout the community.

The voice of the body of Christ is also articulated through sermons and Christian education opportunities; it is proclaimed through the singing of hymns and contemporary songs and through the invitation to Christian discipleship in prayers, sacraments, and the social ministries of local congregations. But the strongest expressions of the voice of the body of Christ is uttered by members of local congregations who tell neighbors, friends, and coworkers the story of their church and what it is doing in the name of Jesus Christ.

One of the local evangelical churches in my town likes to place volunteers in front of a large grocery store. Their task is to encourage shoppers to visit their church. One of the first questions they ask those on the way into the store is "Have you been saved?" While I am sure that this form of evangelism has produced some results for this church, I do not believe it to be the most effective way to bring nonbelievers into the body of Christ.

Television evangelists and "born again" spokespersons have done serious damage to the image many hold of Christians. In their enthusiasm to share the good news, they have often behaved like bulls in china shops, passionately promoting their cause while failing to listen to others' concerns or worries. The mass media often portray all clergy and church members in less than complimentary ways, portraying us in roles that make us appear as nerds, fanatics, or militant activists. We would probably be served well by following St. Francis's advice: "Preach the gospel at all times; use words when you must."

Christianity works best as a faith of attraction rather than promotion. We attract people to our congregations when we proclaim the good news of Jesus Christ through words *and* deeds. As disciples of Jesus Christ, we know the importance of evangelism. John Wesley wrote of the need "to reform the Continent, and to spread scriptural Holiness over these Lands." We are evangelists; how we use our voice will determine how effective we will be. I think again and again of these words of Jesus from the Sermon on the Mount:

> You are the light of the world. A city built on a hill cannot be hid. No one after lighting a lamp puts it under the bushel basket, but on the lampstand, and it gives light to all in the house. In the same way, let your light shine before others, so that they may see your good works and give glory to your Father in heaven. (Matt 5:14–18)

Committee Work: The Skeleton of the Church

The church cannot function without an organizational structure that seeks to coordinate its programs and activities. Having said this, far too many churches and congregations spend far too much time and talent in committee work. The effective church of the twenty-first century will be the one where a bare minimum of church members serve on committees and the vast majority are involved in spiritual growth, Christian education, evangelism, and missional activities and programs.

While there is a need for church members to serve as trustees and other important officers, we sometimes confuse serving the institutional church with actual mission work. Serving on the board of trustees, being a part of the church council, or volunteering for the altar guild does not translate into works of mercy. They are part of the means of disciple making but not the ends. I would hate to watch as countless Christians tried to enter into heaven, pointing to their service on church committees as evidence of their fruit! Committee work may be a necessary ingredient in running a local church, but it should never be confused with the broader purpose of the church.

Social and Fund-raising Events: The Fat of the Church

Nutritionists argue about how much fat the ideal human diet should include. Recent studies have resulted in recommendations of 10 percent to 30 percent. All doctors agree that while humans need a certain amount of fat in their diets, too much fat is a very bad thing. Americans, in general, consume too much fat. According to the National Center for Health Statistics, 65 percent of the adults living in the United States are overweight.

The same can be said of local churches and our social and fund-raising activities. A certain amount of these programs are good for the organism, but too many of them are as unhealthy for the body of Christ as for individual human bodies.

Churches are not social clubs or fund-raising institutions. They are not service organizations like the Kiwanis, the Lions, or the Jaycees. A church should not confuse itself with the local YMCA, or attempt to be the socially "in" place to be. The church is the body of Christ and should, in everything, ask itself this question: Are our programs and activities those Jesus would support? If your church is known throughout the community for your pumpkin, Christmas tree, or Easter chocolate sales, then you should take special note. If your church is known for bingo nights, Victorian teas, or annual fashion shows, a review of the purpose of the church of Jesus Christ is in order.

When church members are more committed to the annual fair than they are that peace and justice be established throughout the world, we have a serious issue. When more volunteers will show up to work at a church tag sale than will volunteer at the local shelter, the church has lost its way. When we are more concerned with the committee structure of the local church than we are that thousands are dying needlessly around the world every day, we cease to be a faithful church of Jesus Christ.

Christian fellowship is a worthy goal. Christian fellowship can and should be achieved through well-chosen means. Fellowship is achieved before or after the worship service where newcomers are introduced and invited to go further in their faith journey. Fellowship takes place in Christian education classes as students learn and grow together. Mission work offers another setting for deeper friendship and commitments between church members. Caring for the sick and elderly can also provide opportunities for fellowship, bonding those who serve others in this way.

When the church is doing its work faithfully, its members will get to know each other in more depth and in more profound ways than they ever will by serving together on committees, working at fund-raisers, or sharing a drink at a fellowship event. Appropriate activities include planning and participating in worship services that inspire, motivate, and challenge members; providing opportunities for church members to go deeper into their spirituality and grow in their faith; leading Christian education classes; and encouraging members to serve the least, the last, and the lost through mission programs.

Churches that focus too much attention on their social and fund-raising activities are churches that have too much fat in their diets! Churches having problems balancing their budgets need to review their overall programs, missions, and activities. Miraculously, a church that is transforming its members' lives through worship, Christian education, spiritual growth, effective evangelism, and mission work will not have financial issues. When a church is dependent on fund-raisers, rents from outside groups, and interest from endowments, it may be better served by closing its doors and allowing another community of faith to take its place.

Concluding Thoughts

It has been said the cabin stewards of the *Titanic* were busy rearranging the deck furniture on the great ship as it was taking on water and about to sink. They were so concerned with the antlike problems they missed the significance of the giant elephant in their midst: their ship was sinking and only a minority of people onboard would survive.

We are living during a particularly difficult time in the history of the world. Many are speaking of the "clash of civilizations" taking place between Western and Arab cultures, of the ongoing, and increasing, conflict between Christians, Muslims, and Jews. The War on Terrorism appears endless. The knowledge to build and possess nuclear weapons is spreading to more nations. Numerous commentators point to the potential of another world war in the near future. Millions of persons have lost their lives in the past decade as wars and violence continue unabated. Many more millions have died from treatable diseases, and poverty continues to take its heavy toll in the developing nations around the world.

Of great concern is the seeming impotence of the Christian church to address these issues. Local churches and clergy are so concerned with their own day-to-day tasks we miss the bigger picture. Equally troubling are those Christians who support the use of violence and military action to achieve national goals. In the past few years, we have witnessed Christian clergy calling publicly for the assassination of foreign leaders. We have elected Christian politicians who have voted in favor of preemptive strikes and aggressive wars against other countries. Church members throughout our nation and the world continue to support and participate in war, and the military-industrial-political complex continues to receive the blessings of the church and its members.

These disconcerting realities indicate that the body of Christ is failing to teach its disciples the ways of Jesus Christ. It is painfully clear we are off the path that Jesus walked. If the church cannot re-educate itself according to the original teachings of Jesus, we will run straight into an oncoming iceberg and have no one to blame but ourselves.

This brings us to a concern of John Wesley, founder of Methodism: "I have no doubt that the people called 'Methodists' shall ever cease to exist in this country [England] or in America, but I do fear they shall become a dead sect, having a form of godliness, but denying the power thereof."[78]

Approximately 75 percent of the citizens of the United States are Christian. There are Protestant and Roman Catholic churches in every town and city. There are men and women who want to follow in the footsteps of Jesus. But most are on a different road. If the churches of Jesus Christ continue to focus their resources of time, talent, gifts, and service on fund-raising, social activities, and debates over trivial issues, Christianity itself will become a dead sect within our country. We may have the buildings, the clergy, the education, and the trappings of the church, but without the passion to follow the Prince of Peace, we will become like museums and tombs, reminders of what we once were as opposed to what we can be.

[78] John Wesley, *Works of J. Wesley,* vol. 13, *Letters and Writings* (Nashville: Abingdon Press, 1984), 320.

Chapter 11

Paradigm Shifters and Agents of Change

Do not remember the former things,
or consider the things of old.
I am about to do a new thing;
now it springs forth, do you not perceive it?
I will make a way in the wilderness
and rivers in the desert.
                    —Isaiah 43:18–21

Twenty years from now you will be more disappointed by the things that
you didn't do than by the ones you did do.
So throw off the bowlines.
Sail away from the safe harbor.
Catch the trade winds in your sails.
Explore. Dream. Discover.
                    —Mark Twain

On December 17, 1903, Orville Wright made the first heavier-than-air flight in a gasoline-powered airplane he and his brother Wilbur had built and named "The Wright Flyer." Off the ground for twelve seconds, he traveled approximately 120 feet. Shot just after takeoff, the picture at the front of this chapter was taken from a camera Wilbur had set up. It is perhaps the most reproduced photograph ever. Later that afternoon, Wilbur himself piloted the plane for fifty-nine seconds, soaring a distance of 852 feet. The two made history. Bill Gates said it well: "The Wright Brothers created the single greatest cultural force since the invention of writing. The airplane became the first World Wide Web, bringing people, languages, ideas, and values together."[79]

The Wright brothers, owners of a bicycle shop and skilled mechanics, were both brilliant and determined. With indomitable spirit and great fortitude, they worked with single-minded purpose for three years before their breakthrough flight. Interestingly, their father, the Rev. Milton Wright, was a bishop in the Church of the United Brethren in Christ. The house in which his children were raised had two libraries: a theological library in the bishop's study and a secular library off the family's living room. Bishop Wright fed his boys a steady diet of books from each collection, balancing their theological studies with contemporary, scientific instruction. He was successful in achieving two important goals for all parents: he gave his children roots and he gave them wings.

For centuries, humanity dreamed of flying. Of course, the common belief was that flying was impossible. It would never be done, people thought. It was considered unfeasible, impractical, hopelessly out of the question, a ridiculous and dangerous waste of people's time and abilities. Those who dreamed and spoke of flying were wasting the time of the realists, who knew it would never happen. But the realists were wrong.

Today, just over a hundred years since those first short, tentative flights along the beach at Kitty Hawk, airplane travel is as commonplace as central heating and indoor plumbing. Boeing's 747 airplanes weigh over five hundred thousand pounds and can carry as many as 480 passengers on cross country or intercontinental trips. Thousands of airplanes take off and land every day in countries throughout the entire world, promoting tourism, trade, business, and international relations. The invention of the airplane was one of the great steps forward in the development of human history. It has radically changed the world. The dream of flying became a reality. Imagine the world we live in without airplanes. It is hard to do.

---

[79] Bill Gates, "75th Anniversary *Time* Salute," speech given in Washington, DC, on March 3, 1998, http://www.microsoft.com/billgates/speeches/gatessalute.aspx.

Now imagine a world without war. Many say it is impossible. Such a world has been, and is, considered unfeasible, impractical, hopelessly out of the question. So-called realists tell us it is a pathetic dream never to be realized. But what if these naysayers are wrong?

The Wright Brothers ushered in a paradigm shift and are credited as the agents of change in developing the first airplane. Paradigm shifts can be evolutionary or revolutionary and involve transformation and/or metamorphosis. These changes do not simply take place; rather, agents of change drive them. Any one of us can be an agent of change to usher in a new way of thinking and behaving. However, this is no easy task, as human nature resists changing the status quo and "stepping into the unknown." Convincing others to follow and take a risk is in itself a risky business.

I recall leading the New Milford United Methodist Church through a paradigm shift soon after I began serving as pastor there in 1993. The church swung from an inwardly looking, closed institution to a mission-oriented service and outreach center. It was a frustrating and, at times, painful change, and several families left the church, but over time this transformation helped us to grow in numbers and in faith.

When I arrived in New Milford, the church was in crisis. Attendance had dropped nearly 50 percent in the past decade. As the attendance and membership of the church declined, so did the income. Budgets were cut, programs eliminated, mission and outreach ended, and the congregation moved into survival mode. The building was kept locked virtually all of the time. With essentially no programs, no activities, and no mission work, the church lost its reason to be. Many in the town whom I met did not realize the church existed.

It was clear a dramatic change would have to take place to stop the church's rapid decline. Following my first year of preaching and pastoral work, an answer came in an unsolicited phone call one afternoon. The caller identified herself as a church member from a neighboring town whose congregation had sponsored a Bosnian family for resettlement in the United States six months previously. It had been a wonderful experience for many in that faith community who had welcomed and provided life sustaining support to war refugees. The father of this family of four had a brother still living in Bosnia whose family was awaiting a sponsor in the United States so they too could resettle here. The caller told me her congregation would be able to officially sponsor the new family, but they could not housing. She said that she was calling all of the churches in the area in the hope someone could help them out. She asked if we would consider providing housing for this family. My immediate reaction was we were not in a position to accommodate her request, and I wished her well with her search.

Later that same afternoon, while visiting a sick parishioner, I learned our church had sponsored a Vietnamese refugee family back in the 1970s. An apartment had been created for this family in an old farmhouse located on our property that was still in use as our Sunday school facility. I immediately remembered the telephone conversation from earlier in the day, and was thankful that the woman had left her name and number "just in case."

The first thing I did after returning to the church office was to call this woman back and get more information. No, she had not yet found housing. The refugee family looking for housing consisted of a mother and father and two teenage daughters. Her church was willing to sponsor this new family; housing was the issue they could not address. Any additional help we could provide would be appreciated but not required or expected.

Equipped with this information, and after a follow-up meeting between myself, the Bosnians who were already living in the United States, the pastor of the church in the neighboring town, and the woman who had initially called me, I set in motion the process of bringing this idea before our governing board for approval. Unknowingly, I was about to become the agent of change for the New Milford United Methodist Church's paradigm shift.

For me, housing the Bosnians was an easy decision. I always believed an important part of being a church was to help others in need. We had extra space in our Sunday school building. The church had made a similar decision and commitment twenty years earlier by opening its doors to a war torn refugee family and allowing them to live in our facilities for several years. It seemed like a no-brainer. But others did not see it the same way.

Two tortuous months of discussion and debate followed, with church leaders eventually voting to recreate an apartment in our Sunday school building and allow the Bosnian family to move in. It was a difficult time for the congregation, as those on both sides fought with determination. Lines were drawn in the sand between members who believed the purpose of the church included reaching out to those in need, and others for whom this seemed to be a foreign concept. Resistance to change was strong and I became the target of personal attacks.

Looking back now from the distance a decade provides, I realize the church was facing the question of what kind of community of faith we wanted to be. Acknowledging anti-Muslim prejudice and the fear of change were also factors, the primary issue seemed to be whether or not we were willing to reach out to others who were in need. If not, if the decision was made to say no to this family in need, we would continue to exist as an inwardly focused institution, unable to take even a small step toward serving the least, the last, and the lost of God's children.

I now see the decision of the church leaders as the planting of a stake in the ground: here we would stand as a community of faith, with open arms, open hearts, and open doors, to serve those in need. This was nothing less than a paradigm shift; it was a turning point for us as we unleashed the good within church members and allowed them to give to others. Although we had never met the family that we were about to "adopt," we mobilized for their arrival. Furniture was donated, volunteers appeared to clean, paint, and prepare the rooms, new appliances were purchased and delivered by an anonymous donor, and clothing, kitchenware, linens, and food began to appear miraculously. Church members came forward to help transport the family around town and to provide English tutoring, driving lessons, and help in finding jobs.

The Seriç family stayed at our church for eighteen months; they remain in New Milford and have assimilated successfully into the community. The decision to provide housing for them led to a decade of growth for the church, as we slowly began to turn the focus of the congregation from ourselves to others.

During those years, worship attendance grew from just over a hundred persons per week to over 270, and we opened a food pantry, built an orphanage in Mozambique, provided food and clothing to homeless persons in New York City, sent our youth group to Virginia with the Appalachian Service Project, staffed the local shelter, and served hot meals every month at the town's food ministry.

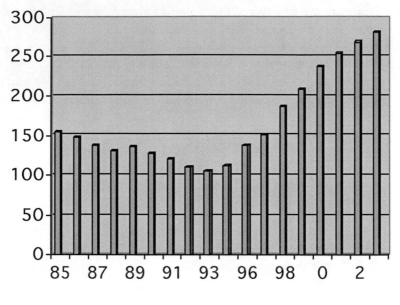

Worship Attendance:

The New Milford United Methodist Church, 1985–2003

The night prior to the vote on whether to allow the Bosnian family to move into our facility, I spoke to my predecessor. Although he had retired eighteen months prior to our conversation, he was still in touch with some church families. Many persons who were opposed to housing the Bosnians had called him and vented their frustration, telling him they were going to vote against this motion. He suggested that I table the idea and drop the whole plan, convinced that if I allowed the motion to be brought forward and if it was defeated, my ministry at the church would receive a severe and perhaps fatal blow. He told me he had never served such an inwardly focused congregation in his lifetime. He suggested if I truly wanted to serve a mission-oriented congregation, I ought to look elsewhere; changing the DNA of this church was unlikely. I thanked him for his input but decided to proceed with the motion, convinced it was the right decision for the church to make.

The next night, following some tense moments and debate, the motion to created an apartment and allow this Bosnian refugee family to move into our facility carried relatively easily. What led to this change in focus and attitude? With the luxury of hindsight, I would like to offer the following reasons.

It was a good decision. The church had extra rooms available. We knew of people in need who could use those rooms. A ministry and mission of the church is to provide food, clothing, and shelter to those in need. We had addressed most of the risks voiced by those who were against this decision. It was a good idea.

Of course, in the history of the Christian church, and specifically in the New Milford United Methodist Church, there have been many good ideas that have not been accepted by the majority. But after several months of debate and discussion, logic prevailed and the good decision was chosen. To vote no would have been to turn our backs on a family of God's children in need; our yes vote said we were willing to offer hospitality to the stranger in need. The majority present that night chose the better route.

The church members acted in faith and love. A popular slogan in church circles is that we are not called to be successful, but to be faithful. The members of this church had an opportunity to be faithful—and they were. While they hoped the decision to house the Bosnians would be successful, the more important fact is they moved forward in faith and love, not knowing how things would turn out.

Each of us has a role to play as disciples of Jesus Christ. Each of us has been given a task, a responsibility, to advance the values and goals of our faith, to build God's kingdom, piece by piece, place by place, no matter where on earth we live. To simply maintain the status quo during one's lifetime would be to miss the opportunity of service—service in God's name leading to true joy, peace, and faith. The church is filled with opportunities to keep members busy and opportunities to "play church," from bake sales to car washes, dinners, and committee meetings. But the church is not called to play church; we are called to be the church, to act courageously in the world through actions of grace and mercy.

The church members were courageous and took a risk. Making decisions involves a level of risk. It has been said the greatest risk is in taking no risks at all. Sitting back behind locked doors and saying no to mission opportunities is a reactive, defensive way of pursuing ministry. Challenged to feed the hungry, clothe the naked, provide water to the thirsty, and visit those who are sick or in prison requires an active, participatory faith that cannot be accomplished safely by staying at home. Believing that Jesus would have said yes to housing the Bosnians was a great argument one of our church leaders made, and it helped set the conversation in the right context.

Although in the greater scheme of things the risk we incurred by housing a family of four was relatively small, the possibility of failure to those church members who made the decision loomed huge. What if the expenses of hosting the new family could not be met? What if this family was dangerous? What if they stole from the church or church members? What if they burned our building down? What if they never left? What if current church members, upset at the decision to house these strangers, left the congregation? Although we did not have the answer to these and other questions, the church was able to take this small step of faith that then helped us with larger steps as time went by.

The church had leaders with a vision that all could follow. Although the church had been through a decade of decline, there were still many caring and compassionate persons within the congregation who were willing to help lead this project. I could not have pushed this motion through without the support of others. These members spoke passionately throughout the two months we took to decide this issue, and they spoke eloquently the night of the critical vote.

Leaders communicate a vision others can follow. A leader helps to recognize and secure the future, and this was accomplished through the decision to reopen our facility and become engaged in mission work once again. Competent leaders do not choose the well-traveled pathways but move in the right direction, even when it is not as popular as other routes.

The church moved away from self-interest and found a higher good. In 1993 the members of the New Milford United Methodist Church were concerned with the survival of their church. Attendance and membership had declined dramatically, and the income was insufficient to meet the expenses. Church members went into survival mode. They began closing their doors and locking everything up so that what they had could be secure. But this mentality was self-defeating and created a vicious cycle. The more the church worried about its own survival and locked the world out, the more the church declined and the more its future was threatened.

But the church cannot simply be concerned with its survival. As Jesus said, "Those who want to save their life will lose it, and those who lose their life for my sake will save it. What does it profit them if they gain the whole world, but lose or forfeit themselves?" (Luke 9:24–25) It is the church's mission and ministry to give. Only through giving do we find ourselves, and only in reaching out in love and service to others will the church of Jesus Christ thrive.

The New Milford United Methodist Church is far from the only mainline congregation to see a decline in membership and attendance through the years. In fact, membership and attendance have fallen in the United Methodist Church for thirty-six consecutive years since the merger of the Methodist Church with the smaller Evangelical United Brethren Church in 1968. Looking at percentages, the mainline denominations in the United States have been in decline since 1940:

The United Methodists dropped from 124.7 adherents per thousand total church members in 1940 to 93.0 in 1960 and to just 64.3 in 1985. For the Presbyterians (USA), the simultaneous decline was from 41.7 to 36.4 to 21.3, while the Episcopalian fall was from 30.9 to 28.6 to 19.2. Meanwhile, the United Church of Christ (Congregationalists) slid from 26.5 to 19.6 to 11.8[80]

Church growth, membership, and attendance are complex issues that have been addressed by authors such as Bill Easum, Adam Hamilton, Lyle Schaller, Michael Slaughter, and Leonard Sweet. It is my belief churches grow when their members are fed spiritually and given opportunities to participate in meaningful mission projects, co-creating with God a just and peaceful global community. Congregations and denominations that do not encourage and offer their church members opportunities in the mission field will continue to decline as seeking Christians will defect to churches and denominations engaged in helping others.

Thinking of Peace with Justice on a Global Scale

What will it take for the nations of the world to embrace peace? What will it take to get the leaders of the world to seek justice for all of God's children?

Using the same criteria I used to document why the New Milford United Methodist Church opted to allow the Bosnian family to live on our premises, I would like to outline five reasons why the United States should move aggressively to be a nation that promotes preemptive peace through a redistribution of our national resources of time, money, assets, and talent.

It is a good idea. The only ones who benefit from war are the manufacturers and dealers of weapons. These "masters of war" are able to reap tremendous profits before, during, and after war, and may even have some influence in policies that lead to war. But no one else wants war. Mothers and fathers, husbands and wives, children and siblings do not want their loved ones to kill and die in wars. Working toward a world of peace and justice for all of God's children is a good idea. We know war means death, but time and time again, we choose it. In order to make us feel better about this choice, we have created ideologies and myths (e.g., the noble sacrifice of our soldiers, who loved country more than self), but the fact remains that throughout the world, war is glorified. Leo Tolstoy wrote about this paradox in *War and Peace:*

---

[80] Kevin Philips, *American Theocracy* (New York: Viking, 2006), 117–18.

The military class is the most highly honored. And what is war, what is required for success in warfare, what are the moral standards of the military world? The aim of war is murder; the implements of warfare—espionage, treachery, and the inducements thereto, the ruination of a country's inhabitants by ravage and robbery to provision the army, the trickery and deceit known as military stratagems; the ethics of the military class—lack of freedom, in other words, discipline, idleness, ignorance, cruelty, debauchery, and drunkenness. Yet in spite of all this, it is the highest class, respected by all. Every sovereign, except the Chinese, wears a military uniform and bestows the greatest rewards on those who kill the most people.

They meet, as we shall meet tomorrow, to murder one another; they kill and maim tens of thousands of men, and then hold thanksgiving services for having slaughtered so many (they even exaggerate the number) and proclaim a victory, assuming the greater the slaughter the greater the merit. How God can look down and hear them![81]

Creating a world of peace and justice for all of God's people will produce a period of economic prosperity. Shifting resources from the creation and maintenance of weapons will provide money that can be used for health care, education, housing, and nutrition. Working for peace and justice is, simply put, a good idea.

The United States needs to lead with conviction and with confidence. The United States is the most dominant nation in the history of the world. Culturally, socially, economically, and politically, we set the global agenda. Where the United States leads, nations follow. Globally, the United States stands for democracy, liberty, and freedom. When we export these products and encourage their proliferation, we are the shining beacons to the nations of the world.

International support for the United States was at an all-time high following the terrorist attacks of 9/11. In fact, the headlines of a leftist French newspaper carried these words under the heading, "We Are All Americans":

In this tragic moment, when words seem so inadequate to express the shock people feel, the first thing that comes to mind is this:

---

[81] Leo Tolstoy, *War and Peace,* trans. Ann Dunnigan (New York: New American Library, 1968), 933.

We are all Americans! We are all New Yorkers, just as surely as John F. Kennedy declared himself to be a Berliner in 1962 when he visited Berlin.[82]

It is unlikely a similar article could be written like this one today. We have squandered the empathy and good will of our global neighbors we held September 12, 2001, and have taken a path that has led to more violence and more death. Returning to our core values can restore the international reputation of our nation, and we can be the leaders in ushering in a time of peace and prosperity.

The United States needs to break the current cycle of violence by taking a risk. For far too long and far too often, national leaders have used the tactic of fear to manipulate their people. Clearly, fear of the enemy is not an effective and healthy national policy!

I grew up being told that I needed to fear communism and the Soviet Union. Hundreds of billions of dollars and rubles were wasted on the senseless policy of mutual assured destruction. Although the Cold War ended with the collapse of the Soviet Union, there remain enough nuclear weapons to destroy the earth many times over.

I grew up during the Vietnam War. The war was described to the American public as a war against communism. We were told that if communism won in Vietnam, a domino-like effect would take place, with nations falling to this evil way of life one after another until the United States itself would be threatened.

Over 58,000 American soldiers were killed in Vietnam. The estimates of the "enemy" that were killed during the war range from one to two million persons. We had superior forces, controlled the skies completely, had tremendous technological advantages, and killed far more enemy soldiers than we lost, but we could not win over the hearts and minds of the population. As a result, we lost the war.

Contrary to the fear instilled into us by our elected leaders, communism did not spread. In fact, in 1991, sixteen years after the fall of Saigon, the Soviet Union collapsed. China, the world's largest remaining communist country, has introduced many free market reforms. Capitalism, rather than communism, is spreading throughout the world.

As of this writing, our nation is involved in wars in Iraq and Afghanistan that the Bush administration considers two fronts in a larger War on Terror.

---

[82] Jean-Marie Colombani, *Le Monde,* September 12, 2001.

Over 3,100 Americans have lost their lives in Iraq, and the estimates of Iraqis who have been killed range from 60,000 to 650,000.

Our governmental leaders have told us this is now a war for civilization. We have been told if we do not win the battle being waged on the streets of Baghdad, there will be fighting in the streets of our cities. We have been told this war is similar to World War II, where the lines between good and evil are clearly defined and the enemy must be defeated. We have succumbed to a campaign of fear.

We must break this cycle of fear and violence by working to create peace. Courageous leaders must step forward and take us down a different path. They will come under personal attack and will be criticized as naïve, weak, and foolish. Doing the right thing will be difficult, but the rewards demand the effort.

The United States must generate and support agents of change. History is filled with the names of men and women who have led their nations through good and bad times. From the earliest pages of the Bible through today's newspapers, we encounter leaders who have improved the conditions of their nations and people, and those who have made things worse. In today's world, we must find leaders who can plot a course that will lead toward peace and justice; failure to do so could result in the onset of World War III, a war waged by governments, sanctioned by religious leaders, and fought with weapons of mass destruction.

The United States has been blessed with some of our greatest leaders when we needed them most, as at the time of our founding (Franklin, Washington, Adams, Jefferson, Hamilton, Madison, and Monroe) and during the Civil War (Lincoln), World War I (Wilson), and World War II (Roosevelt). Most of these led during times of conflict and warfare, but now it is imperative we find leaders who can guide us toward a future of peace and prosperity for ourselves and for the people of the world.

All across our nation I see a rising tide of peaceful, gentle men and women who are greatly concerned with the aggressive response our nation reverts to when threatened or attacked. But the military solutions we offered in previous centuries will no longer work today. Violence, poverty, disease, and oppression are not new phenomena in our world. As we enter the twenty-first century, however, there seems to be an escalating trend in human suffering. Around the world, extreme poverty, AIDS, civil war, and corrupt or incompetent governments have plunged nations into downward socioeconomic spirals. These conditions have created a vacuum in which hate has been allowed to breed; this void has created incredible hopelessness, providing incubators for terrorists and fodder for more wars and acts of violence.

The future will belong to those courageous agents of change who can reverse these trends, offer life-sustaining technologies and innovations, and move the world toward peace and justice. We must find and support the men and women who will stand up to those committed to violence, hatred, and destruction and instead forge a path of reconciliation, forgiveness, healing, and understanding.

We must move away from self-interest and find a higher good. In today's global village, it is no longer possible to worry only about our national interest. Our self-interest now includes the safety and security of people all over the world. When the citizens of foreign nations are fed, clothed, housed, educated, and cared for, they are far more likely to be peaceful. Being a good neighbor to other nations of the world will lead to their being better nations to us as well; we must understand it is in our interest to eliminate extreme poverty and create hope among the world's poor.

We need to establish a new Declaration of Independence and launch a new global vision that recognizes these commitments: Every child born in the twenty-first century should be entitled to a twenty-first century education. Every person alive today should have access to modern medicine. There should be no economic worries for the elderly. Every person alive should have a warm, safe, and dry place to live. No one should be treated differently because of his or her race, religion, sex, sexual orientation, nationality, or any other difference.

Do We Have the Courage to Work for Change?

Eugene Jarecki, producer of the movie *Why We Fight,* says the military-industrial complex has placed defense industry jobs in every one of the 435 districts from which members of the House of Representatives are elected. He believes cuts to the military budget of the United States will not happen because every senator and every representative to Congress defend every dollar that comes into their state or district as though they were sacred. Bringing home the "pork" is seen as an important role our politicians fill; keeping military bases and defense-related jobs in their jurisdictions is proof our elected officials are busy protecting their districts and states. Protected with campaign contributions from defense contractors and always concerned with re-election, our most politicians cannot see another path.

A better example was set in 1996 by agents of change at the closing of the Fort Devens military base in Massachusetts. The Massachusetts legislature established the Devens Enterprise Commission to lure businesses and create jobs in the wake of the base's closing. Today the 4,400-acre site boasts more than eighty companies with 4,200 workers—double the base's employment in 1991 when the closing was first announced. "In just a decade, Devens, as it's now called, has gone from basket case to showcase, a transformation underscored last week by Bristol-Myers Squibb Co.'s decision to build a $660 million manufacturing plant there."[83]

Building a world of peace with justice will require the transformation of many bases and many communities from a defense-based economy to a peace-based economy. We must encourage our elected leaders to begin to move resources away from military spending and toward life-sustaining work. When we find the courage to say no to the military-industrial-political complex, we will open the door to the many possibilities a peace economy can bring to the world, and we will be working to fulfill the prophet's words:

> He shall judge between the nations,
>> and shall arbitrate for many peoples;
> they shall beat their swords into plowshares,
>> and their spears into pruning hooks;
> nation shall not lift up sword against nation,
>> neither shall they learn war any more. (Isa 2:4)

* * * * * *

We fly from city to city, state to state, and country to country without a second thought. It is hard to imagine what the world would be like without this modern convenience. We experienced a brief time without commercial airfare in the United States in the wake of the 9/11 attacks, when the skies over the United States were closed as new security measures were put into place. Men, women, and children were stranded all over the nation without ways to get back home. Business meetings were canceled, shipments were delayed, vacations lost, and plans ruined. We take air travel for granted these days.

Orville and Wilbur Wright had a great idea, and they worked hard to make their dream a reality. They devoted themselves to building the world's first airplane. They were courageous, and they opened the doorway for others to stand on their shoulders and continue the development and evolution of airplanes. I wonder what Orville and Wilbur Wright would say if they could come back and spend a few hours at a modern airport and watch how their efforts unleashed a technological and transportation revolution.

---

[83] Robert Gavin and Charlie Russo, "Devens Thriving as Old Fort's Leaders Put Businesses at Ease," *Boston Globe,* June 9, 2006.

What will historians write of the decisions of the United States at the dawn of the twenty-first century? Will we be seen as a nation that chose to work for peace and embraced it with our full commitment? Will we be seen as the nation that broke the ongoing cycle of violence? Will our leaders be regarded as having offered a higher, global vision of peace and justice? These are the questions we must seek to address now.

Chapter 12

A Call to Action

The man who dies thus rich, dies disgraced.

—Andrew Carnegie

For the love of money is a root of all kinds of evil, and in their eagerness to be rich some have wandered away from the faith and pierced themselves with many pains.

—I Timothy 6:10

In February 2006 I traveled to Mozambique for the third time. Once again I went as a guest of the United Methodist Church and at the invitation of Bishop Jao Samoe Machado. I stayed in the capital city of Maputo for three days before moving up the coast approximately 250 miles to the United Methodist mission site in Cambine. There, I worshipped with the seminary students and attended their classes. I played with the children of the Carolyn Beleshe Orphanage. I visited schools and churches in the area and met with agriculturists, doctors, nurses, and teachers who were working to improve the living conditions of people in this poor, developing nation.

One Sunday morning I worshipped at the large United Methodist Church in Cambine. The three-hour worship service was filled with joy and thanksgiving, with heartfelt singing, prayers, and powerful preaching. The time came for the offering.

I had learned from previous trips that church offerings in Mozambique are taken in a manner different from most North American churches. Instead of ushers passing plates, baskets are placed at the front of the church, and those present are invited to come forward in small groups of ten to twenty. The men, women, and children who present their offerings together are members of the same house church, divided within the larger congregation as a small group ministry. The worshippers bring their offerings forward and place them in the basket, singing and dancing as they come forward and return to their seats. After each small group is finished presenting its offering, the money is removed, counted separately, and announced later in the worship service.

I had brought with me a thousand dollars to give to several organizations and projects. The exchange rate at the time of my trip was 27,000 Mozambican meticais to every U.S dollar. Soon after arriving in Maputo, I exchanged six hundred dollars and received 16.2 million meticais!

I decided to present two million meticais, the equivalent of fifty-four dollars, to the church that morning. It seemed a fair and modest offering. When they called for the offering of the guests, I moved forward, along with my host and a friend, and placed twenty 100,000 meticais notes in the basket. We sang a simple praise song, "God Is So Good," and returned to our seats.

Later in the service the offering totals were announced. It was reported the church leaders had met the day before and had prayed for an offering of at least a million meticais. They shared the information that they had exceeded that amount, and proceeded to read the totals from each separate group. When they announced the total for the "guests," loud cheers went up throughout the building. The total for that morning came to three million meticais, triple the original goal. It was a good morning for the church treasurer.

But I felt embarrassed. Everyone knew what my offering had been and realized my gift alone was double what the entire congregation had given—and on this morning there were approximately two hundred persons present. I was reminded of the following story of Jesus, standing next to the treasury in the Jerusalem temple:

> He looked up and saw rich people putting their gifts into the treasury; he also saw a poor widow put in two small copper coins. He said, "Truly I tell you, this poor widow has put in more than all of them; for all of them have contributed out of their abundance, but she out of her poverty has put in all she had to live on." (Luke 21:1–4)

For the rest of the day and throughout the next week, I was treated as a celebrity in Cambine. I was warmly greeted, acknowledged, and hailed as the rich American who had given so generously to the church. People wanted to shake my hand, speak to me, and even have their pictures taken next to me. It was an odd situation given that, having lived most of my life on a pastor's salary in rural and suburban Connecticut I have never thought of myself as a wealthy person. In Mozambique, however, I was a rich man. I was a millionaire—literally—walking around with ten million meticais in my wallet. When I calculated the money and assets I had back in the United States, I came to the realization I was actually, in the currency of Mozambique, a billionaire! I alone was worth more than the population of entire villages!

I am materially a rich man. The truth of this statement hit me right between the eyes. It was not long before I went to my Bible and looked up the story of the rich man and Jesus. The story still makes me uncomfortable:

> Then someone came to him and said, "Teacher, what good deed must I do to have eternal life?" And he said to him, "Why do you ask me about what is good? There is only one who is good. If you wish to enter into life, keep the commandments." He said to him, "Which ones?" And Jesus said, "You shall not murder; You shall not commit adultery; You shall not steal; You shall not bear false witness; Honor your father and mother; also, You shall love your neighbor as yourself." The young man said to him, "I have kept all these; what do I still lack?" Jesus said to him, "If you wish to be perfect, go, sell your possessions, and give the money to the poor, and you will have treasure in heaven; then come,

follow me." When the young man heard this word, he went away grieving, for he had many possessions. (Matt 19:16–22)

Then Jesus said to his disciples, "Truly I tell you, it will be hard for a rich person to enter the kingdom of heaven. Again I tell you, it is easier for a camel to go through the eye of a needle than for someone who is rich to enter the kingdom of God." When the disciples heard this, they were greatly astounded and said, "Then who can be saved?" But Jesus looked at them and said, "For mortals it is impossible, but for God all things are possible."

* * * * * *

Andrew Carnegie was one of the more interesting men in American history. Born in Scotland in 1835, he immigrated to the United States with his family in 1848. To raise payment for the passage, his parents were forced to sell all of their possessions and borrow an additional twenty pounds from friends, a considerable sum in 1848. From Glasgow the family traveled to New York; from there, they journeyed up the Hudson River, through the Erie Canal to Lake Erie, and eventually to Allegheny, Pennsylvania, where Andrew's father found work in a cotton factory. The young Andrew Carnegie found a job in the same factory, working as a "Bobbin Boy" for $1.20 per week.

Soon after taking his first job, Carnegie found another position as the telegraph messenger boy in the Pittsburgh office of the Ohio Telegraph Company, doubling his salary to $2.50 per week. This in turn led to a job with the Pennsylvania Railroad Company as a secretary and telegraph operator in 1853 that paid the relatively large sum of four dollars per week. Carnegie was only sixteen, but he began to advance rapidly through the company, eventually becoming the superintendent of the Pittsburgh division.

Carnegie's success did not end here. His involvement in the railways led to investments and shrewd business decisions that allowed him to accumulate some capital. As the railroads continued to expand, Carnegie's interests extended into the iron and steel industries. He traveled to Great Britain and met with the world's leaders in steel production including the inventor of the Bessemer steel process, Sir Henry Bessemer. With Bessemer's consent, Carnegie brought his technology to the United States in 1868. In 1873 he made his now famous gamble. He decided to "put all his eggs in one basket, and then watch the basket." That year he sold all of his holdings in the railroad and other stocks and concentrated his wealth in the making of steel. The rest, as they say, is history. He built an empire of steel and, in 1892, combined all of his steel-making assets and companies together to form the Carnegie

Steel Company. His business dominated the national market and brought him millions of dollars.

But Carnegie had strong opinions regarding wealth and society. Born and raised in relative poverty, he did not believe the accumulation of wealth was the ultimate purpose of humanity. Carnegie wrote *The Gospel of Wealth,* in which he stated the rich should use their wealth to help enrich society. He believed great leaders should earn all that is possible during their careers so it could then be given to projects benefiting the public, which is what he proceeded to do upon his retirement in 1901. He had grown his company into the world's first billion-dollar corporation, and he sold his share of it for $230,000,000. He spent the remainder of his life giving this money away.

Among his many philanthropic projects, the building of public libraries in the United States, the United Kingdom, and other English-speaking countries was especially important. Carnegie libraries, as they were often called, were built everywhere. His plan was to build and equip the libraries, but only on condition that local authorities provided the sites and maintenance. Carnegie funded three thousand libraries, located in every U.S. state except Alaska and Delaware, as well as in Canada, Britain, Ireland, Australia, New Zealand, the West Indies, and Fiji.

Although Carnegie benefited financially during the Civil War through his shrewd deals with the federal government, the experience of transporting soldiers to the front line where they killed and were killed had a major impact on him. Later in life he developed a passion for peace work. In addition to his other humanitarian works, he established the Carnegie Endowment for International Peace, contributed $500,000 in 1903 for the erection of a Peace Palace at The Hague,[84] and was one of the first to call for the League of Nations. His influence with Woodrow Wilson can be seen in Wilson's adoption of the League of Nations as one of the keys to establishing a world of peace following the First World War.

Carnegie wrote a book, spoke and lectured widely, and advised presidents and foreign leaders. In this speech he seemed to sum up his personal philosophy regarding wealth:

> Man does not live by bread alone. I have known millionaires starving for lack of the nutriment which alone can sustain all that is human in man, and I know workmen, and many so-called poor men, who revel in luxuries beyond the power of those

---

[84]The Peace Palace today serves as the headquarters of the World Court.

millionaires to reach. It is the mind that makes the body rich. There is no class so pitiably wretched as that which possesses money and nothing else. Money can only be the useful drudge of things immeasurably higher than itself. Exalted beyond this, as it sometimes is, it remains Caliban[85] still and still plays the beast. My aspirations take a higher flight. Mine be it to have contributed to the enlightenment and the joys of the mind, to the things of the spirit, to all that tends to bring into the lives of the toilers of Pittsburgh sweetness and light. I hold this the noblest possible use of wealth.[86]

In the eighteen years from his retirement to his death on August 11, 1919, Andrew Carnegie gave away $350,695,653, over 90 percent of his wealth. Following his death, the remaining $30,000,000 was given to foundations, charities, and public works per instructions in his will. Although he had retained enough to live in great luxury, his intention was clear: to give everything away. Being a literate man who read extensively, it is likely Carnegie was familiar with the conversation between the rich man and Jesus. Did he see himself in this story? Was he able to slip through the eye of the needle and enter into the kingdom of heaven?

More importantly, how do we respond to the story of Andrew Carnegie? Can we simply dismiss him because he was so incredibly wealthy that his life bears no resemblance to ours? Or is he a stewardship role model for American Christians living at the beginning of the twenty-first century?

* * * * * *

As the director of Passing the Peace, a non-profit organization dedicated to creating a world of peace and justice for all of God's children, I have had the opportunity to travel to many different locations to discuss church and state, poverty and terrorism, war and peace. In some places, I have found people to be extremely supportive. In other settings, however, I have encountered hostility and anger. It is ironic how talking about peace can get some people so upset.

Although I have received both positive and negative reactions to my work on peace, both those who agree with me and those who don't often ask the same questions, which boil down to something like this:

---

[85] In Shakespeare's *Tempest,* Caliban is a grotesque, brutish slave.

[86] Andrew Carnegie, "Mr. Carnegie's Address," in Presentation of the Carnegie Library to the People of Pittsburgh, with a Description of the Dedicatory Exercises, November 5th, 1895 (Pittsburgh: The City of Pittsburgh, [1895]), 13-14.

- Do you, Wayne Lavender, think that you can make a difference in the world, bringing peace and justice to all of God's children?

- Do you believe that I can make a difference?

- Do you believe that the church of Jesus Christ can make a difference?

- Do you think that the United States and other nations can change the way they have operated for centuries?

Of course, there are no simple answers to these questions. On a daily basis we hear of war, murder, genocide, and corruption; there are always new stories of sexual abuse, disease, and natural disasters. No matter which way we turn, there are more victims to help, worthy causes to support, rallies to attend, and rights to protect. The needs are greater than our resources. Because we cannot address all of these issues, we sometimes retreat and neglect to address any of them. Instead of using our time, talents, and resources to help where we are capable of helping, we flee the mission field altogether and choose, instead, to mulch our garden, renovate the kitchen, or build a new storage shed in an effort to feel that we are at least accomplishing something.

We are living during a time of disillusionment, decline, and apathy among Christians living in the industrialized nations. Many contemporary persons of faith are more loyal to their college than to God; many are more faithful to a favorite sports team than to their church. Instead of tithing out of our abundance, we miserly tip churches and charities while we purchase more products and use more resources. Can we expect the church of Jesus Christ to awaken and address the pressing issues of our day? Can we eliminate war and destruction and channel the resources squandered in these endeavors for life-sustaining endeavors?

I love these words of Daniel Berrigan: "One cannot level one's moral lance at every evil in the universe. There are just too many of them. But you can do something, and the difference between doing something and doing nothing is everything."

This book is a call for Christians and persons of faith around the world to unite and use our moral lances to do some good. Individually, no one Christian can solve all of the world's problems; even together we have not been called to be the world's savior. However, we are called to follow the one we do believe was the world's savior—Jesus Christ. Collectively, if every Christian were to do his or her part to resist evil and oppression, war and terror, hunger and extreme poverty, the results would be spectacular. Contrary to the prevailing practice of ignoring the problems that face the world, we must show as much love and compassion as Christ. We must love as much as the terrorists responsible for the attacks of September 11, 2001, were able to hate.

In his "Serenity Prayer," Reinhold Niebuhr acknowledged the great dilemma humans confront:

God grant me the serenity

to accept the things I cannot change;

courage to change the things I can;

and wisdom to know the difference.

It is time for Christians to develop the courage needed to change the things we can. In working together we will learn there are few things we cannot change.

How do you eat an elephant? One bite at a time! We will need to work for peace and justice with small steps, increasing incrementally as we go. We will need to become peacemakers first as individuals and then as congregations and communities before finally progressing to the national and international level. We will need to remember, as the saying goes, Rome was not built in a day. It will take many acts of love and kindness to change the momentum evil, hatred, intolerance, ignorance, and bigotry have created. But unless we start to make changes, nothing will change. If we continue to live and act as we have always lived and acted, the world will continue on its present course.

Paul tells us "the one who sows sparingly will also reap sparingly, and the one who sows bountifully will also reap bountifully" (2 Cor 9:6). To put it more simply, "You reap what you sow." As I grow older, this seems to me more and more true. If we sow seeds of hatred, we will receive hatred back. If we sow seeds of love, we will reap love. When we plant the seeds of war, we will reap war. If we truly seek peace, we will begin by planting the seeds of peace. We must begin the process of planting these seeds of peace now as individuals, using our personal resources in life-sustaining and life-giving programs. We must re-center the work of the church around the themes of peace and justice, sowing seeds of peace within our local congregations, denominations, and across Christian circles and broader, interfaith communities. And we must, as citizens of the United States, help our nation exchange its militaristic mentality for one that sees the promise in sowing peace.

We are living in one of the most exciting times in history. The innovations in science and technology that exist at the beginning of the twenty-first century continue to define and transform the world around us in new and exhilarating ways. We have the resources, the technology, and the ability to eliminate poverty and create everlasting peace and harmony between all of the world's people and religions. What we currently lack is the desire. But for perhaps the first time in world history, we have the capacity to truly build God's kingdom on earth. We can sow peace now, and our children and grandchildren can reap the rewards of peace during their lifetime.

Men like Andrew Carnegie are few and far between. I do not expect, nor do I desire, to have even a fraction of the wealth he possessed. But his writing and his determination move me. Carnegie believed in giving, and he dedicated the final years of his life to giving his wealth to individuals, communities, and organizations that were working to improve the world. He understood that inner peace and happiness cannot be bought or purchased; true fulfillment and richness in life come through giving, through serving others and working to improve their lives. Twenty years ago I learned the following rhyme from my district superintendent, the Rev. Barber Waters:

> It's not what you would do with millions if fortune should be your lot, but what you are doing right now with the dollar twenty-five you've got.

It has been said, "We must live more simply if others are simply to live." There is something profoundly wrong with a world in which the four hundred highest income earners in the United States make as much money in a year as the entire population of twenty African nations—more than 300 million people. Those 300 million live in conditions of severe poverty, where death is a constant companion. Such conditions are unfathomable to most Americans.

The facts of the gap between rich and poor are unbelievable. According to the United Nations, about 2.8 billion people—some 45 percent of the world's total population—live on the equivalent of two U.S. dollars a day or less, 1.2 billion of whom live on one dollar a day or less. Roughly two-thirds of those living on a dollar a day or less are female. Worldwide, the poorest 20 percent have access to only 1 percent of the total Gross World Product (GWP).

On the other side of the equation, the richest 20 percent of the world's people possess 86 percent of the collective GWP. Although you may not consider yourself to be wealthy, by global standards, if you were able to purchase this book you are among the richest people who have ever lived! If you are living in a family that earns $100,000 or more, you are among the world's richest 1 percent and you are richer than 99.9 percent of all the people who have ever lived!

We live rich and extravagant lives that were unimaginable a few generations ago. You and I have more stuff in our homes, attics, garages, and basements than we will ever need and more than almost anyone in history prior to the twentieth century ever accumulated. Far from taking up our crosses and following Jesus, we choose the path of trying to up with our neighbors in shopping, buying, and spending.

But Jesus returns over and over again to the issues of wealth and resources. He uses a variety of ways to tell us the following truth:

> Do not store up for yourselves treasures on earth, where moth and rust consume and where thieves break in and steal; but store up for yourselves treasures in heaven, where neither moth nor rust consumes and where thieves do not break in and steal. For where your treasure is, there your heart will be also. (Matt 6:19–21)

It is clear where the hearts of thousands, even millions of American Christians are: with their checking accounts, homes, and investments. This prompts me to think of the rich man and Lazarus. I know which character I play in this vignette.

> There was a rich man who was dressed in purple and fine linen and who feasted sumptuously every day. And at his gate lay a poor man named Lazarus, covered with sores, who longed to satisfy his hunger with what fell from the rich man's table; even the dogs would come and lick his sores. The poor man died and was carried away by the angels to be with Abraham. The rich man also died and was buried. In Hades, where he was being tormented, he looked up and saw Abraham far away with Lazarus by his side. He called out, "Father Abraham, have mercy on me, and send Lazarus to dip the tip of his finger in water and cool my tongue; for I am in agony in these flames." But Abraham said, "Child, remember that during your lifetime you received your good things, and Lazarus in like manner evil things; but now he is comforted here, and you are in agony. Besides all this, between you and us a great chasm has been fixed, so that those who might want to pass from here to you cannot do so, and no one can cross from there to us." He said, "Then, father, I beg you to send him

to my father's house—for I have five brothers—that he may warn them, so that they will not also come into this place of torment." Abraham replied, "They have Moses and the prophets; they should listen to them." He said, "No, father Abraham; but if someone goes to them from the dead, they will repent." He said to him, "If they do not listen to Moses and the prophets, neither will they be convinced even if someone rises from the dead." (Luke 16:19–31)

The Individual Christian as Peacemaker

Peace with justice demands there be a more equitable distribution of the world's resources. To live in a world where the richest 20 percent of the population are in possession of 86 percent of the world's resources and the poorest 20 percent own less than 1 percent is morally unacceptable. There is enough food for everyone in the world to eat abundantly; there is enough medicine for everyone in the world to receive proper medication for treatable diseases; there are enough resources for everyone in the world to receive an education and live in adequate housing.

American Christians have the resources to make a tremendous impact on the world's population. However, those who claim Jesus Christ as their Lord and Savior have also fallen prey to the consumer mentality so dominant in our culture. We have allowed advertising agencies and marketing firms to dictate what the priorities of our lives should be. Tragically, the more income we receive, the less we give on a percentage basis to churches and other nonprofit organizations. Unless we start sowing seeds of peace with our personal resources, others simply will not live at all.

When you travel to an undeveloped nation and see how much a hundred dollars can purchase, you become acutely aware of our economic disparity. By living simpler lives, we can increase our savings and thus have extra resources for sharing. Most of the Americans I know live up to and beyond their means; no matter how much we earn, we spend a similar, if not larger, amount. Families routinely complain that they cannot possibly tithe to the church, even when their income exceeds $100,000. Between the mortgage and car payments, grocery bills and vacations, clothing and so many other expenses, there is simply nothing left at the end of the month to give to those in need.

John Wesley's first job as an assistant professor at Oxford paid an annual salary of £30. Wesley discovered he could live on £28.50 pounds per year, and he gave the remaining £1.50 pounds to charity. The next year he was promoted to associate professor and his salary increased to £60, but he kept the same budget and was able to contribute £31.50 to charity. The following year when he was promoted to full professor and his salary was elevated to £90, Wesley continued his great discipline and held his expenses to £28.50, allowing him to give away £61.50.

Although Wesley's radical discipleship may be hard for us to duplicate, it stands in great contrast to the stewardship we Americans demonstrate today. Andrew Carnegie, quoting Jesus, who was quoting Deuteronomy,[87] was correct: we do not live on bread alone. Americans are spiritually bankrupt, looking for material "things" to fill us up and, conveniently, for a short time, they do. We then need another "fix," another purchase to satisfy our insatiable appetite. "I shop, therefore I am" can be the theme for the lifestyle of the typical American.

As a United Methodist pastor, I have a personal pension account that has been accumulating funds for the past twenty-two years. Through the contributions of the churches where I have worked and my own giving, this account has grown to more than $300,000. I have sixteen more years until I reach the standard retirement age of sixty-five. Depending on the investments, interest rates, and growth of the stock market, it is possible my pension account could grow to a million dollars by the time I retire. Payments from my pension, combined with Social Security checks and supplemented by other savings could lead to a comfortable retirement even taking into account future inflation.

I learned this past year that United Methodist clergypersons can withdraw some of the money in their pension accounts before they retire, under certain conditions. We can borrow up to $50,000, or make a one-time hardship withdrawal, also up to $50,000.

There are approximately forty thousand United Methodist clergypersons in the United States. While some have fewer years in ministry and less in their pension accounts than I do, others have more. If every clergyperson were to withdraw a thousand dollars from his or her pension account and combine it for mission work in a developing nation, the resulting amount would be $40 million! Imagine if every clergyperson were able to take out $10,000 from his or her pension account and donate it to a mission project. That would enable us to have $400 million for mission work! Few if any of us would even feel the effects of this transfer.

---

[87] Matthew 4:4 reads: "But he [Jesus] answered, 'It is written, "One does not live by bread alone, but by every word that comes from the mouth of God."'" Deuteronomy 8:3 reads: "He humbled you by letting you hunger, then by feeding you with manna, with which neither you nor your ancestors were acquainted, in order to make you understand that one does not live by bread alone, but by every word that comes from the mouth of the LORD."

Think now of *every Christian pastor* in the United States donating a small percentage of his or her pension account to mission projects around the world. Imagine them making a real commitment to helping the world's least, last, and lost by donating real money to their favorite project or cause.

We clergy have fallen victim to the sin of consumerism. I know of clergy who retire as millionaires. I personally know clergy who own two and even three homes. There are pastors who spend more time on the golf course worrying about their handicaps than they do in the mission field. When the church's leaders have their priorities confused, it is no wonder that the church has lost its way.

What then can we do? We can sow seeds of peace and justice through numerous programs and activities, including:

- For nineteen cents per day, the World Food Program and UNICEF provide meals for children in impoverished schools, a program that has greatly increased school attendance and is often the only meal these children have during the course of the day. It is one of the most successful programs administered by the United Nations.

- For $10 a mosquito net can be purchased that can reduce the odds of a child becoming infected with malaria by 60 percent. An average of three thousand children die every day in Africa from malaria. That is equal to the deaths from the terrorists' attacks on September 11 every single day of the year, year in and year out. Often a mosquito net will provide overnight protection from mosquitoes for two to four children who all squeeze into the same bed and who can all be safe under one net.

- For $60 per year, a student's tuition, room, and board can be taken care of at a secondary school in Mozambique, where the public education provided by the government stops at grade six. Because extra funds are so scarce, only 5 percent of Mozambican children advance beyond the sixth grade.

- For $2,000 a well can be dug in an African village that will provide water to hundreds of individuals. Women and children routinely walk six to eight miles per day to bring water back to their homes from the village stream or well. More wells will create safer, cleaner water that is desperately needed by millions of Africans.

- For $25,000 a library can be built in many of the world's developing nations. In the spirit of Andrew Carnegie, we can provide for libraries to become the center of learning for thousands of villages currently lacking this resource that every American city, town, and village takes for granted.

- For $50,000 a tractor can be shipped to an African country where the green revolution has yet to take place. African fields are ready to provide the crops that can feed and sustain their own populations. What they often need are irrigation and fertilizers combined with modern farming equipment. Watching men and women manually work the fields (without even the help of farm animals) drives home to the observer how great the needs are and what a tremendous blessing a tractor would make to nearly any village or community.

Churches Can Sow Seeds of Peace

The New Milford United Methodist Church, where I served as the pastor from 1993 to 2005, was typical of many suburban, mid-sized congregations in the United States. We grew to an average attendance of approximately 270 per week, and the total annual budget came to roughly $300,000 per year. We struggled to reach this goal every year but generally managed to achieve it one way or another.

Following a mission trip to Mozambique in 2002, church leaders made a commitment to build a new orphanage and relocate roughly twenty-five children from a facility where the living conditions were intolerable. The old orphanage was adjacent to a swamp, where malaria-carrying mosquitoes lived in abundance, leading to continual sickness. It had no running water or electricity. The closest school and health clinic were miles away. A missionary center thirty miles away had extra land and could provide the children with access to schools, health care, running water, and a limited supply of electricity. Most important, this would bring the children out of isolation and into a larger communal setting.

Initially, we were given an estimate of $50,000 to build a new orphanage, and we began raising funds toward that goal. As with building projects everywhere, the estimate was too low, but we were able to construct two dormitories and two additional buildings for the workers and infants for a total of $65,000. The church raised this amount in less than three years, and the new home provides a safe and secure location for the ever growing number of orphans, which now totals forty. These children are now being raised in an environment where hope has replaced despair and the future is not something to be feared. Seeds of peace have been sown, and members of the church continue to be in touch with the children, sharing e-mails, resources, blessings, and joys.

Imagine if every congregation in the United States was able to take on a significant mission project as we did. There are approximately 400,000 churches in the United States. Many are smaller than the New Milford United Methodist Church, but others are larger. Even if small congregations were to join together for mission, tremendous results could be achieved if church leaders, clergy and laity, put their minds to it.

Churches reap what they sow. Pastors who steer their congregations toward mission work see their members fed as Christ is encountered in the feeding, clothing, sheltering, and visiting of those in need. Mission trips provide many Americans their first genuine opportunities to save human lives.

Churches that are inwardly focused institutions debating theology and doctrine and worry about their organizational rules and policies will find an absence of spirit-filled members. Division, strife, discord, and schism have been a constant in the life of the church of Jesus Christ and one way the forces of evil have prevented the church from reaching its full potential.

If I were the devil and wanted to design the most effective way to inhibit the church from fulfilling its mission and purpose, I would concentrate on creating conflict—among members of local congregations and denominations, and between denominations. The early church argued about whether its members needed to be circumcised and what foods were permissible. The churches of the Middle Ages argued over how many angels could sit on the head of a pin. The Reformation saw the church at war over issues of papal authority, priestly celibacy, the number of sacraments, and other doctrinal matters. The nineteenth century saw the church split over slavery. In the twentieth century we fought over the ordination of women and the civil rights of minorities. Today the pressing issues seem to be abortion, homosexuality, and biblical interpretation. Our elevation of these secondary issues over the more pressing mission of the church is clear proof that the church is often distracted by ants while the elephants march by.

While church members and clergy contest the authority and nature of the Scriptures, the exclusivity of the Christian pathway to God, and the qualities necessary for serving the church as an ordained person, millions of God's children are suffering and dying. Their cries of despair and their hopelessness demand the action of justice-seeking disciples.

The United States Can Sow Seeds of Peace

In the early 1940s, the United States secretly launched the Manhattan Project, a governmental endeavor to develop and build atomic weapons. The goal was achieved. At a cost of $2 billion dollars (about $20 billion today), the United States was able to create two atomic bombs, which it detonated over cities in Japan.

During the late 1940s and early 1950s, the United States unleashed the greatest humanitarian effort in human history—the Marshall Plan. As described in chapter 1, the Marshall Plan was successful in helping Europe get back on its feet after the terrible destruction of World War II. Totaling $20 billion, it helped us win friends and greatly influenced the world in which we live.

The time has come for a new Marshal Plan. We can call it the End to Poverty Plan, or the Jeffrey Sachs Plan,[88] or any other name our leaders can agree to. The new Marshall Plan could be a $200 billion development plan, led and administered by the United States that would reestablish our place in the world as the good neighbor. Additionally, it would do more to stop terrorists in their tracks than any military solution currently being discussed or actively being waged. Investing in the "Big Five"—agriculture, health and education, electricity, transportation and communications, and safe drinking water—is in the short-term and long-term interests of the United States and is an international policy every citizen of our country should support.

In addition to the creation of a master plan to eliminate global poverty, a strategy must also be developed to reduce the number of Americans who themselves are living below the poverty line. We live in the wealthiest nation in the history of the world, but we still have people living in substandard housing and sleeping in shelters or on the streets. An estimated forty-five million Americans lack health care. Soup kitchens and food pantries help feed millions of persons across the nation every day, but others go without food. Many public schools do not receive the funds they need to provide an adequate education, and millions of young people are denied access to college because scholarships and loans are not available. Addressing the needs of Americans may be the first step in creating a world of peace with justice, but it will not remove our moral obligation to help our brothers and sisters in developing nations as well.

A nation that sows seeds of war will reap war. As long as the United States continues to be the world's largest arms exporter, we should expect wars

---

[88] Jeffrey Sachs's book *The End of Poverty* (New York: Penguin, 2005), provides the blueprints for the systematic elimination of severe poverty from our planet.

to continue; sometimes, in fact, those arms we sell will be aimed back at us. But if we shift tactics, if we concentrate our efforts on sowing seeds of peace, we will reap peace. Albert Einstein understood this dilemma when he said, "You cannot simultaneously prevent and prepare for war."

Of course, there will be those who insist that we cannot afford to sponsor a new Marshall Plan. My response is twofold:

1. Can we continue to afford virtually unchecked military increases in spending? Can we continue to spend on our military an amount equal to the total all of the other nations in the world spend on their military combined?

2. Can we afford to miss this opportunity to change the world during our generation? Can we afford to travel down the road we have taken, determined to impose our will on other nations, even when it is not in their or our interests?

Joseph Stiglitz, a Nobel Prize–winning economist at Columbia University, and Linda Bilmes of the Kennedy School of Government at Harvard, estimate that the true cost of the war in Iraq will be more than $1 trillion, and probably more than $2 trillion.[89] Can we afford this war? Can we afford another war?

* * * * * *

John the Baptist streaks across church history as a shooting comet. Each Advent we read again of this wild man who, from the margins of human society, preached a message of repentance and preparation. The people flocked to see him, caught between curiosity and desire to see a prophet of God in person. His message was as harsh as the environment in which he lived:

John said to the crowds that came out to be baptized by him, "You brood of vipers! Who warned you to flee from the wrath to come? Bear fruits worthy of repentance. Do not begin to say to yourselves, 'We have Abraham as our ancestor'; for I tell you,

---

[89] Joseph Stiglitz and Linda Bilmes, "The Economic Costs of the Iraq War: Appraisal Three Years after the Beginning of the Conflict," National Bureau of Economic Research Working Paper 12054, February 2006, http://www.nber.org/papers/w12054.

God is able from these stones to raise up children to Abraham. Even now the ax is lying at the root of the trees; every tree therefore that does not bear good fruit is cut down and thrown into the fire.'" (Luke 3:7–9)

Strangely enough, John's audience did not seem put off by this message. Instead, they asked him a simple question—"What then should we do?"—to which John provided a series of simple, ethical living standards:

In reply he said to them, "Whoever has two coats must share with anyone who has none; and whoever has food must do likewise." Even tax collectors came to be baptized, and they asked him, "Teacher, what should we do?" He said to them, "Collect no more than the amount prescribed for you." Soldiers also asked him, "And we, what should we do?" He said to them, "Do not extort money from anyone by threats or false accusation, and be satisfied with your wages." (Luke 3:11–14)

John's clear-cut, down-to-earth answers and his straightforward, uncomplicated yet demanding instructions for how to prepare for God's kingdom offer wisdom to us two thousand years later. We who have too much food, too many coats, too many televisions and computers, and too much china and silverware need to be reminded of the beauty of simplicity and sharing.

What then shall we do?

Those who have the opportunity to travel to Africa for a safari usually go to see the "Big Five." This list was developed by hunters during the nineteenth and early twentieth centuries and consists of the following animals: rhinoceros, lion, leopard, buffalo, and elephant. No one goes to see the ants. The termites, likewise, are ignored. A safari guide once told me that when people ask him the names of some of the small birds they see, he usually tells them that the birds are LBJ's, his acronym for "Little Brown Jobs." Few people are interested in them, so he spends little time trying to learn their true names and identities.

But the elephants dominate the landscape and demand your attention. The largest land animal on the earth, they are a force of nature and command respect and admiration. A mother elephant defending her child or a bull in musk is an unpredictable animal that can cause great harm when threatened. Far from being ignored, the elephants are the true sovereigns of the African plains. They are the masters of their domain.

We live in a world where an average of 20,000 children die each day from a variety of preventable diseases and related problems caused by extreme poverty. Our nation spends forty times more on military expenses than we spend on development and aid. In the church we debate and divide over polity, the interpretation of Scripture, the appropriate pathway to God, and various ethical issues. Because we live thousands of miles from those in severe and extreme poverty, their concerns are out of sight and out of mind. Feelings of despair and disillusionment over the direction of the local church and the policies of our national government lead us to the belief that we are powerless to make any effective changes. We retreat to issues that we do have control over, surrendering our moral responsibilities to others.

How can we change this behavior? By eating the elephants, one bite at a time. By finding mission projects we are interested in and giving ourselves to them. We become part of the change we are looking for when we assume leadership positions in the local church and speak out about the elephant sitting in the middle of the room. We become part of the solution every time we write our elected officials and express our opinion. We have the power of elections and the ability to choose leaders who reflect our opinions. We can write letters to newspapers, attend rallies, and let our voices be heard.

I cannot tell you, or anyone else, what to do. But I do know that our faith and tradition is one of actions and deeds. When we read the Gospels, we see Jesus as a man of faith and action. Jesus came preaching and teaching; he healed the sick and fed the hungry. He called a group of fishers to follow after him and made them fishers of people. He ate with the sinners and tax collectors and showed them how to live lives that were more faithful. He welcomed women, and he addressed Samaritans and Romans, the perceived enemies of his day. He shared his vision of the kingdom of God and invited his followers to join him on his journey.

In the two thousand years since his death, the church has alternated between following in the footsteps of Jesus and forging our own way. Only by consciously deciding to follow his vision now will the church be faithful in these difficult times. Shortly before he was killed, John Lennon shared these words of wisdom in a song: "Life is what happens to you while you're busy making other plans." We are too busy making other plans—but we have the ability to change, to turn, to move back toward the cross. We can sow the seeds of peace by offering life to our brothers and sisters. When people have food, adequate shelter, and access to health care and education for their children, they have hope. A world filled with people of hope is our greatest asset in the war against the terrorists.

Epilogue

An ancient common law in England declares individual civilians, in the absence of sheriffs or law enforcement officials, must do all in their power to capture and hold suspected criminals. Known as "hue and cry," the concept is based on the principle that n order to create a just society every person is morally responsible for doing his or her civic duty. The law encourages the use of horns, bells, and voices in sounding the alarm so neighbors will "join the chase." Criminals caught in the act are subject to immediate justice. Hue and cry was part of the official law of England in the centuries following the Norman Conquest and existed into the nineteenth century.

For many years I have been wondering why affluent Christians in developed, industrialized nations seem so unconcerned about their global neighbors. What will historians say about this generation? Will they write we lived in the richest of times and the poorest of times? Will they write millions ate and drank extravagantly while others starved and died? What will be written about the church of Jesus Christ? Where can we find the faithful Christians of our day? Will future students of history wonder why so many persons of faith so enthusiastically supported war and the military-industrial-political complex?

Ironically, we are perhaps the most informed society in the history of the world. The information age is upon us: we are bombarded by news and knowledge provided to us through a variety of media ranging from newspapers, magazines, books, television, movies, and the Internet. The devastating effects of extreme poverty are regularly reported in the mainstream press, which often provides the name, phone number, and Web addresses of organizations that are making a difference. Those responsible for raising the "hue and cry" regarding the needs of the world's poor are doing their part to raise awareness. Why is it we are not hearing this distress signal? What is the force so powerful that we are deaf to the sound of these alarms ringing in our presence?

We all experience fear. Fear can be a healthy emotion; it warns us of dangers like stepping into a busy street, jumping off a cliff, or touching a hot stove. Its purpose it to keep us safe. But fear in too large a dosage is harmful when it becomes the overriding factor in our decision-making. Too much fear will create paralysis. There is an irrational fear of change and of the unknown. We fear public speaking, death, and taxes. Many are afraid of the dark or of trips to the dentist. We fear for the safety of our loved ones and for the security of our jobs, pensions, retirements, and health. Fear is an emotion and characteristic that inhibits risk and variation. It locks humanity into the status quo and limits prophets, mavericks, and risk takers emerging from the crowds to lead in an alternate direction. Fear is a powerful force!

God knows human fear. Often in biblical stories when angels appear, the first words spoken are "Fear not." Overcoming fear and hearing God's voice is a step in faithful discipleship.

Moses experienced moments of fear. After killing an Egyptian supervisor, he feared for his life and fled to the wilderness. Confronted later by the burning bush, he resisted God's command to return to Egypt and offered a list of excuses. But Moses was able to control his fear, return to Egypt, confront Pharaoh, and lead his people out of Egypt and through the wilderness for forty years.

The spies Moses sent to the Promised Land were afraid of the people living there and reported back to the children of Israel that giants who could not be conquered resided there. Only Caleb and Joshua overcame their fear and advocated an immediate campaign.

Time and time again the call narratives of biblical characters demonstrate their fear. The stories of Elijah, Gideon, David, and Jeremiah, likewise the disciples and Paul, show how these persons who became effective leaders controlled their fear and allowed God to work through them.

One of the most famous sound bites of American politics was spoken by Franklin Delano Roosevelt, at his first inauguration on January 20, 1933: "We have nothing to fear except fear itself." His words were comforting to Americans who were experiencing the economic uncertainty of the Great Depression. He set the tone of courage and optimism in the midst of human suffering and helped Americans face their conditions with hope, fortitude, and resolution.

Contrary to the messages of old, the communication from today's White House is this: Be afraid! Since the terrorist attacks of September 11 2001, we have consistently been told to support the Bush administration because they are doing all within their power to protect Americans and keep us safe. The Terrorist Alert Code represents the absurd lengths our government will go to in order to frighten its people and coerce us to support the administration's policies. Predictably, the alert status often moves to a higher stage just prior to elections or important votes in Congress. Fear as a public policy has never been as well managed as it is now, and it is being used to manipulate national and international debates, discussion, and decisions. Cultivating the population's anxiety and trepidation over future terrorist attacks has produced a near panic

200

among many in our country leading us to abandon long-held traditions and moral values. In the first few years of the twenty-first century, forsaking over two centuries of tradition and established practices, our nation has accepted a preemptive, unprovoked invasion of a sovereign nation, has concurred with the sanctioning of torture, and has acquiesced to the curtailment of basic civil liberties.

As I write on peace and share thoughts with individuals, small groups, and congregations, I consistently hear the same theme: We hear you, we agree with you, we know that you are correct, but what about the terrorists? These people want to kill us. If we lower our guard and stop fighting them, they will attack us here, and many more will die. We must fight them over there so they will not fight us on our streets. We don't want the smoking gun to come in the form of a mushroom cloud. Such statements are made out of an unreasonable amount of fear.

It is true that there are those out there who want to kill innocent Americans. I can only imagine that, given the opportunity, there are those would take the controls of an airplane and fly it straight into another skyscraper. It seems likely there will be more terrorist attacks within the United States. We probably cannot stop all of these attacks from taking place. But we can implement policies to reduce future attacks. Providing food, clothing, decent shelter, education, and adequate health care will offer more real protection to us than guns, bombs, tanks, fighter jets, and missiles. Proverbs 25:21 instructs us, "If you enemies are hungry, give them bread to eat; and if they are thirsty, give them water to drink." Enemies are thus transformed to allies, hatred is diffused, and terrorists are disarmed.

Opening a dialogue with those who hate us would be a better defense than military tactics designed to silence them. "Keep your friends close, and your enemies closer" is the approach advocated by Sun-tzu, the great Chinese general and military strategist who lived 2,400 years ago. A policy of keeping our enemies closer could make a profound change possible. Jesus also spoke about the reality of enemies but offered a different path: "But I say to you, Love your enemies and pray for those who persecute you, so that you may be children of your Father in heaven" (Matt 5:44–45).

Fear should not be our governing emotion. Courage and moral fortitude provide us with the ability to confront our fears. Courage is one of the four Cardinal Virtues (along with prudence, justice, and temperance). "Cardinal" here means "pivotal" and is applied to courage because to possess any virtue, a person must be able to sustain it in the face of difficulty.

During the call of the disciples, Luke reports that Jesus challenged Simon Peter to have faith and courage: "Put out into the deep water and let down your nets for a catch" (Luke 5:4). The term for the main section of a church is "nave," a word derived from the same root as "navy." The church is to be seen as a ship, traveling through the water under the wind of the Holy Spirit.

But Jesus did not intend his ship to hug the coast and remain in the shallow waters. Churches that refuse to go deep content themselves with inwardly focused programs and events. They offer fund-raisers and fellowship events. They provide for themselves and the families who worship within. But they miss the greater catches possible when the decision is made to lower our sails and leave the safe harbor by serving God through outwardly expressed ministries and missions.

I love the line of clothing called No Fear. Marketed to members of Generation X, the name promotes a can-do approach to life. Maybe this is a modern way to state what biblical writers have been telling us for centuries: Humans have fear, but we cannot allow that emotion to prevent us from living as faithful Christians. We need to check our fear at the entrance of the church by the baptismal font, remembering that "there is no fear in love, but perfect love casts out fear" (1 John 4:18).

A generation following her husband's famous warning against fear, Franklin Roosevelt's widow Eleanor wrote these words when our nation was in the midst of the Cold War and potential nuclear confrontation. They are great words to remember today:

> Once more we are in a period of uncertainty, of danger, in which not only our own safety but that of all mankind is threatened. Once more we need the qualities that inspired the development of the democratic way of life. We need imagination and integrity, courage and a high heart. We need to fan the spark of conviction, which may again inspire the world as we did with our new idea of the dignity and worth of free men. But first we must learn to cast out fear. People who "view with alarm" never build anything.[90]

* * * * * *

I am a new deep-sea sailor. For twenty years I have sailed churches too close to the shore. For too long I have failed to hear the "hue and cry" raised regarding the world's poor. I confess to years of preoccupation with institutional

---

[90] Eleanor Roosevelt, *Tomorrow Is Now* (New York: HarperCollins, 1966), xvii.

enhancement and a very limited personal agenda. I have not been a good neighbor. I have abdicated my prophetic voice. I have not heard the cry of the needy. But hearing their cries now, I pray I can cast out the fear that has held me back and head for the deep seas. There will be much to learn out there beyond the lighthouses, but I am determined to embrace it.

It is my hope to see you there as well. Let us sail the course laid before us by the one who tamed the storm and still calls us to walk on the waters.

Wayne Lavender
March 19, 2007